By the Sweat of Their Brow

Unloading at the Pit Brow, Lancashire

By the Sweat of Their Brow

Women Workers at Victorian Coal Mines

Angela V. John

CROOM HELM
LONDON

© 1980 Angela V. John
Croom Helm Ltd, 2-10 St John's Road, London SW11

British Library Cataloguing in Publication Data

John, Angela V
    By the sweat of their brow.
    1. Women – Employment – Great Britain – History
    – 19th century
    2. Coal mines and mining – Great Britain – History
    – 19th century
    I. Title
    331.4'82'2330941   HD6073.C/

ISBN 0-85664-748-9

Printed and bound in Great Britain by
Redwood Burn Limited
Trowbridge and Esher

CONTENTS

ACKNOWLEDGEMENTS

This book originated as a doctoral thesis for the University of Manchester. Its shape and size have since altered considerably, but my first and greatest debt is undoubtedly owed to my supervisor, Dr Iorwerth Prothero. I am also grateful to Professor Royden Harrison and to my former tutors, Dorothy Thompson and Professor Ieuan Gwynedd Jones. Thanks are due to those who organised and attended the lectures and seminars where I tried out some of my ideas, and particularly to the staff and students of Thames Polytechnic, especially Paul Stigant. The staff of record offices, libraries and museums in areas which employed pit women have come to my aid, as have the National Union of Mineworkers and the National Coal Board. Dr Gaskell and his staff at the Wren Library, Trinity College, Cambridge, have been particularly helpful and I am grateful to the Master and Fellows of Trinity for permission to use the Munby collection. I also wish to record my debt to the late Dr A.N.L. Munby who allowed me to consult unpublished family papers relating to his great-uncle and to Leonore Davidoff and Pat Bradford for numerous discussions about Munby. The following have kindly granted me permission to use papers in their possession: The Rt Hon. the Earl of Crawford and Balcarres (Haigh Collieries and Estate Papers, the John Rylands University Library of Manchester), His Grace the Duke of Sutherland (Loch-Egerton Papers), the Trustees of the Broadlands Archives Trust (Broadlands Manuscript, Royal Commission on Historical Manuscripts), and Chorley Public Library (Mrs Holden's Manuscript).

Thanks are due to the Editor of the *Bulletin* of the John Rylands University Library of Manchester for permitting the use of a small amount of material which originally appeared in an article, and to the Social Science Research Council for a grant to study women's pit brow work in the Wigan coalfield. These acknowledgements would not be complete without thanking the following former pit women for their contributions to the book: Isabella Adams, Lottie Barham, Mary Bolton, Jane Carroll, Mrs Foster, Polly Gee, Ellen Gregory, Ethel Hindley, Minnie Holdcroft, Jane Oakley, Ann Ogden, Annie Prior, Elizabeth Rigby, Alice Simm, Mary Smalley, Miss Tyrrell, Martha Unsworth and their successors the women coal miners of the United States, especially Barbara Angle and Carol Jean Naland. My thanks also

Acknowledgements

to the relatives and friends of pit women and to all others, too numerous to mention by name, who helped this venture in some way.

I would like to thank Sue Harris and Liz Staff for their typing. Donald Anderson C.Eng, FI Min.E, FRICS, FGS and Dr Kate Tiller read Chapters 3 and 4 respectively and Francis Duke kindly read through the entire manuscript. I am extremely grateful to them for their comments. The faults that remain are my own.

TO MY MOTHER
AND THE MEMORY OF MY FATHER

PREFACE

This book is an attempt to recover from obscurity a group of nineteenth-century women workers who have been virtually ignored by historians yet who, in their lifetime, became the centre of a spirited and protracted debate about their right to continue working. They were the 'pit brow lasses' who sorted coal and performed a variety of jobs above ground at British coal mines. Although this Lancashire term referred to the area surrounding the pit mouth, it was extended by critics to cover all surface jobs performed by women and girls.[1] Attempts to restrict the work culminated in exclusion proposals in the 1880s which became channelled through coal mines bills.

Studying the efforts to prohibit their employment enables a penetration of contemporary conceptualisation of the problems of women's work. The pit brow debate encapsulates the ambivalence of nineteenth-century attitudes towards working-class female employment and it highlights the dichotomy between the fashionable ideal of womanhood and the necessity and reality of female manual labour. The pit brow woman appeared as a direct contradiction to the deification of the home. Viewed as the example *par excellence* of degraded womanhood, she was portrayed as the ultimate in defeminisation, an aberration in a masculine domain, cruelly torn from her 'natural sphere', the home. The attention paid to her, helped by comparison, to define the 'perfect lady'. In practice this was merely reinforcing an ideal image of woman, creating another stereotype. It failed to recognise the realities of pre-industrial society or the problems facing many middle-class women.[2] Yet the symbolic emphasis on the pit woman as the antithesis of the bourgeois ideal, extended the notion of what the diarist Munby (see below) called the 'Dresden China' type of lady.

This book has been organised into three sections. The first part is devoted to the exclusion of women from work below ground. Part II looks at the life and work of the pit brow women. Though these are in themselves discrete fields of enquiry, they are used here to coalesce into the third, and major part, which concentrates on the significance of the attempts to exclude women from the pit brow in the 1880s. The implications of this pit brow debate can best be understood by a prior examination of contemporary attitudes towards the mining industry and more particularly, of the early-nineteenth-century experience of women colliery workers. The fact that the pit brow woman was the descendant of generations of women and girls who had worked *in* coal mines was to permeate attitudes towards surface work. The First Report of the Children's Employment Commission investigated the conditions of girls, boys and women working in mines and collieries and in 1842 revealed subterranean terrors to a shocked public. As Marx commented, the scandal was so great that Parliament had to salve its conscience by passing the Mines and Collieries Act.[3] This legislation, enacted at 'railroad speed', forbade the employment of boys below ten and of all females in British mines of any kind though they were permitted to continue working above ground. The pit brow women were associated with this earlier unsavoury employment (and the even more distasteful fact that nothing had previously been done about the situation). This helped to stigmatise the female surface worker so that she was depicted as the remnant of an undesirable past which had been rightfully swept away. In fact her work was often less debilitating than many other fields of employment which attracted less attention and actually employed more people. The furore caused by the pit woman's work in the 1880s must however be viewed in the light of the memories which helped to shape critics' opinions. This is more fully realised by looking not just at 1840-2 (the years when the work of the colliery women was officially scrutinised) but by also considering the experience of the period following the legislation. The difficulties of finding alternative employment and the frequent evasion of the law were further crucial determinants of later attitudes.

Having placed the pit brow debate in its historical perspective in Part I, it is essential to examine the lifestyle of the pit brow lasses before proceeding to a critical discussion of it. Part II does this by considering firstly the work experience and, secondly, their social life and position within the local community. The chapter on the work place discusses changes within the industry in the second half of the nineteenth century. It looks at the diversity of jobs, the differing degrees of skill, regional variations, the pace of work and both ordinary and extraordinary demands and expectations. It demonstrates how legislation and mechanisation might affect numbers and improve or hinder opportunities for women and girls. By showing what their daily work involved, some impression can be gained of how they might have viewed their employment. This also helps to elucidate the complex economic and social relations which existed between the women and the rest of the colliery workforce. This theme is explored further in the following chapter which concentrates on one district, the Wigan coalfield. A third of the country's pit brow women worked in West Lancashire, mainly in the Wigan area. The attempt to remove women from the surface became concentrated here, Wigan assuming a symbolic role as an industrial town and employer of women.

Even today mention of Wigan still invariably provokes outsiders to comment about its pier. George Orwell became the best known of British social explorers of the first half of this century. Like a considerable number of his predecessors, he sought to penetrate worlds hitherto unknown to him by attempting to become temporarily one of the poor.[4] Yet, less well known is the fact that, in the nineteenth century, Wigan was subjected to far closer scrutiny by another upper-middle-class gentleman, Arthur Joseph Munby.[5] For over thirty years Munby travelled around the Wigan coalfield, conversing with the pit brow lasses. Like Orwell, he was a stranger to Wigan yet anxious to be accepted. Though he did not adopt Orwell's disguises, Munby was, as a gentleman, automatically given a passport, an unspoken recognition that he might talk to the women at home and at work, as he wished, by virtue of his status. This was helped by the fact that pit girls were literally more accessible than mill girls and many other women workers since they were mainly employed in the open air. Yet ironically, Munby's very gentility which, on the one hand permitted freedom in communication with working-class women (and he could never have talked to women of his own class in the same way), on the other hand erected a permanent and impenetrable barrier. As with Orwell, he was inevitably socially distanced from the women and could not transcend the boundaries of class.

Munby's background, motives and expectations are analysed critically in Part II in order to assess his contribution to our understanding of pit life, particularly in Wigan. In a number of respects his views provide an important corrective to the blanket condemnations of so many critics of pit brow work. Munby offers a useful focal point for surveying the women's position within the community. By looking at an area which was not just dependent on one industry, it is also possible to consider the question of how far the pit lasses interacted with and were accepted by both miners and mill women.

The final and longest section broadens out from the micro-level to encompass the exclusion campaign of the mid-1880s. It questions how and why opinions became polarised at this particular time. The development of the debate is traced, the fusion of local and national interests and the convergence of apparently disparate concerns. For example the early suffragists upheld the pit women's right to work, their involvement helping to mark a transition from relatively inchoate ideas about working-class female employment, to more systematic feminist attacks on protective legislation. The pit brow debate acted as a spring-board both for questioning and for asserting the rights of adult women to work in outdoor manual occupations. One newspaper explained that it was the 'first instalment of a crusade against all field work for women' whilst another paper presented it as a test case for the rights of these women to work.[6]

Part III, then, focusses nationally on some of the issues raised in the context of Wigan society and relates the specifics of female pit brow work to the more general implications for women's employment. With the aid of literary and visual evidence, it concentrates on the three major contemporary questions of physical, moral and economic suitability. It shows how arguments about the work were rehearsed and extended and pays particular attention to the views of the miners and coal masters and the women's position in the class struggle. The conclusion is followed by an epilogue which places the debate in another, still wider context by briefly considering twentieth-century developments within and beyond Britain.

It is true that four to five thousand pit brow women represented only a fraction of the total colliery workforce and less than seven per cent of surface workers. They were, however, concentrated in certain areas – in parts of West Lancashire, Scotland, South Wales, Cumberland, South Staffordshire and Shropshire. Yet what is more important is the fact that, although numerically insignificant as colliery workers and indeed as women workers, they managed to cause such a stir. The interest which they aroused in the 1880s was out of all proportion to their numbers. This book takes up this contradiction and examines its origins, nature and implications. It aims wherever possible to view the problems of the pit women from their own perspectives, a daunting task exacerbated by highly mediatised evidence, though aided by some oral testimony for the end of the period.[7]

As Sally Alexander and Anna Davin have explained, most social history books today contain sections on women but they are still 'tagged on, not integrated into the overall understanding of a society or even of its parts'.[8] Although this problem is increasingly being recognised, coal mining history has not yet demonstrated such an awareness.[9] In this field women have been accorded only scant attention. Not only have they been ignored as waged workers (except for the 1840-2 period when they have been invariably linked with children) but even in the many districts where they did not work at the pit, their position has tended to be viewed solely in terms of the wife's 'back-up support' for the male miner. Admittedly this was vital but accounts of mining communities have not only forgotten the single woman and the widow, but have internalised the male miners' 'eye-view'.[10] The intention of this book is to depict the pit brow lasses not just as crucial members of the family in an industry where familial support was extremely important, but to show them as women and as part of a working class involved in production. While the numerous complex problems of the pit brow debate cannot begin to be answered here, questions can at least be formulated about the significance of the work and the implications of prohibiting it for both women and men. Thus they can provide another way of looking at one of the nineteenth century's most important growth industries.

Notes

1. Within different coalfields local terms were used. South Wales had its tip girls, Scotland pit head women, Cumberland screen lasses and South Staffordshire pit bank women.
2. Several recent studies have examined the demands of the Victorian family, especially for lower-middle-class women. See T. McBride, *The Domestic Revolution. The Modernisation of Household Service in England and France 1820-1920* (London, 1976), and P. Branca, 'Image and Reality: The Myth of the Victorian Woman' in M. Hartman and L. Banner (eds.), *Clio's Consciousness Raised* (New York, 1974).
3. K. Marx, *Capital*, 1 (London, 1976 edition), p.626.
4. See G. Orwell, *The Road to Wigan Pier* (London, 1972 edition) and Introduction to P. Keating (ed.), *Into Unknown England 1866-1913. Selections from the Social Explorers* (London, 1976 edition).
5. See Ch. 4 for biographical details of A.J. Munby.
6. *St. Helens Newspaper*, 8 May 1886; *The Spectator*, 27 March 1886.
7. Interviews with 18 women who formerly worked at Lancashire, Cumberland and Pembrokeshire pits from the 1890s onwards. I am grateful to Cliff Webb of the *Wigan Observer*, and to Richard Keen of the National Museum of Wales for permitting me to use the information from one taped interview made in 1970. All the other interviews were conducted by the author between 1974 and 1978.
8. Editorial, *History Workshop Journal* (Spring 1976), p.4.
9. For a discussion of such problems by American historians see the seminal collection of theoretical and critical essays, B.A. Carroll (ed.), *Liberating Women's History* (Urbana, 1976), especially the essay by Gordon, Buhle and Dye on 'The Problem of Women's History' where it is argued that the historians' neglect of women has been a 'function of their ideas about what is historically significant', p.75. See also P. Hollis, 'Working Women', *History*, 62 (1977), pp.439-45, and Hartman and Banner, *Clio*, Preface.
10. For a critical consideration of the classic community study by N. Dennis, P. Henriques and C. Slaughter, *Coal is Our Life* (London, 1956) in these terms see R. Frankenberg, 'In the Production of their Lives, Men (?). . .Sex and Gender

in British Community Studies' in D. Barker and S. Allen (eds.), *Sexual Divisions and Society. Process and Change* (London, 1976). See also H. Smith, 'Feminism and the Methodology of Women's History' in Carroll, *Women's History* and J. Mitchell, *Woman's Estate* (London, 1971).

PART I: THE LEGACY

Its echoing noises, its tremendous gloom
To her are all familiar and benign;
A child of toil, a daughter of the mine

> A.J. Munby 'Leonard and Elizabeth', unpublished MS poem

Winding: the Children's Employment Commission, 1842

Winding: *The Westminster Review*'s version, 1842

1 BELOW GROUND

The stalwart frame of robust man,
The sylph-like form of women frail,
The tender flesh of children wan
Come all within the mining pale
To work for ducals' grand regale.

A. Wilson 'Slaves of the Mine' in *Lays, Tales
and Folk Lore of the Mines* (Perth, 1944 edition).

The tradition of women working in coal mines had a profound effect
on attitudes towards their work at the surface or pit brow. Contemporaries simply confused the two, believing that anything under
the label of women's work at mines must be similar to the situation
described in the Children's Employment Commission of 1842. This
perpetuated a false link between very different types of work. As late
as the 1880s respected journals such as the *Lancet* could condemn this
'disgusting' work, making the basic mistake of assuming that women
still worked *in* pits when in fact they had been prohibited by law from
such work nearly fifty years earlier![1]
Even for those who knew slightly better, the legacy of the earlier
memories remained strong. Accounts of pit brow women invariably
began with descriptions of saturnine caverns. A mention of the picking
belts where women sorted coal from dirt was frequently prefaced by
an account of the better known belt and chain which had harnessed
women and children to their tubs of coal underground. Female surface
work was therefore portrayed as an anachronism, a sad vestige of the
barbaric days before the legislation of 1842.[2] The late-nineteenth-
century attempt to prohibit pit brow work was seen as the necessary
completion of a process begun many years earlier, a natural corollary
to an investigation which had revealed profoundly disturbing facts.
Such a social evil clearly ran counter to the feminine ideal and must be
completely blotted out. Until 1842 'civilised society' had remained
blissfully ignorant of women's work in mines. Fear of a repetition of
the complacency which had existed before Lord Ashley's shock
exposures of pit work meant that there must be no opportunity for
falling into a similar trap — being caught unawares again. Yet this does
not mean that those concerned individuals came any nearer to
understanding the nature of colliery communities, or even recognising

19

that it might be important to do so. It does however explain how people could busy themselves with enquiries into pit work which purported to be fulfilling a duty and moral obligation. In the 1840s the revelations of coal mining horrors were unfolded in the midst of economic depression and political unrest. In the wake of the anti-slavery campaign they produced striking parallels which the press eagerly seized upon.[3] By the 1880s a country steeped in imperial forays had developed a sense of mission at home, another belated catharsis. The new campaign to remove colliery women was also a concatenation of memories of 1842 and part of the continuing dilemma of the right of women to work.

Women had worked in coal mines for centuries, wives and daughters playing a vital role in the family economy, helping husbands and brothers to extract coal from easily accessible holes. The family organisation makes it difficult to obtain precise information about its origins or the way in which it adapted as coal mining techniques became more sophisticated. It is significant but frustrating to note that the Sub-Commissioners for the Children's Employment Commission did not recognise the value of questioning the background to the work which they so readily condemned. Nor are there any national statistics of female colliery labour prior to 1841. In fact the paucity of early sources means that we know far more about women ceasing to work underground than we do about how long and where they had worked in the first place. Descriptions of conditions must therefore remain largely conjectural. The earliest known reference to a woman working concerns an Emma Culhare (or Culhaxe) who lost her life at a lead mine in Derbyshire after a firedamp explosion in 1322.[4] Several cases are documented of women working in coal mines in the sixteenth century but they need to be treated with caution as sporadic references must not be confused with knowledge of regular work. There is however some evidence that women were working at Winlaton colliery in the north-east as early as 1587.[5] Further information about early employment can be gleaned from reports of colliery disasters and coroners' inquests.[6]

In the eighteenth century the employment of women was still part of a family concern, male members utilising the help of their female relatives wherever possible. Since the hiring and payment would be the responsibility of the male collier, women were not usually recorded in colliery accounts.[7] Their main task was to work as drawers. This involved pulling sledges or tubs along the pit floor or on planks from the coal face to the bottom of the shaft. (Drawers were known

as putters in Fifeshire and in Yorkshire they were called hurriers.
Terms varied from district to district and in the following pages
the terms peculiar to the district being discussed will be the ones used.)
Frequently working in wet, cramped conditions, the severity of the job could
be intensified by the degree of the incline of the roof which followed the
rise and dip of the seam. Age, strength, size, the weight of the load,
state of the atmosphere and demands of the collier could also make a
considerable difference. Drawers crawled along the floors harnessed to
their tubs by a belt of leather or rope. This passed around the waist
or shoulder and from it a chain passed between the legs and was hooked
on to the tub. Such a primitive form of haulage survived in certain areas
until the 1840s.[8]

Some districts appear to have employed female labour before but
not during the nineteenth century. Women had ceased to work in the
Northumberland-Durham coalfield by about 1780.[9] They may also
have worked in Shropshire coal pits — they had certainly been
employed in stone and iron pits there.[10] In Cumberland women's work
was actually more extensive and diversified before the nineteenth
century than it became later. Women worked as bearers, fillers, hookers
of baskets, cleaners and as horse drivers. Yet by 1841 such work was
unknown in all but one colliery there, due to the 'general odium it
excites'.[11] Women were not employed below ground in the coalfields
of Gloucestershire, North Somerset, Warwickshire, Leicestershire or
Staffordshire though in the southern part of the last county, they did
work on the surface as was the practice in North Wales. In Yorkshire
and Lancashire women worked below ground before and during the
nineteenth century. A story based on a true situation at a Lancashire
pit in the late eighteenth century describes how a female drawer did a
daily double turn (shift). *The Lancashire Collier-Girl*, written by Joseph
Budworth but published anonymously in the *Gentleman's Magazine*
(May 1795) was later reworked and printed as one of Hannah More's
cheap religious tracts — with a typically strong moral exhortation.[12]
After her father's death and financial troubles, Betty Hodson had to
work in the pit to rescue her family from the ignominy of the
workhouse. She eventually received her reward by gaining a place as an
under-servant in the household of the charitable Benevolus of
Hospitality Hall (in reality the coalowner William Bankes of Winstanley).
By 1798 her exemplary behaviour had earned her promotion to the
position of head cook.[13]

The work of Lancashire pitwomen was not however as widespread
or severe as that in Scotland. Women here worked mainly in the eastern

part of the country though there are scattered references to female work in Ayrshire and Lanarkshire prior to the nineteenth century. It was part of a system of slavery which had been imposed by an act of 1606, was reinforced in 1641 and lasted until 1799 since an early emancipation act of 1774 was virtually ineffective. Whole collier and salter families were bound in servitude to employers, lacking any real freedom. Originally designed to cope with a shortage of labour during the expansion of the coal and salt trade, this attempt to prevent owners appropriating miners meant binding families for life. It ensured that 'wives, daughters and sons went on from generation to generation under the system which was the family doom'.[14] Some women drew baskets of coal from the face to the pit bottom but the most arduous work was done by bearers who carried coal on their backs, climbing up steep, winding staircases to the pit hills.[15] Armed with a short stick and a candle held between their teeth they would work for eight or ten hours without a rest. The coal was carried in wicker creels or baskets with supporting straps which went around the forehead. 120 lb might be carried on a single journey over a distance of a hundred and fifty yards, followed by an ascent of about a hundred feet and a further twenty yards to the pit hill. This might be repeated twenty-four times in a day. The hewer who extracted the coal from the face generally engaged two bearers and perhaps shared a third 'fremit' (non-relative) with a fellow worker. Bearing had developed through the difficulty of working the edge seams but it had, unjustifiably, also spread to the neighbouring flat collieries. Some attempts were made to substitute windlasses but they were costly and the Sub-Commissioner finding the practice still in force in 1841 described it as 'unexampled in severity and most revolting in nature'.[16]

Bearers had been employed in South Pembrokeshire but by the turn of the century the system was obsolescent. Even in the seventeenth century some pits had boasted primitive windlasses known locally as a 'druke and beam'.[17] The 1842 report described women using windlasses above and below ground. The considerable depth of some pits meant that they were used to haul tubs up steep slopes, a number being fixed at convenient intervals on the incline of the vein. Women would turn the handles of these wooden rollers, the system sometimes being called 'pitching veins'. With some veins nearly upright, women might haul in one day about four hundred loads each weighing between one and a half and four cwt. They also helped with pouncing or boring when a new shaft was being sunk. Three women and two men would position themselves opposite each other and press the ends of two logs which

operated on a circular bore and acted as levers. They also drew coal
here and further east. In the Sirhowy district they were known as
dragger girls. Young Welsh girls were also door keepers and carriers of
tools.[18]

The fact that female pit work was unknown by 1840 in some areas
which had formerly employed women, suggests that it may have been
at its height before the nineteenth century. Added to the fragmentary
evidence of earlier employment and the accepted use of women as part
of the family economy in pre-industrial society, is the fact that though
modernisation increased some types of work for males (particularly
youths) it reduced opportunities for females below ground. The
introduction of horses and a few wheeled vehicles by the mid-eighteenth
century saw boys taking over haulage jobs. This meant that in the more
advanced pits drawers now had only to pull the coal down the passages
as far as the main roadways. It was then transferred to four-wheeled
trams running on wooden rails. These were pulled by horses and guided
by trammers or horse-drivers.[19] Apart from a few female horse-drivers
in the Cumberland pits, adults did not do this job which became the
prerogative of boys aged between fourteen and seventeen. Such a sexual
division of labour may have arisen because the work was envisaged as
part of the apprenticeship of the future miner. Since women did not
graduate to being hewers such a job would not have been seen as a
necessary stage in a training process. Possibly too a distinction was
perceived between the traditional haulage work performed by women,
rough and arduous but well-established, and the creation of a new job
which raised the question of choice and the suitability of employing
female labour. Perhaps there was also a feeling that while women might
be acceptable performing non-dangerous heavy work, there was a
difference between that and more hazardous activities. Present and
future mothers should not be unduly threatened. This job did not deal
with inanimate objects but with live beasts and a rudimentary
distinction might be drawn between drawing which required physical
strength, and horse-driving which demanded the control of animals and
the possibility of dealing with the unpredictable behaviour of powerful
creatures.[20]

From the mid-1770s the introduction of cast iron rails in place of
wooden ones lightened tasks further and meant a reduction in the
number of females.[21] Innovation was, however, expensive and rails
were only adopted gradually. All such changes were piecemeal and pits
with thin seams (for example many of those in the West Riding) or
little capital were slow to adapt.[22] Ultimately conditions were largely

determined by the finances, whims and concern of coalowners who enjoyed virtual immunity to external pressure. The process of modernisation reduced the proportion of jobs open to women and was the reverse of the trend in factory employment. In mining the expansion of the industry brought with it new opportunities for adult male colliers. The women were not threatening to replace the miners' skilled work nor were the females' jobs coveted by adult males, this work complementing rather than competing with men's jobs.[23] Only with the development of surface jobs did the situation alter radically, the women becoming rivals to the adult males.

The decline in female pit labour by the early nineteenth century coincided with an increased opportunity for work in other industries. In 1841 it was noticed that Yorkshire women did not work in the pits near the large towns of Sheffield and Leeds.[24] In East Lancashire there was no opportunity or encouragement to employ women as miners since they could get work in mills. When one collier who had moved from West Lancashire to Oldham took his wife underground he was forced to leave the area, the men threatening to leave if she remained.[25] By the 1840s there were four major areas where women worked in the pits: West Lancashire, Yorkshire (though not the extreme north or south-east of the coalfield), East Scotland (the Lothians, Clackmannan and Fifeshire) and South Wales (Pembrokeshire, Glamorgan and Monmouthshire). With the exception of Yorkshire this was to remain the pattern for surface work.

The first full occupational census which counted miners was taken in 1841. Coincidentally this was also the year when coalowners were asked to disclose the numbers they employed to the Children's Employment Commission. The census returns show only 118,233 employed in coalmining in England, Wales and Scotland. 2,350 of this number were female. Yet these figures are incomplete and misleading. Ambiguous instructions had resulted in a number of coal miners being omitted. A more realistic national figure would be closer to 150,000.[26] The census figures for women and girls were seriously deficient. They returned 767 Scottish female workers yet the Commission report shows 2,341 women and girls in East Scotland, 1,189 of them adults. Some of the omissions seem to have arisen from the non-inclusion of miners' wives who were in fact working. The census showed 1,321 English women and girls to have been employed yet just one part of the Yorkshire coalfield contained 388 female pit workers according to the Commission. And the Commissioners themselves admitted that their own figures were incomplete as a number of owners were reluctant to fill in their questionnaires. A reasonable estimate of the number of women and girls employed both in and at the top of coal mines would seem to be between 5,000 and 6,000 or about four per cent of the amended total figure.

The shifts in female employment cannot be computed accurately due to the lack of figures prior to 1841. In addition to the possibilities of new and alternative employment gradually reducing numbers in some areas, other factors may have influenced the regional distribution. The influence of Methodism in the north-east may have encouraged resistance to women working in the pits and helped promote the domestic ideology, though single women did continue to work in South Wales despite its strong commitment to nonconformity. The higher wages paid to miners in the Great Northern coalfield would have acted as a deterrent since miners would have been able to afford to engage older boys in place of females.[27] This helped encourage the idea of a man earning a family wage sufficient to keep his wife and children, a concept which was rapidly gaining ground and found ready acceptance in the north-east where miners were better organised than in other coalfields. The safety question may also have had some influence. Experiments to make mines safer were chiefly concentrated in this area although there were many disastrous explosions as deeper shafts were sunk. The South Shields Committee was set up in 1835 to investigate safety and openly condemned female pit labour. Meanwhile the rest of the country had higher rates of accidents from roof falls and gassy seams. This may have indirectly affected the perpetuation of female employment elsewhere. The likelihood of a high percentage of colliery widows and the presence of ailing miners suffering from unhealthy conditions, would have increased the need for women to work. Miners' wives in Scotland testified to the high degree of respiratory diseases caused by the breathing of impure air. A large number of these women were working because they had been widowed or had to support disabled husbands and a family.[28]

Therefore by the 1840s female colliery labour appears to have been declining slowly and to have become concentrated in more clearly defined areas. Meanwhile the coal industry was undergoing a phenomenal increase. By this time there were about 2,000 collieries though many individual pits remained small, frequently employing under thirty people. The increase was however threatening the traditional structure of the industry though a striking feature of the Children's Employment Commission is the extent to which coal mining had remained so closely bound to the family. This was in part a reflection of the solidarity and self-sufficiency of pit life. The very fact that female labour could have remained unheeded for centuries emphasises the way in which women were traditionally accepted as part of the family economy. It is also a reflection of the autonomous nature of colliery communities and the ignorance of the world beyond. Such a situation helps explain the full extent of the shock produced by the Commission's revelations.

By 1800 Britain was producing 80 per cent of the world's coal. Yet, though this coal was so renowned, those who worked it were unknown. The nature and isolation of the work secured its folk from outside interference. Physically out of sight, they were also conveniently out of mind. But there was more than physical separation isolating the male and female collier from other people. Admittedly this feature was important — for example, in the Welsh valleys — but colliery communities were also segregated socially. This could result in a mutual suspicion. A.J. Munby's wife Hannah, a Shropshire servant, visited the Wrekin one 'reckoning' Monday (the time when the colliers rested after their wages had been paid). Chatting to her friends, she commented on the blackbirds who were stealing nuts. The mining women immediately took offence and presumed that this was a personal insult. Hannah was upset — 'they reckon'd we thoughten they are fules' — and all her subsequent attempts to be friendly were rebuffed.[29]

Miners were regarded as an outcast group, not conforming to the habits of 'respectable' society. Critics adopted the 'savage' metaphor constantly drawing comparisons with 'civilised' behaviour. Sheer ignorance of their lives lays behind much of this. When Cumming Bruce, a Scots MP, made a plea on behalf of the women excluded from pit work by the 1842 legislation, he explained that mining folk were

> looked on as a separate race, they seldom inter-marry with other labouring classes, the nature of their employment prevents such intercourse.[30]

Separation was enhanced by the perpetuation of pre-industrial organisation and customs. Family employment persisted whenever possible and shift work meant unsociable hours. The colliery worker was generally only seen leaving work when he or she would be dirty. Their clothes, or rather, the lack of them, caused further uneasiness. Much of the later outrage against pit brow woman emanated from disgust at the trousers worn by women in the Wigan district. Daily toil in the bowels of the earth suggested eschatological images in art and fiction. Their infernal world produced a plethora of Dantean fantasies. It provided the setting for John Martin's illustrations of *Paradise Lost* while surrealistic interpretations culminated in Emile Zola's novel *Germinal*.[31] The language used by visitors to the coal mine was highly charged with Romantic overtones. One American who saw the Lancashire pit brow women at work described them as

> weird swarthy creatures, figures of women, half clad in man's and half in women's attire, plunging here and there, as if engaged in some bedlamish saturnalis. It is one of the most picturesque scenes of labour I ever beheld, and it has the element of wild and awful grandeur in it.[32]

The development of a community around the pit itself further enhanced this separation — rows of colliery houses, perhaps a truck shop and the all-pervasive influence of the management. Meanwhile the coalowner's entrenched position in Parliament helped to keep his empire inviolate. Miners were also traditionally nomadic and, as with navvies and canal boatmen, their peripatetic lifestyle and work habits were causing increasing uneasiness amongst those with property to protect.[33] There were worries that the rapidly expanding coalmining force might in some way instigate social and political upheaval. Thus whilst they might be ridiculed for what *Knight's Magazine* called their 'primitive simplicity', they were only to be integrated into the wider community on certain terms.[34] In other words they must be prepared to accept clearly defined standards of behaviour and respectability. The constant proximity to death distanced them even further from more mundane occupations and produced some grudging respect for their fearlessness combined with the knowledge that their corresponding camaraderie and interdependence within the community distanced them still further from the world outside. The encroachment of change seems to have produced a reinforcing of the traditional image of exclusiveness and a retreat into a subculture with its own heroes and forms of self-celebration.[35] The miner worked in the pits as a result of family background and early training. A marked hierarchy of skills and a stress on learning from a young age were an essential part of an industry which needed such protection against inexperience and outsiders. Aware of the problems of depressed workers in other industries and of the necessity of being trained to appreciate potential danger, the early miners' unions deliberately extended an image of craft pride and mutuality. The symbiotic relationship between the mine and all those who depended on it defied interference and made it extremely difficult to penetrate from outside.

The Children's Employment Commission temporarily exposed this world. It uncovered not just a self-contained working community which outsiders found difficult to comprehend though easy to condemn, but one in which females worked indistinguishably from males. Moreover, they were employed in what was traditionally portrayed as the most masculine of domains, as far removed from the Victorian drawing room as could be imagined.

The investigation was made possible by a number of developments. The rapid increase in the size and importance of the industry meant that sooner or later some publicity would be forced upon it. Pit explosions received coverage in the illustrated newspapers which were becoming so popular. The 1841 census and early trades union activity began to draw more attention to the coalfields. Meanwhile Whig legislation was seeking to regulate the hours of work for children. The 1833 Factory Act proved to be the spring-board for further intervention. In 1837 Nassau Senior wrote to the President of the Board of Trade explaining that

> the factory act, by driving many children into other employment makes the expediency of adopting a general system of education for all children even more urgent than it was before.[36]

He related the case of a small boy working in a coal mine who, when questioned, had explained that he was working there because he was not old enough to work in a factory. H.S. Tremenheere's report on elementary education in Wales (1840) drew attention to backward conditions in the mining areas.[37] Victorian inquisitiveness therefore began to penetrate the industry. Yet in spite of the percolation of information, details would have to be spelt out before any positive action would be deemed necessary. The prospect of comprehensive legislation for coalmining was a daunting one. The huge variety of concerns, the power of the owners and the difficulty of exercising control over underground operations precluded easy intervention. The man who undertook to spell out the details of colliery work possessed few practical qualifications for the task. Anthony Ashley Cooper was a southerner from an influential landed family and Tory MP for the county of Dorset.[38] A philanthropist dedicated to the plight of the downtrodden, he saw himself primarily as the champion of children. His leadership of the Ten Hour Movement was fortuitous — there had been nobody else available after Sadler's death. Motivated by an unwavering evangelical sense of mission, Ashley had placed an almost deterministic trust in God's will which goes a long way towards explaining his crusading zeal and desire to help the less fortunate.

His statements such as 'my business lies in the gutter and I have not the least desire to get out of it' reflected his desire to further rather than destroy social harmony.[39] Possessing a deep-rooted belief in the existing structure of society he was convinced that the rich man's survival might best be ensured by helping the poor. Thus he maintained that 'distinction is of God's appointment'.[40]

When on 4 August 1840 he requested an enquiry into the condition of children in employment (including those working in mines and collieries), Ashley had never been underground himself.[41] Moreover the eventual size and implications of the enquiry were not evident from his initial demand. Although likely candidates to receive his sympathy, colliery children were not singled out for special treatment. The motion to establish a Children's Employment Commission sought to bring a number of industries under the umbrella of limited protection. The list was long and mining was placed eighth, following accounts of the exploitation of children in industries such as tobacco manufacture and framework knitting. The extension was a logical one. As Ashley explained,

I had long been taunted with narrow and exclusive attention to the children in factories alone. I was told that there were other cases out of the factories equally grievous, and far more numerous that just as much deserved attention; and I was told, too, that I was unjust in my denouncement of the one and my omission of the other.[42]

His description of colliery labour was based on E.C. Tufnell's account of conditions in Lancashire which had been included in the first report on the Employment of Children in Factories (1833). Tufnell claimed that

the hardest labour, in the worst room, in the worst conducted factory, is less hard, less cruel, and less demoralising than the labour of the best of coal mines.[43]

This was now to be put to the test. The House of Commons could not easily refuse a mere request for an enquiry and the motion was granted. Tufnell had mentioned that girls worked and the Commission was instructed to examine the work of both boys and girls. At this stage no mention was made of adult women.

Several individuals had in fact already raised the question of women's work but their views had not been widely broadcast. The emancipation from slavery in Scotland had presented an opportunity for some limited publicity. The 9th Earl of Dundonald had set an example by prohibiting bearers from his Culross pits in 1790.[44] He denounced the 'barbarous and ultimately expensive method of converting the colliers' wives and daughters into beasts of burthen', linking the system to the 'present scarcity and irregular mutinous and disorderly conduct of Scottish colliers'. He predicted that prohibition would reduce the extravagant wages earned by colliers as well as benefiting domestic life. Robert Bald, a civil engineer and mineral surveyor at Alloa, published in 1808 'An Inquiry into the condition of those women who carry coals underground in Scotland, known by the name of Bearers'. He included the words of one old woman who told him 'O Sir, this is sore, sore work. I wish to God, the first woman who tried to bear coals had broken her back and none would have tried it again'.[45] Bald's indictment still exonerated the masters from any blame though at least it did persuade the Earl of Mar to ban female bearers at the Alloa coal company. Opposition from miners did however force a resumption of the work for all except married women.

Elsewhere conditions were not deemed sufficiently opprobrious to merit interference. The Reverend John Evans travelling through Pembrokeshire in 1803 noticed some women coal bearers but did not attack the practice.[46] The first condemnation of the work in England appears to have been made by the writer Richard Ayton who visited the William pit at Whitehaven in 1813.[47] His account of women working typifies a layman's horror at a totally alien experience. Ayton's remarks were all the more forceful because he prefaced his account with an explanation that the pit was reputed to be 'the best planned work of its kind and the most complete in all its conveniences of any in the Kingdom'. Predictably the subterranean surroundings gave vent to Romantic imagery. It was a place where

> A dreariness pervades. . .one felt as if beyond the bounds allotted to man or any living being, and transported to some hideous region unbles't by every charm that cheers and adorns the habitable world.

Horrified at the lack of sanitary arrangements, the scanty clothing and the blackness, his imagination took flight. He saw girls driving horses

ragged and beastly in their appearance and with a shameless
indecency in their behaviour, which, awe-struck as one was by the
gloom and loneliness around one, had something quite frightful in it,
and gave the place the character of a hell.

He was surprised by their mirth since the work made 'not the slightest
account of human life in its calculations'. He conjured up scenes of
'most bestial debauchery' and even incest. But it was the effect on
femininity which above all affronted him. Such women he felt

lose every quality that is graceful in women, and become a set of
coarse, licentious wretches, scorning all kinds of restraint, and
yielding themselves up, with shameless audacity to the most
detestable sensuality,

Ayton's sentiments of lugubrious gloom expressed the extremity of
contemporary fears yet in a milder form were to continue to pervade
much of the reasoning behind the pit brow agitation of the 1880s.
He repeated that such 'dismal dungeons' were not fit places for women
and children. His fears were summed up in his statement that

The estimation in which women are held is one test of the
civilisation of a people; and it is somewhat scandalous in a country
of gallant men, to see them sacrificed to the rough drudgery of coal
mines.

In 1795 the contribution of the Lancashire collier girl had been viewed
rather differently. Whereas it was appreciated that her work did
eventually have a debilitating effect, it had not been condemned on
moral grounds. Her contribution had been valued. The miners not only
allowed the 'hapless female to sleep her hour in rest and safety, but
return unsullied to the world'. She was 'both beloved and protected'
by the men and her work had evidently not disqualified her from
adapting to domestic service. Yet by the 1840s it was the potentially
destructive effect of colliery work on the acquisition of these very
domestic skills which was foremost in the minds of those who, faced
with the widespread employment of women in unskilled wage labour,
sought to remove them from underground and, in later years, from
surface work.[48]
Ayton's attack helped persuade the owner of the William pit to stop
recruiting women miners after about 1827. Beyond this there was little

immediate response. The attack had been made in an esoteric volume of travels and, notwithstanding the popularity of topographical tours, its influence was limited. Pressure was however beginning to emerge from a new direction. Some miners were now voicing opposition to female colliery work. In 1841 for example, Barnsley colliers voted for a resolution which stated that 'the employment of girls in pits is highly injurious to their morals; that it is not proper work for females, and that it is a scandalous practice'.[49] Such sentiments were to become commonplace during the later pit brow agitation. At this stage however the miners were not yet organised in a union powerful enough to express their views collectively and forcefully. Their attitudes towards female employment in the pits were complex and at times appeared contradictory. Moreover the Commission was essentially an enquiry 'from above'. However, the aftermath of the 1842 act was to give the miners an unprecedented opportunity to see how easily legislation might be abused by those in control of their destinies.

Notes

1. *Lancet*, 9 January 1886.

2. A letter in the *Wigan Observer*, 8 June 1867, deplored the fact that women still worked *at* coal mines and urged that this female slavery which was 'a relic of barbarism' be removed. John Plummer (see Ch.4) described pit brow work in the 1860s as one of 'the few remaining links by which our present civilization is united to a barbaric past'. *Once A Week*, XI (1864), p.280.

3. For example, *Halifax Guardian*, 14 May 1842; *Northern Star*, 21, 28 May 1842. See Ch.2.

4. I. Pinchbeck, *Women Workers and the Industrial Revolution* (London, 1969), p.240.

5. R.L. Galloway, *Annals of Coal Mining and the Coal Trade*, I (Newton Abbot, 1971), p.11. The Winlaton collieries had been suffering from labour shortages and had introduced some Scottish miners and women.

6. For example, see F.A. Bailey, 'Coroners' Inquests held at the manor of Prescot 1746-1749', *Transactions of the Historic Society of Lancashire and Cheshire*, 86 (1934), p.26.

7. There were some exceptions. See J.U. Nef, *The Rise of the British Coal Industry*, 11 (London, 1966), p.432 and Sir A.M. Bryan, *Health and Safety in Mines* (Letchworth, 1975), p.32.

8. *Reynolds's Political Instructor*, 9 March 1850.

9. E. Welbourne, *The Miners of Northumberland and Durham* (Cambridge, 1924), p.128; T. Wilson, *The Pitman's Pay and other Poems* (Gateshead, 1843), p.XII; *Newcastle Weekly Chronicle*, 9 May 1874. Parliamentary Papers (henceforth PP) 1866, XIV, p.341, qu. 10120.

10. B. Trinder, *The Industrial Revolution in Shropshire* (Chichester, 1973), pp.352-4; Munby MS, Wren Library, Trinity College, Cambridge University, Visits to Hannah, 1891, XIV, p.79. Evidence from a Black Country informant born in c.1909: 'Now I remember as a little lad two women who were very old

then, so this is bringing them back to be born in the 1830s and to have been little children in the 1840s. Now both these women worked down the pit. And I remember the harness of one of the women who used to crawl on all fours with her brother, dragging tubs along; and the harness used to hang on the wall.' Interviewed 17 April 1970 by Roy Palmer to whom I am grateful for the information.

11. T.S. Ashton and J.S. Sykes, *The Coal Industry in the Eighteenth Century* (Manchester, 1929), p.22; O. Wood, 'A Cumberland Colliery during the Napoleonic Wars', *Economica*, 21 (1954), pp.255, 261. PP 1842, XVI, no.1, p.875; no.314, pp.302, 306.

12. 'The Lancashire Collier-Girl. A True Story', *Gentleman's Magazine* (March 1975), pp.197-9. Joseph Budworth (1758-1815) was a minor poet and writer and a native of Lancashire who lived for many years at Upholland. The story was reprinted in 1797. See also *Gentleman's Magazine* (April 1795), p.336 (June 1795), p.486 (December 1798), p.1030. It sold for 1d as a cheap tract.

13. She was left £50 in Bankes's will in 1800. P.E.H. Hair, 'The Lancashire Collier Girl 1795', *Transactions of the Historic Society of Lancashire and Cheshire*, 120 (1968). See the Appendix for family reconstitution. The pit has been identified as Halliwell's Engine pit. D. Anderson, *The Orrell Coalfield* (Buxton, 1975), p.133.

14. From Lord Cockburn's memoirs quoted in NCB publication *A Short History of the Scottish Coal Mining Industry* (Edinburgh, 1958), p.58; B.F. Duckham, 'Serfdom in Eighteenth Century Scotland', *History*, XLIV (1969); Anon., 'Slavery in Modern Scotland', *Edinburgh Review*, 189 (1899), pp.119-48.

15. Ashton and Sykes, *Coal Industry*, p.24; R. Bald, *A General View of the Coal Trade of Scotland* (Edinburgh, 1808), p.128.

16. PP 1842, XV, p.128. In parts of India where coal mining remained a family occupation, women were still working as bearers as recently as 1940. One of the methods of payment was based on the number of baskets of coal they carried. B.R. Seth, *Labour in the Indian Coal Industry* (Bombay, 1940), p.130.

17. PP 1842, XVII, pp.573-80. For the eighteenth-century employment of women at the Moreton, Begelly and Ridgeway collieries see Picton Castle collection 4076, National Library of Wales, also disbursements of the Spence Colby papers 1138, NLW, for Hook colliery.

18. O. Jones, *The Early Days of Sirhowy and Tredegar* (Risca, 1975), pp.35-6; PP 1842, XVII, for Jones's and Franks's reports on Wales.

19. T. Ridd, 'Truck, Trappers and Trammers' in S. Williams, *Glamorgan Historian*, III (Barry, 1966), pp.138-44

20. PP 1843, XX, pp.165-82, 194 for examples of males being in charge of horses in agriculture even though females performed extremely arduous field work. See also G. Ewart Evans, *The Horse in the Furrow* (London, 1960); P. Frank, 'Women's Work in the Yorkshire Inshore Fishing Industry', *Oral History*, 4, no.1 (1976), p.67. I am grateful to Peter Frank for discussion on this topic.

21. Halls's introduction of light malleable iron edge rails helped to improve haulage as did the use of flanged wheels. The adoption of rails most probably reduced the number of young children pushing vehicles − by 1841 the areas with most rails had the lowest proportions of children. This could however have been compensated by the new job of trapping (controlling the opening of air doors as a result of Buddles's compound system of mine ventilation introduced in 1810). See A.R. Griffin, *Coalmining* (London, 1971).

22. Corves (baskets) were still in use at the end of the 1860s at Birket Bank, Wigan. Munby MS, Notebook IV, 1869.

23. Only very rarely did women become hewers and extract coal themselves.

In such cases a shortage of male labour, rather than promotion, appears to have been the reason.

24. PP 1842, XVII, p.3.

25. PP 1842, XVI, pp.24, 294. See a petition from 1,062 Oldham miners and inhabitants presented in 1842. Hansard LXIII, House of Lords, 6 May 1842, p.126. Resistance to women working in East Lancashire persisted in the early twentieth century. See Lancashire and Cheshire Joint District Committee, 'Arbitration on the Scale of Minimum Wages for Females' (NUM Bolton, 1919), p.9. In Belgium women were ceasing to work in the Liège pits as alternative employment opportunities developed in the area.

26. The term 'coal miner' had not been clearly defined in the census. See P.E.H. Hair, 'The Social History of the British Coalminer', D.Phil. thesis, Oxford University, 1955, pp.2-3. This estimates that out of a total amended number of about 5,000 females, about two-thirds worked in Scotland, one-fifth in Lancashire and another fifth in Yorkshire. PP 1842, XVI, pp.166, 210. Appendix B, pp.379-81. See Ch.2, note 9.

27. Hair claims that average wages for hewers in the early nineteenth century were slightly lower than in the north-east where they were about 3/9d a day by 1841. Hair, 'Social History', p.363.

28. P.E.H. Hair, 'Mortality from violence in British Coal Mines 1800-1850', *Economic History Review*, 2nd series, no.21 (1968); J. Mather, *The Coal Mines, their dangers and means of safety and the report of the South Shields Committee* (London, 1868). The results were collated by 1839 and the first report was published in 1843.

29. Munby MS 98, Hannah's Diary, 31 August 1863.

30. Hansard LXIX, House of Commons, 16 May 1843, p.34. The Newcastle Glass-makers excluded from membership of their Friendly Society in 1800 'persons that are infamous, of ill character, quarrelsome, or disorderly', pitmen, colliers, sinkers and watermen. Quoted in E.P. Thompson, *The Making of the English Working Class* (London, 1968), p.458.

31. See for example 'The Hollow Deep of Hell' (1826) in F. Klingender, *Art and the Industrial Revolution* (London, 1968) and illustration 53.

32. *Wigan Observer*, 12 September 1891.

33. See H. Hanson, *The Canal Boatmen 1760-1914* (Manchester, 1975); T. Coleman, *The Railway Navvies* (London, 1968). In *Capital*, Marx discussed miners under the heading 'The Nomadic Population'.

34. *Knight's Magazine*, 1, no.2 (1835), p.300.

35. See R. Colls, *The Colliers' Rant* (London, 1977), p.54; J. Holland, *The History and Description of Fossil Fuel* (London, 1968), pp.287-8, 291.

36. N.W. Senior, *Letters on the Factory Act as it affects the Cotton Manufacture* (London, 1837), p.23. W.E. Hickson repeated this – PP 1840, XXIV, pp.48-50. See also PP 1842, XVI, no.268, p.292, XVII H10.

37. PP 1840, XL.

38. For details of Anthony Ashley Cooper, see E. Hodder, *The Life and Work of the Seventh Earl of Shaftesbury* (3 vols., London, 1886); G. Battiscombe, *Shaftesbury* (London, 1974); G. Best, *Shaftesbury* (London, 1964); and G.B.A.M. Finlayson, 'Shaftesbury' in P. Hollis (ed.), *Pressure from Without in Early Victorian England* (London, 1974).

39. See his anonymous article on 'Infant Labour' in *Quarterly Review*, CXXXIII (1840), p.173.

40. The Earl of Shaftesbury. Broadlands Archives. Royal Commission on Historical Manuscripts SHA/PD/2. Diary 1, 20 May 1841; Diary 8, 2 March 1867.

41. He did go underground in 1842. Hansard LV, House of Commons, 4 August 1840, p.261. *Mirror of Parliament*, 1840, pp.5203-11.

42. *Mirror of Parliament*, p.5203.
43. PP 1833, XX, p.82.
44. A. Cochrane, *A Description of the Estate and Abbey of Culross* (Edinburgh, 1793). Sir John Clark II had erected a horse gin at Loanhead in the 1720s but it was unpopular since part of the colliers' earnings had been used to pay for it.
45. Bald, *Coal Trade*, p.142.
46. Rev. J. Evans, *Letters written during a Tour through South Wales in 1803* (London, 1804), p.276.
47. R. Ayton, *A Voyage round Great Britain in the Summer of 1813* (London, 1814), pp.152-60. Another visitor to a Whitehaven pit saw girls at work driving horses. He too commented on the sepulchral effects but added that 'one may reasonably claim a right to be imaginative on such an occasion'. Sir G. Head, *A Home Tour through the manufacturing districts of England in the Summer of 1835* (London, 1965), p.408.
48. *Gentleman's Magazine* (March 1895), p.199.
49. PP 1842, XVI, p.204. Galloway, *Annals of Coal Mining*, 11, p.152. Scottish miners were also attempting to exclude women.

2 EXPOSITION, EXCLUSION AND EVASION

My name's Polly Parker, I come o'er from Worsley
My father and mother work in the coal mine.
Our family's large, we have got seven children
So I am obliged to work in the same mine.
As this is my fortune, I know you'll feel sorry
That in such employment my days I shall pass
I keep up my spirits, I sing and look merry,
Although I am but a poor collier lass.

By the greatest of dangers each day I'm surrounded;
I hang in the air by a rope or a chain.
The mine may fall in, I may be killed or wounded,
May perish by damp or the fire of the train.
And what would you do if it weren't for our labour?
In wretched starvation your days you would pass,
While we could provide you with life's greatest blessing —
Then do not despise the poor collier lass.

> The 'Collier Lass', verses 1 and 2. Broadside printed
> by Harkness of Preston, quoted in R. Palmer,
> *Poverty Knock* (Cambridge, 1974), p.44.

The Children's Employment Commission came into existence on
20 October 1840 headed by a central Board of four Commissioners.
By March of the following year a team of twenty Sub-Commissioners
had been recruited. Instructions required them to

> look into the employment and condition of all Children of the
> poorer classes, not under the protection of the Factories Regulation
> Act who are employed in any description of mining and
> manufacturing labour whatsoever in which they work together in
> numbers.[1]

The first undertaking was to be an examination of children's work in
mines and collieries. This was soon extended to include 'Young
Persons' (boys and girls aged between thirteen and eighteen). Advice
was given about the collection and collation of evidence but none of
the terms of reference specified an investigation of the work of adult

females. The Sub-Commissioners must therefore have been sufficiently horrified by the women's conditions to have included them in their reports on their own initiative. Those who visited areas where adult females worked were shocked by their employment and all, without dissent, condemned the practice.

Thus that misnomer, the *Children's* Employment Commission, examined far more than its name implied. And total female exclusion from the pits became the *first* clause of the Mines and Collieries bill. The results of the enquiry covered four volumes (two of evidence and two general summaries, one of which considered moral and educational aspects of the work and was not published until 1843).[2] Unlike some commissions which prescribed possible solutions (for example the enquiry into Handloom Weavers' plight), this commission was restricted to describing conditions. It could then be used as a basis for deciding what changes might be needed. The task facing the Sub-Commissioners was nevertheless a daunting one. The speed with which investigations were made is impressive yet raises doubts about their thoroughness.[3] Imbued with middle-class notions of respectability, attacks on morals were to some extent the product of an ignorance of a different lifestyle and a readiness to condemn anything which deviated from the familiar pattern of conformity. Yet this was true of all such undertakings and was also to prove a problem for the less formal examinations of pit brow work.[4] Such scrutiny inevitably imposed high standards. A petition from Newbattle colliery, Scotland attacked the errors and 'falsehoods, exaggerations and antipathies' of the reports and claimed that instead of comparing miners with other workers 'we have been compared with perfection itself, consequently we have been found wanting'.[5]

Economic pressure and the demands of coalowners were underestimated, female employment being readily attributed to miners' laziness. The backgrounds and diligence of the Sub-Commissioners did however vary. Robert Franks who reported on East Scotland and parts of South Wales appears to have been the most thorough in his coverage of female work and since, in the eyes of owners like the Marquis of Londonderry, this was synonymous with unwarranted interference, he was also the most criticised.[6] Insinuation into local communities without much disruption was not easy yet was imperative. One Sub-Commissioner Scriven found his arrival in the Bradford-Halifax area so little understood that he donned flannel trousers and clogs before going underground. He visited nearly two hundred pits, descended seventy and conducted some interviews in public houses. His predecessor Wood had taken pits at random and then privately examined every child and sometimes every adult working there. Symons, the third of the reporters for Yorkshire, used local people to help him. One old Barnsley resident questioned five female pit workers for him. He also acted on the advice offered by the Board and used magistrates and clergy and even tried performing the work himself.[7]

Following the precedent set by the Poor Law Commission, evidence was not taken on oath. This made interviews less formal but inevitably raises some questions of reliability. Not only interpretations but factual answers to the same question could vary dramatically from person to person. Difficulties arose, not so much from a desire to deceive (as Londonderry would believe), as from bewilderment and a natural caution. It must have been an intimidating experience, especially for children, and colliery officials were sometimes nearby. The reports stressed their abysmal ignorance though this may be attributed not so much to stupidity as to local dialects, nerves and the young age of many informants. Lack of technical knowledge (not helped by the fact that there was as yet no standardisation of weights and measures) and lack of time in which to check on details, exacerbated the difficulties. Co-operation was hindered by the coalowners' suspicion. Moreover the Sub-Commissioners do not appear to have been particularly disturbed by opportunities for briefing employees prior to interviews.[8] Although a circular letter urging co-operation was distributed to all employers, the answers to the queries and requests for statistics were very disappointing.[9]

Table 2.1: Proportion of Females to Males in Female Employing Districts[10]

District	Adults		13-18		Under 13	
	Male	Female	Male	Female	Male	Female
Yorkshire	1,000	22	352	36	246	41
Lancashire	1,000	86	352	79	195	27
Midlothians	1,000	333	367	184	131	52
East Lothians	1,000	338	332	296	164	103
West Lothians	1,000	192	289	154	180	109
Stirling	1,000	228	283	129	184	107
Clackmannan	1,000	202	246	213	142	87
Fifeshire	1,000	184	243	109	100	34
Glamorgan	1,000	19	239	12	157	12
Pembrokeshire	1,000	424	366	19	196	19

The information that was provided showed a varying ratio of male to female workers in the major areas of female employment. Work began at a young age — in Kennedy's Lancashire area two-thirds of the 828 boys and girls started work before they were nine and in some cases children were employed as early as six years of age.[11] In Wales there were five-year-old door keepers — one girl at Dowlais recounted how she used to be carried to work. At Hirwaun miners could get an extra allowance for taking down a young girl. Franks was told that Scottish girls traditionally began working younger than boys because they reached an understanding of their duties earlier. Some worked for many years — Margaret Winstanley had been down the pits for over fourteen years yet she was only twenty four. In the West Lothians there was a fifty-year-old woman hewer and another woman had continued bearing coal until she was sixty-six. A number of widows in Scotland worked until their children were old enough to replace them.[12] Hours were long — frequently at least twelve hours daily — and night work was common. There were discrepancies in the information — Scottish owners claimed that women worked between eight and ten hours yet Franks found instances of fifteen to sixteen and occasionally eighteen hours continuous employment.[13] Though most women were young and single or colliery widows, there were still many married women and, like Nell Carter, the heroine of Mrs Tonna's story *Forsaken Homes* (1843), they returned to work very soon after the birth of their children.[14] Drawing was done in low, cramped and damp spaces. There were cases of deformed spines and swollen legs and those who pushed trams from behind (known as thrutchers) complained of tiredness and a listless feeling. The lack of fresh air gave them constant headaches.[15] Although the relationship between health and work was not seriously explored, some of the Sub-Commissioners believed it to be healthier than manufacturing work. However, surgeons connected with collieries tended to endorse owners' favourable opinions whereas those who could afford to be more critical, did stress the evil effects, particularly for growing girls.[16] As with pit brow investigations, physical dangers involved the risk of accidents as well as health hazards. Work below ground was dangerous for all. The absence of coroners in Scotland made the system of investigating deaths there particularly haphazard though elsewhere too records were not yet very efficient.

In many parts of Lancashire and Yorkshire drawers or hurriers were still working in unrailed roads. Scriven interviewed seven girls at Tinkers' Day Hole pit where they all wore the belt and chain and pulled tubs along the pit floor. Drawing uphill was particularly difficult.[17]

Yorkshire females hurried an average of twenty to twenty-four corves over distances of about two hundred yards each way. Some Scottish strappers drew hutchies (oblong square-sided boxes with four wheels) but where there were no rails they pulled slypes (wooden-framed boxes, curved and tipped with iron). Female pumpers found their work places so wet that they had to be relieved every six hours. Others carried buckets of water (leaders) or helped rede (clean) the roadways at night. Coal-bearing remained barbarous. Six-year-old Margaret Leveston performed between ten and fourteen rakes (one rake was the complete journey from the surface to the face and back) daily.[18] A seventeen-year-old girl might do thirty rakes a day carrying at least two cwt on her back. In Pembrokeshire girls might begin separating coal from culm on the surface but by the age of twelve would graduate to windlass work below ground, a job which men refused to do as they apparently found it too hard![19]

Most female workers were hired by the colliers and paid by them though a small number had their own contracts and so were paid by the company. By 1842 bearers received about 1/- a day or 12/- in a fortnight of eleven working days. Scottish drawers or putters earned 1/- to 1/3d daily and supplied their own oil. In England rates were a little higher — 1/6d to 1/8d daily was usual though it was very rare for a woman to receive over 10/- a week.[20] Such rates reflected a distinct improvement from the late eighteenth century, were higher than payment for agricultural work and commensurate with the rates being paid for woman's surface work in the second half of the century. Yet they did fluctuate tremendously and the rates for girls were low. Since the hewers who engaged them were generally fathers, brothers or husbands they would not have seen themselves as independent wage earners but as contributors to the family wage.[21]

The moral implications of the work were however to have familiar echoes in the 1880s. The Sub-Commissioners were shocked when they saw how little the women wore — particularly in Yorkshire where in the very hot and cramped atmosphere they sometimes worked naked to the waist. It was the ragged state of one girl's trousers which prompted Symons's claim that 'no brothel can beat it'.[22] However, girls frequently worked for close relatives and could be protected by them. The industry was far more family-oriented than it became later. In Scotland it was actually claimed that wives were chosen for their strength, hence the saying 'she is like the collier's daughter, better than she is bonny'.[23] Many girls claimed that the men respected them, though even if this were not the case, they might not have dared admit otherwise. A number of colliers did hint at personal knowledge of 'immorality' below ground although on the whole claims seem to have been based more on hearsay than on actual evidence.[24] Symons's statement that coal mining was a 'nursery for juvenile vice' seems to require some modification and factual evidence was much weaker than that given to the *Commission du Travail* which investigated women's work below ground in Belgium in the 1880s.[25] Physical punishment did take place though it is interesting to note that those who were flogged were generally employed by non-relatives. Selina Ambler declared that boys never dared to touch her because her brother would 'plump' them.[26]

Much of the evidence about male and female relationships in the pit was based on accounts from local gentlemen who had some limited knowledge of miners but who were also eager to fulminate against their unorthodox lifestyles though not necessarily prepared to do anything to remove the ignorance which they deplored. Tales were relayed of the lack of religious training – one girl stated that Jesus was Adam's son. However, not only were informants often very young but the enquiry was obviously going to concentrate on the more disturbing information it received. Anyway, children in other industries were no different – a young mill worker told Symons that Jesus came to earth in order to commit sin.[27] For pit workers Sunday was the one day of freedom, rest and light and chapels, churches and schools might be some distance away. Informants may also have felt that they were expected to say they went to school and in so doing only betrayed their ignorance when questioned further. There was a tendency to attribute ignorance to parents' greed for money. Yet teaching was frequently of a low standard and even those who attended classes were not very well informed. Mary Reed went to Sunday School yet told Franks, 'The man in the sky made me, but I do not know who he is: never heard of Jesus Christ.'[28] Of eighty-six females at eighty Yorkshire collieries, twenty-four specifically stated that they could write their names yet Symons found 'in nineteen out of every twenty instances the mind of the child is as much uninformed even after a couple of years tuition as before it went to school'.[29] Yet formal education must have seemed of little relevance to these girls. Local schools did not provide an appropriate training for the exigencies of life in the pit. Only experience could teach about the dangers below ground. Nor would it help in the rearing of children or provide a vehicle by which they might easily alter their pattern of life.

Coalowners exonerated themselves from any real responsibility for educating their workforce. There were a few exceptions — for example the Crawfords (Haigh), Evans (Haydock) and Guests (Dowlais), but most of the tabular returns on literacy were highly inflated. Attempts to educate the workforce only really developed from the mid-1840s and were motivated by the unease generated by trades union activity and, in particular, the miners' strike of 1844. Disturbed also by the educative influence of Chartism and its formidable autodidactic impulse, colliery day schools were a response of the 'if you can't beat 'em join 'em' variety. They sought to inculcate deference and obedience from an early age. They also served to combat physical as well as political danger — a workforce with a rudimentary standard of literacy was increasingly important — particularly with the spread of printed safety rules.[30]

Prior to 1842 the colliery owner was conveniently oblivious of his workforce. His world was so far removed from the pit that ignorance of conditions was hardly surprising. At Norwood Green the coal master Emmett knew so little about his pits that he readily admitted to having no idea about the possible ill effects on females.[31] A *Punch* cartoon by John Leech in 1843 depicted a rich owner surrounded by wealth, relaxing with a drink. Below him was a caricature of a pit with wretched children in baskets, girls pushing tubs and women with babies. These infernal creatures who were 'not intended for the light of day' were compared with the 'very pleasing picture of aristocratic ease'.[32] Some coalowners admitted that they preferred girls as they found them cheaper, less ambitious and more reliable than boys.

The majority of the women and girls who actually expressed opinions about the work were resolutely opposed to it.[33] Their reactions were markedly different from those of the pit brow lasses. Women who worked in the pits emphasised that the work was hard, tiring and frequently frightening. Yet they also knew that there were few alternatives. Anyway familiarity had produced a degree of resignation. In *Germinal* Zola explained that Catherine, a haulage worker in the Montsou pits, never complained

> for familiarity had brought apathy, and you would have thought that being doubled up like that was part of the normal course of human suffering.[34]

In Yorkshire fifteen out of fifty-four women and girls claimed that they did not like the work but badly needed employment which was now being threatened. When Mary Ann Watson of Flockton heard that exclusion was imminent she was so 'overpowered by fear' that she could not complete her evidence.[35] The Sub-Commissioners were convinced of the need to act. Franks, in words reminiscent of Tufnell, asserted that the hardest daylight work was infinitely superior to the best colliery work.[36] It was the potential danger to the domestic ideology which he and his colleagues found most disturbing. Worried about the lack of knowledge of domestic economy Kennedy feared that 'a large portion of the evils that prevail in the class of colliers' could be attributed to the women being absent from their homes. Certainly colliers' wives did face special problems — constant washing of filthy pit clothes, the exigencies of shift work and in certain areas, they might be circumscribed still further by the presence of truck shops. The proposed remedy was to remove the women from underground work to fulfill their domestic roles and to see to the socialisation of their children. Though many were still very young, such girls were being forced into premature womanhood and could be perceived as embryonic mothers. Scriven was echoing Ayton when he made a plea for exclusion:

> The estimation of the sex has ever been held a test of the civilisation of a people. Shall it then be said that in the heart of our own country — from which missions are daily sent to teach God's law, and millions upon millions have been generously poured forth for the manumission of hosts in a distant land — that there shall exist a state of society in which hundreds of young girls are sacrificed to such shameless indecencies, filthy abominations and cruel slavery as is found to exist in our coal pits?[37]

Not only were such conditions deemed highly inappropriate for the female sex but the possible threat to home life goaded the investigators and those who read their reports into a demand for the suppression of all underground female labour. Woman was seen to be the saviour of the nation and must be placed back in the home. Such an emphasis was timely. Not only would her removal from work help resolve certain demographic imbalances but it might help restore harmony to a country threatened by Chartism. At a time when Bronterre O'Brien was proclaiming that an entire transformation of society was essential it was felt important to reaffirm the value of matriarchal control. The emphasis must be on the family as a point of stability in the midst of the upheaval caused by industrialisation. When the church's grip upon the nation appeared to be threatened yet education had not yet succeeded in 'forcing civilisation downwards', it was vital that the influence of the wife and mother on the family be emphasised.[38] As Samuel Smiles explained, in the home it was woman who

> in all spheres of life and stations of life, there regulates those influences which operate the most powerfully on the physical, moral and mental constitution of man.[39]

Women held the family together and the family in turn could bind society: — 'nations are but the reflex of Homes: Peoples of mothers'. But

> As surely as you make women day labourers with men, and efface the peculiar modesty and delicacy of the female character so you will produce a ferocious, regardless and desperate population ready for any mischief.

He went on to describe woman as the 'great civiliser', and urged:

> Let us, in short, make the most of woman, by so directing her power as to increase the amount of the general happiness.

This might best be done through the family. In this way the natural order of society would not be disrupted and the state must intervene to ensure this and to bring about the moral improvement of the working class.

Now a more extreme case could be made out against a system which, though not new, was a novel revelation for the majority of Victorians. Thus Kennedy was able to argue that females must stop work in order to protect the state from 'the growth of an ignorant, depraved and dangerous population'.[40] He and other Sub-Commissioners had exceeded their briefs by their recommendations for the prohibition of a system which they believed was pernicious. The cumulative effect of this message was such that it could not be ignored.

The first report of the Children's Employment Commission appeared in print on 7 May 1842 after an unsuccessful attempt to delay publication at a time of severe economic distress and overt Chartist activity.[41] 2,000 copies of the two volumes of evidence and a further summary were produced. There was also a ninety-page book which summarised the main report.[42] The end product was praised by Ashley. It was a 'noble document' showing that 'perhaps even civilisation itself

never exhibited such a mass of sin and cruelty'.[43] Yet Ashley doubted
whether the obvious initial impact on public opinion could be sustained.
He need not have worried. The press, reactionary and radical, deplored
the revelations. The *Morning Chronicle* depicted the findings as a
'volume of travels in a remote and barbarous country'.[44] Despite
centuries of coalmining history, the *Quarterly Review* could comment
that

> the earth seems now for the first time to have heaved from its
> entrails another race to astonish and to move us to reflection and
> to sympathy.[45]

Comparisons with slavery abounded and it was stressed that more was
known about blacks abroad than about those who were black from
their subterranean toil at home. A land which had sent Christian
missions to remote parts of the world was ignorant that

> the backs and limbs of their own countrywomen are being broken
> and their moral nature corrupted, by a species of slavery in the coal
> mines more cruel, more degrading and more profligate, than any
> that obtains among serfs and slaves in any part of the world which
> the anti-slavery zealots of missionary enterprise has yet discovered
> to claim British sympathy and cash.[46]

Whereas the Commission had refrained from blaming the coal masters,
the main torrent of abuse was now heaped on them by the press.
Perhaps the most vitriolic attack came from the *Penny Chronicle*, a
Sunday newspaper:

> Of the bloody and unsparing cruelty of CAPITALISTS we have
> already held and expressed a tolerably strong opinion; the cotton
> lords of the North are not much in our debt for complimentary
> expressions. . .but alas!. . .we were directing our enmity against a
> mere wart on the smallest finger of the fell and bloody moloch
> CAPITAL. . .they are mild and moral as compared to those of the
> mine lords and their subordinates.[47]

Many papers regurgitated extracts from the reports, particularly those
relating to women's work and they took care to emphasise the moral
implications. The mere fact that males and females worked in such close
proximity must, according to the *Leeds Mercury*, produce immorality —

'no other result could accrue'.[48] The women's work was used as
demonstrable proof of the absolute necessity of intervention by the
state. A short-lived Owenite paper the *Union* explained that society
had been

> startled from its propriety by the sudden announcement of the fact
> that women, mothers of families, were employed underground to
> do the work of brutes; the thing was too barbarous to be tolerated
> for a moment longer in this our Christian country.[49]

The accounts of the work spelt the antithesis of the bourgeois concept
of appropriate feminine pursuits. The *Halifax Guardian* commented on
the lamentable effects of taking woman from her proper sphere and
degrading her to the dress of man and the drudgery of the mine.[50]
E.W. Binney, a Manchester geologist who personally visited some
Lancashire pits, wondered whether a woman collier could ever be a
good wife. Such work was surely more likely to

> destroy that purity and delicacy of character which ought ever to
> invest her with a hallowed atmosphere; and to lay the foundation
> for a life of sensual indulgence, domestic thriftlessness, dirt,
> dissipation and quarrels.[51]

Such criticism failed however to ask how possible it might be for an
ordinary working-class woman to live in a 'hallowed atmosphere'. It did
nevertheless perform a service in helping reveal kinds of conditions to
which colliery workers might be subjected. The exposition was
completed by the use of illustrative material. All four areas which
employed women in any numbers had, in addition to the text, included
along with the evidence, graphic wood engravings. The original
instructions had not mentioned pictorial representations and their
addition was apparently made at the request of one of the
Commissioners, Dr Southwood Smith.[52] Familiar with the value of
anatomical drawings, he recognised that an illustration could at a glance
convey the necessary information. In addition to maps of coalfields,
individual seams and methods of ventilation, there were drawings of
the women and children at work. Scriven, Kennedy and Franks may
have done the original sketches of the women themselves. Binney
helped Kennedy by sketching below ground, experience in the
execution of geological drawings no doubt aiding him.[53] The use of
wood block engravings was not new — the process had already been
used to effect by Thomas Bewick and his followers and had been

eagerly espoused by the press. It was however unique to include them in a Parliamentary Paper and their realism provided a direct contrast to the more conventional artistic portrayal of woman as mother or heroine.[54] Not surprisingly this new direction caused some uneasiness. Londonderry roundly condemned the engravings as 'beastly', they were the 'most disgusting pictorial illustrations that ever were seen'.[55]

Delighted by such a scoop, the press hastened to defend them. Douglas Jerrold explained that far from being exaggerations they were inadequate to convey the full extent of wretchedness.[56] In fact although the original drawings were probably not on the whole a gross exaggeration of actual conditions of work, this cannot be said for all the reproductions in newspapers and journals. For example one engraving designed to show the use of winding with a well winch and fly wheel demonstrated in the report how colliers were at the mercy of a winder. Will Dyson and Ann Ambler who worked for Ditchforth and Clay at Elland were being drawn up cross-lapped on a clatch iron. It is hard to believe that the old woman winder could perform such a task. Yet in the reproductions of this, it was not the superhuman strength which invited comment or the precarious situation for the children. Instead the original was considerably embellished, directing attention to the near-nakedness and close proximity of the boy and girl, thus enhancing sensationalism and helping to canalise moral fears.[57]

A few newspapers and journals felt the whole subject to be lacking in taste. The *Quarterly Review* simply provided a prose account of conditions while the new *Illustrated London News* did not feel it to be appropriate reading matter for its readers. Yet as with the pit brow lasses, the subject provided many papers with material which they could not afford to miss. There was a similarity in the prurient nature of the accounts of both underground and surface work and in the morbid curiosity and fascination which they aroused. The *Penny Chronicle* claimed to be the first to dare to drag the enquiries into the open, accusing other papers of plagiarism.[58] They were however in agreement on one matter. There was almost unanimous support for banning female work in the pits. Even those papers generally opposed to the principle of intervention endorsed this and the Chartist *Northern Star* commented how the issue was

far removed beyond and above the narrow range of party bickering; it is a great question of social and moral interest; it demands the exertions of all, and no one can henceforth refuse to aid in the rescue of those victims of oppression without incurring the guilt of innocent blood.[59]

With such mobilisation of public opinion and supported by numerous petitions demanding the exclusion of women and other colliery reforms, Ashley felt sufficiently fortified to introduce a Mines and Collieries bill.[60] After some delay the House of Commons was eventually treated to a memorable two-hour speech on 7 June. Basing his comments on the summary of the reports, he explained that

> nothing can be more graphic, nothing can be more touching than the evidence of many of these poor girls themselves — insulted, oppressed and even corrupted, they exhibit not infrequently a simplicity and a kindness that renders tenfold more heart-rending the folly and cruelty of that system that has forced away these young persons, destined in God's providence to holier and happier duties, to occupations so unsuited, so harsh and so degrading.[61]

His demand for intervention was based on an appeal to public humanity and sympathy and his first request was for total female exclusion. The first reading passed easily. Ashley, always a perfectionist, was delighted by its unqualified success.[62] Yet although the oratory produced universal acclamation, the bill was not guaranteed an easy passage. The novelty of the revelations had taken members by surprise and produced a sense of urgency which was soon dissipated. The committee stage forced a reduction in the age of boys entering mines (from twelve to ten). Already Ashley found himself in a precarious position. Not being a government measure it was difficult to whip up support and he was particularly disappointed by Peel's failure to intervene on its behalf. It took some time to find a suitable person to take charge of the bill in the Lords but eventually Lord Devon undertook the responsibility. Ashley recognised the changed and charged atmosphere in the upper house where coalowners sought to defend their rights.

> Never did one body present such a contrast to another as the House of Lords to the House of Commons — the question seemed to have no friends; even those who said a sentence or two in its favour spoke coldly and with measure.[63]

The bill was badly disfigured in the Lords. The northern coalowners, concerned about interference and the implications for child employment, produced *Notes on the Report of 1842* and met to discuss the subject with Ashley. Not being employers of females, they were not unduly concerned about this subject. The undisputed leader of the anti-Ashley faction was Londonderry who challenged the wisdom of novel legislative interference. Londonderry's concern for his own interests was exemplified by the fact that he was quite content to accept the Sub-Commissioners' statements about females since they implied condemnation of other districts, not of his own. [64] Clearly he would not tolerate any criticism of practices in which he indulged. Personal involvement also made a significant difference in the 1886-7 Parliamentary debates on pit brow work. Mining representatives from the north-east where women did *not* work were foremost in condemning the practice.[65]

Petitions urging or opposing exclusion proliferated during the final stages of the bill's progress through Parliament. There were some compromise proposals — one from Edinburgh suggested that women should declare their willingness to work to a Justice of the Peace and the system be extended for another five or six years. The more drastic proposal that single women over twenty-one continue to work was quickly scotched.[66] In spite of the Lords' modifications of the bill, the female clause remained virtually intact.[67] One alteration was however to have repercussions. Originally women had been forbidden to enter mines at all. This was amended to permit them to enter as long as they did not work there. This looked innocuous but, as Ashley recognised, it increased the possibilities for evading the law. And, much to his disappointment, a plea to Peel failed to alter the situation.[68]

Just how far the cause of the women had taken over from the original concern of the investigation is demonstrated by Ashley's comment in agreeing to amend the age of the boys employed in mines. He admitted that he was disposed to sacrifice the children in order to save the women. The bill received the Royal assent on 10 August. Ashley appreciated his 'undeserved measure of success' and hoped that it would be the beginning of good to all mankind — 'the more I labour, the more I see of labour to be performed and vain to the last will be the labour of us all'.[69]

The Mines and Collieries Act has been seen as the first triumph in the movement for labour legislation.[70] Clearly it had exposed one problem. In its place however it posed another — what was to happen to the women and children forcibly excluded from their work? Although the state had assumed responsibility for legislating against them, it provided no subsequent machinery to control or direct the fate of those affected. The executive clauses of the act were vague, excepting the rule that within six months all females must leave underground work. The law was unique — it was to apply to all mines and collieries on a national basis and with such varying conditions, problems of enforcement soon became apparent. A memorial from a meeting held at Polmont, Scotland on 24 March 1843 explained:

> We question not the policy of legislating on this subject, where abuses are proved to exist, but we humbly question the policy of framing a general measure applicable to all collieries without distinction.[71]

It also left very little time for adaptation and conformity.[72] Worry on this score had been evident during the debates when some procrastination had been urged. The Earl of Crawford's agent also recognised the need for gradualism:

> Unless the measure is very slow and gradual in its operation — the immediate misery it will produce will be greater than the vice and immorality it is certainly well calculated to check.[73]

Such a fear was also to permeate the reasoning of the defenders of pit brow work — Josephine Butler was available to emphasise the immorality that might well ensue should women be thrown out of regular work.[74] The Belgian Labour Commission of 1886 recognised a similar problem of isolation, specialisation and moral danger:

> élevées dans un milieu spécial, sans éducation, ni instruction qui leur permettrait de se suffire à elles-mêmes. N'y a-t-il pas là pour la moralité un danger bien plus grand que celui que présente la situation actuelle?[75]

> (brought up in a peculiar environment, lacking the education and instruction which would allow them to be self-sufficient. Surely that represents a far greater danger to morality than the present situation?)

Londonderry's threat of a league to force repeal did not materialise but the opponents of the work made one last bid in 1843. Petitions against exclusion were presented almost daily from early in February for over two months and continued at intervals for the next two years. They expressed concern about the lack of alternative work and the intensification of the problem due to the adverse economic situation and stringent application of the 1834 Poor Law Amendment Act. 180 colliers and other workmen from Newbattle colliery, Midlothian 'shuddered to contemplate' the 'horrifying miseries, destitution, profligacy and starvation' which would follow. They predicted that 'an untimely grave will be the lot of hundreds of fine young females who now live usefully and happily'.[76]

One argument which was urged forcefully in the petitions was that colliery women would not stand much chance of obtaining any available employment. Not only was there the traditional suspicion of pit folk but the women themselves felt that, being bred to such special work, they were accustomed to it and fit for nothing else.[77] Seventy-three petitioners from Townhill near Dunfermline emphasised the peculiar nature of the employment which made them 'in a great measure incapacitated from performing the duties of domestic servants or even from acting as ordinary out of door labourers'.[78] The situation in Scotland was particularly disturbing since the Poor Law there made no provision for relief for the able-bodied on the assumption that the latter could all find employment. Thus the majority of females could receive no parochial assistance and were in danger of losing their cheap or rent-free cottages and fuel. Many women had small children at home or elderly or sick relatives who relied on them for financial assistance. At Wellwood colliery where eighty women were forced to cease work, nineteen were supporting fifty-nine dependants and thirty-four supported sixty-three at Fordel colliery.[79] Some of these dependants now claimed relief and the reports of the Poor Law Commissioners in 1844 included complaints about this drain on parish funds.[80] One isolated charitable scheme provided £110 for the alleviation of distress in Scotland but there was no formal compensation.[81] Harriet Martineau who recognised that the work had deserved condemnation nevertheless deplored this 'partial legislation' which failed to substitute alternative work and therefore did not represent social progress for women.[82] Thomas de Quincey agreed that one could not expect Parliament to pay permanent wages to the women but he felt that some responsibility should have been accepted:

> I do contend that in the act of correcting a ruinous social evil that never could have reached its climax, unless under the criminal negligence of Parliament, naturally and justly the duty fell upon that purblind Parliament of awarding to those poor mining families such an indemnification once for all, as might lighten and facilitate the

harsh transition from double pay to single pay, which the new law had suddenly enacted.[83]

The *Edinburgh Review* explained that Ashley's act should go beyond removing the women and concentrate on removing the need for them to work below ground in the first instance.[84] In practice no money was forthcoming — in spite of the handsome compensation paid to West Indian slave-owners and the sums of money given to landowners by railway companies. Nor was advice proffered. Recognising the gravity of the situation, one Scottish MP, C.L. Cumming Bruce (a colliery owner who had made his own preparations for excluding women some years earlier) attempted to amend the first clause of the act. In 1843 he proposed to the Commons that adult single women and widows in Scotland be reinstated in their former work.[85] Sheriffs could grant licences for this purpose. His attack centred on the Commission. Meanwhile Roebuck characteristically asserted the argument from a rather different angle, stating that each adult must be the best judge of the manner of disposing of his or her labour. He asked whether there was anything in the female sex which rendered women incapable of judgement and seriously questioned the right of men to interfere with women's labour. Such remarks were quite common by the 1886-7 pit brow debates but in the early 1840s were quickly and conveniently ignored. More persuasive was Ashley's speech condemning retrogressive tendencies. Cumming Bruce's proposal was rapidly defeated.

Never again in the course of the century did Parliament seriously consider repealing or amending the clause prohibiting female labour in the pits. Those who supported the pit brow lasses, even the most ardent of nineteenth-century suffragists, deplored women's work *in* coal mines and did not urge its resumption. They saw surface work as something rather different, as a pointer to the future when women might receive equal status with men in work. Their opponents however viewed it in a very different light. For them it represented a backward step and must therefore be wiped out completely. Yet paradoxically both sides drew on the experience of 1842 to substantiate their arguments. Pit brow attackers regurgitated the morality arguments propounded *before* the passing of the 1842 law. Pit brow defenders on the other hand concentrated on the act's immediate aftermath. For them the ensuing difficulties were sufficient warning that legislating about women's work at mines could have dire consequences, particularly if the legislation was hastily enacted.

Prospects of finding alternative employment were severely limited. In

Scotland there was some domestic service, seasonal field work and small textile mills which occasionally might have some work. By 1845 it was estimated that about 200 out of 4,200 Scottish colliery women had found work.[86] Problems of finding employment were compounded by the fact that the women were in competition with each other. 147 had to leave the Alloa collieries at the same time, similarly 105 were turned out from Clackmannan and 96 from the Devon coal company.[87] In 1844 out of 126 made redundant at the Carron company's Stirling pits, about eight had been provided with surface work and a further dozen had been placed in country service. Some others had tried service but soon abandoned it. Others were being supported by families while some had to resort to hawking goods around the farms. P.M. Steward, the MP for Renfrew, received a deputation of pit women and their husbands who explained that they were 'in a state of great destitution, they were deprived of an employment with which they were perfectly satisfied, and were reduced to a state of idleness and misery'.[88] The reports of the Commissioner of Mines reiterated the problems – many could only find odd jobs such as collecting manure from the roads or making and selling camstone (a white clay used for washing earthen or stone floors). Such work paid only a pittance – camstone-selling fetched about 3d a day if one was prepared to walk many miles.[89]

A few owners recognised some responsibility – Geddes at Bannockburn added 3d a ton to the men's wages to compensate for the loss of seventy-three women.[90] In the Lothians Sir George Clark provided financial assistance for those totally unable to work, while at Fordel five or six widows were placed on the poor list and fed until other jobs could be found.[91] A few of these women found work in the brickfields, in sewing and in agricultural work. The same tale of privation could be told for West Wales where job opportunities were minimal and colliers' wages extremely low. Pembrokeshire pits had employed the highest proportion of adult females to adult males in Britain – for every hundred adult males there were forty-two adult females. Apart from a little turnip picking and milking and knitting there was simply not remunerative work available and many of the women were widowed. They had explained to the Sub-Commissioners, that they had only taken up pit work in the first instance because of this absence of other jobs.[92] In the West Riding of Yorkshire and in West Lancashire there was at least some mill work though the dire economic conditions of the early 1840s meant that it was the worst possible time to be in search of a job. A study of the effects of exclusion in Lancashire has highlighted the problems for these women.

Excepting Sumner's Haigh Moor brewery which offered some work to women as a result of the legislation, there were simply not the openings to absorb them.[93] Munby, who idealised colliery work (and was suspicious of the motives of male miners), nevertheless recognised the problems inherent in such intervention:

> Never with your leave or by your leave, they tell'd us all to go;
> They've took the bread clean oot on oor mooths, aye, every
>   mother an' maid,
> An all for to pleasure the menfolk, as wants to steal oor trade!
> Well, if it's hard an mucky, who knows that better nor me?
> But I liked it, an it was my living – an so it had to be
> Surely, a wench can choose her work![94]

The intentions of Ashley and his supporters were not that the women should replace unsavoury work with more pleasant employment. Instead there was the implicit assumption that the women should be removed from the labour market and remain at home. The gap between the pit and the home could be bridged by promoting a limited form of suitable education which emphasised domestic economy. Girls could then be prepared for looking after their own homes. In addition, since female domestic service was one form of employment which significantly was not to be probed, subjected to investigation or controlled (even though by 1851, 40 per cent of the female labour force were employed in domestic service), an appropriate education could also provide a valuable training for this. The Commissioner of Mines, H.S. Tremenheere put forward plans which emphasised a sexual division of education. He felt that girls should be taught separately from boys and that the former should learn 'cleanliness, neatness and propriety of manners'. He advertised Baird's Gartsherrie and Eglinton industrial schools which trained women for the duties of housekeeping. At Eglinton there was a course for girls in economy and neatness in cooking, washing and sewing.[95] He also praised the scheme devised by Robert Brown, principal agent of the Hamilton estates in Scotland. This proposed special schools for women and children and it was hoped that their education would have a beneficial effect on their husbands who would become sober, steady workmen, prepared to work longer hours and produce more coal.[96]

In only a few instances was the harshness of the act relieved by prior planning. At the Haigh collieries in Lancashire the 24th Earl of Crawford and Balcarres took steps to soften the effects of exclusion by adopting a policy of gradualism.[97] The most successful efforts were made by a neighbouring coalowner, Lord Francis Egerton whose work at the Worsley collieries showed how the act might have been made more humane.[98] The combined efforts of Egerton and his wife, aided by his superintendent James Loch produced a somewhat suffocating paternalism but none the less at least assumed responsibility for the consequences of directives. Controlled exclusion was considered desirable not just on moral grounds. It was also carefully tailored to fit in with economic needs. Plans were devised to monitor numbers carefully and reduce them before and during 1842. In addition to providing temporary work for adults on the estate, Lady Francis Egerton was responsible for establishing a servants' school at Walkden Moor for former pit girls. Even more surprising was the 1/- paid weekly for a year to those who were excluded. A rudimentary form of unemployment benefit, it was a far cry from the reaction of most owners. Although the latter were frequently wealthy landowners who exerted extensive influence over a number of concerns, in the main they abdicated any real responsibility for the women. Not only did they not phase out female employment in advance of the act, but they barely accepted the consequences of that legislation.

The use of older boys in place of women and young children rebounded in economic terms directly or indirectly on the employers. Altering roadways for horses was also costly and took time. Many pits had not been adapted by the time the women had to leave and this, coupled with the lack of alternative work, only too frequently meant that the help offered by the majority of owners amounted to a silent condonement of evasion, thus helping to perpetuate the system which the law was meanwhile attempting to eradicate. Financial difficulties made the possibility of remaining at home extremely difficult. As Ray Strachey remarked:

> Everyone wanted to put an end to the scandal but no one, not even Lord Shaftesbury himself, remembered that when these pit women could no longer crawl through the bowels of the earth to earn their daily bread it might happen that they would starve.[99]

Hundreds of women therefore continued working underground. The very secrecy of such action makes it difficult to obtain information though accidents and informers revealed part of the story. Tremenheere was the sole person appointed to supervise the enforcement of the law throughout the century.[100] He not only never went underground but he always gave notice of an impending colliery visit. These were anyway infrequent and he considered his main task to be the compilation of annual reports (there were fifteen in all) on the progress of the act. He did believe that everything would work out for the best and accepted that in the meantime some dislocation was inevitable. Engels wrote in 1844 that the act was a 'dead letter in most districts due to the lack of a proper Inspectorate'.[101]

The act lacked precise and detailed executive power. Magistrates had no power such as they possessed under the factory legislation. They were unable to summon witnesses in prosecutions and anyway these magistrates were themselves frequently coal and/or iron masters or their close associates.[102] The policing of the provinces in the 1840s left a lot to be desired — for example, the Wigan Watch Committee set up in 1836 was hopelessly inefficient — one historian has likened its minutes to the scenario of a Will Hay comedy.[103] One of its number, Bradley, did play a part in providing information but like some of his colleagues, he was soon dismissed for being drunk. Coalowners cleverly exculpated themselves from responsibility for the women and transferred blame to the miners.[104] It was difficult, as the management knew, for the prosecution to provide evidence of 'consent, concurrence or knowledge' yet the law required this. Fines were not sufficiently high to deter the wealthy coalowners — the maximum was £10 per person.[105] And some proprietors even went so far as to get the women to cover the cost of possible fines in anticipation of trouble! In 1842 and 1843 Peace, the agent to the Earl of Crawford complained about this practice — 4d a week was being deducted from wages at one colliery and paid into a fund to defray the cost of future fines.[106]

The evasion of the law was aided further by alternative forms of descending the pit. In Scotland stairs meant that women could enter them relatively easily and at some Lancashire pits ladders were placed at the pit mouth for this purpose. In South Wales many pits were entered by levels or tunnels in the hillside. Moreover they were usually worked by sub-contractors, a system which made it harder than ever to apportion blame and to secure effective control as mineral agents might only go down a particular pit about once a month. In Yorkshire the thin seams encouraged the continued use of small children. Since the women and girls wore men's clothes, detection was anyway difficult and many of them slipped down at night. If Tremenheere decided to prosecute, the procedure was lengthy. The Home Office was anyway reluctant to spend much money. Some contact was made via local officials and paid informers but it was difficult to get reliable evidence.[107] Tremenheere knew that there were at least 200 females evading the law in the Wigan area alone in 1845. There were instances in Lancashire, Monmouthshire and around Stirling of girls starting work for the first time *after* 1842 and as late as the mid-1850s the law was being evaded by girls and women in West and South East Wales.[108] Munby heard that they were working illegally around Pontypool and Nantyglo in 1864 and two years later an accident at the Tunnel pit, Nantyglo revealed that females were still being employed underground — twenty-four years after the act had been passed.[109]

The eventual decrease in evasion was due in part to the passage of time and in part to incidental adverse publicity from accidents. Some coalowners also began to enforce measures against miners more rigidly. They threatened dismissal for those who employed women — at the Carron works in Scotland the pit was stopped every time a woman was found below ground.[110] The tactic of punishing all for the action of some may have caused some ill-feeling between the miners but it also served to demonstrate to them the way in which the management could use the law as and when they chose.

The most effective and convincing pressure to make the legislation meaningful seems to have emanated from the miners themselves. Their propaganda drew attention to the shortcomings of the executive clauses of the act. The newly-formed Miners' Association of Great Britain and Ireland (dating from 1842), took up the issue, recognising that here at least was the beginning of improvements for mine workers. The Commission had spelt out the situation and now it was the responsibility of the miners' own union to see that the law was not thwarted. The women could be seen as part of a system which perpetuated the payment of low wages. And although the issue of cheap labour was to become much more significant in the pit brow debates, the removal of the women miners in 1842 was interpreted as a progressive step. The *Northern Star* urged:

> Keep them at home to look after their families; decrease the pressure on the labour market and there is then some chance of a higher rate of wages being enforced.[111]

Meanwhile the dismissal of union leaders and a stringent enforcement of contracts in the 1840s deepened the divisions between masters and men. Now these masters seemed experts at breaking the very laws which they and their colleagues had helped devise. Yet if trouble arose they simply implicated their employees! The Duke of Hamilton who owned

collieries where evasion of the law was rife was a prime target,
subjected to especial derision due to his being 'an hereditary law maker;
a commissioned law administrator, the head of the magistracy of a whole
county, being the Lord-Lieutenant and as such the Queen's
representative'.[112]

The belief in the idea that the women should remain at home was
made clear in the miners' organ the *Miners' Advocate*. Yet it did not
reflect a percolation of middle-class doctrines down to the working
class but was rather evidence of the popularity of the idea that a
working man should earn a family wage, enough to keep his wife and
children. An essential part of this was the consciousness that members
of the miner's family should be as entitled to remain at home as the
wives of wealthy men such as the Duke of Hamilton. Miners were also
critical of the legal authorities and felt that Tremenheere did not exert
enough pressure and was only too willing to listen to the coalowners.[113]
In 1848 David Swallow, Secretary of the Miners' Association informed
Tremenheere of cases of evasion at a number of pits in the Dunfermline
area. Yet the local Fiscal refused to take action although Swallow
supplied him with names. Nothing was done so Swallow wrote again.
In a final bid to get something done, he communicated directly with
the Home Secretary. Eventually Tremenheere tried to get witnesses and
wrote to the Fiscal. The Commissioner was however highly suspicious
of Swallow and once he had been reassured by the colliery managers
that the law was being observed, he was prepared to believe them and
let the matter drop. To his surprise he later received a letter from the
Fiscal explaining that he had not taken any action because he had
discovered that he would not have had his expenses paid had the
prosecution failed! In fact the Lord Advocate had also upheld this
decision. Not surprisingly Tremenheere chose not to convey this
information to Swallow! It later transpired that the Fiscal was
personally connected with some of the local collieries.[114]

The miners had wanted a professionally qualified team of
Inspectors yet they had been given only one Commissioner.[115] They
therefore sought to exert their own pressure. They publicised cases of
evasion and attacked the popular press which had 'wept bottles of ink'
at the Commission's revelations but now refused to print incriminating
evidence against individual owners.[116] Miners' agents spoke at meetings
about the need to stop women working and drew up petitions. Some
miners (at Lochgelly, for example) instigated proceedings against coal
masters for employing women. Similarly the 'miners' attorney', the
Chartist W.P. Roberts, and Peter Brophy of the Miners' Association took

legal action against the employment of women on pit banks in Staffordshire (see Chapter 3).

Yet the situation was not clear cut. While the miners' union might officially oppose the continuation of women's pit work and succeed in exposing the coalowners (themselves the law makers) as the law breakers, many miners must have found themselves in an ambivalent position where practice might of necessity differ from principle. The speedy execution of the act, lack of planning and the need for miners to foot the additional expense of hiring older boy assistants militated against an attempt to disrupt the traditional family work. At the Carron company work ceased for a month due to objections to exclusion.[117] And whereas some Wigan miners were following up cases of evasion themselves in an attempt to enforce this part of the law, in the same town a policeman and a watchman were beaten up 'in a most brutal manner' for giving information against those coalowners who allowed women to continue in their pits.[118] Although this might have been a case of the owners in question simply hiring a gang to teach a lesson to those who interfered, it is none the less likely that economic circumstances may have forced many heads of families to abandon their ideals and continue deploying their own womenfolk.

The problems raised by the legislation of 1842 proved crucial in determining later attitudes towards pit brow work. Some coalowners had been exposed as hypocrites, able to turn the law to their advantage. The experience and shortcomings of the act had helped to formulate union responses to women's pit work and to confirm the idea that the working world of the miner should be a completely male world. There was also evidence of more direct competition. Some former women miners were now given work at the pit top. While this might resolve some of their immediate difficulties, it could be disastrous for male workers. At some Scottish pits men were discharged from the pit head in order to give work to women — they were told that they could get alternative employment more easily than women. At Clackmannan men lost their jobs because twenty-four women were taken on and some of these surface men were still idle in 1844. An attempt to please all could result in universal dissatisfaction. At some pit brows work was divided between old employees and women but all had their wages halved.[119]

Such action served as a lesson which made it hard for male miners to accept pit brow work. Unlike many of its critics, the miners understood only too well the differences between the gruesome work of drawing below ground and the very different jobs on the surface. Yet many of them were embittered by the experience of female exclusion.

Their respect for the coalowners diminished as their dependence upon them both legally and even illegally, increased. The women who worked at the pit brow therefore found themselves at the centre of a deep-rooted and complex controversy and the debate about their right to work must be viewed both in the light of the shocking conditions to which women and girls had been subjected underground and also in the context of the problems posed by their enforced exclusion from this work in the 1840s.

Notes

1. Its full title was 'An Inquiry into the Employment of the Children of the Poorer Classes in Mines and Collieries, and the various branches of Trade and Manufacture in which numbers of Children work together, not being included in the provisions of the Acts for regulating the Mills and Factory.' This survey will be restricted to coal mines and the collieries attached to ironworks. The Commissioners were Thomas Tooke, Dr Thomas Southwood Smith, Leonard Horner and Robert John Saunders. All had experience of factory legislation. The first six Sub-Commissioners were appointed in November 1840. Instructions dated from 16 November 1840 and 11 February 1841. They were to investigate twelve major features of the work including the physical and moral condition of children. PP 1842, XVI, p.1; PP 1843, XIII, pp.IV, 205-11.

2. PP 1842, XV, XVI and XVII; PP 1843, XII. For a more detailed analysis of the report as it affected women see A.V. John, 'Women Workers in British Coal Mining 1840-90, with special reference to West Lancashire', unpublished PhD thesis, University of Manchester, 1976, Ch.2, Section A.

3. The pressure for quick results in the Poor Law enquiry of 1834 had meant that the report was written before all the evidence had arrived, let alone been studied. Only six months elapsed between the circulation of the questionnaire and the evidence being sent to the printers. S.G. and G.O.A. Checkland (eds.), *The Poor Law Report of 1834* (London, 1974), p.31. The attitudes expressed in the 1867 Royal Commission on the Employment of Women and Children in Agriculture were attacked in the *Saturday Review*, 27, no.161 (1869), p.78. It drew attention to the 'lofty canon of virtue in their minds, that everything they witness or are told, shocks them as falling short of their ideal. This high moral tone detracts somewhat from the value of their opinions and suggestions.'

4. See Chapter 6.

5. Appendix to 1st Report on Public Petitions (1843). Appendix 25, p.19.

6. Londonderry drew attention to the fact that Franks was a former retail hatter who had once been imprisoned for libel. Hansard LXIV, House of Lords, 24 June 1842, p.538; 14 July 1842, p.118; House of Commons, 16 May 1843, p.439. C.W. Vane, *A Letter to Lord Ashley M.P. on the Mines and Collieries Bill* (London, 1842), p.37.

7. PP 1842, XVII, p.57, HI and XVI, pp.179, 181, 196. Southwood Smith and Saunders made personal underground visits to Yorkshire coal mines. PP 1842, XV, p.5.

8. Symons did however admit that one girl was 'evidently crammed with her evidence'. PP 1842, XVI, p.181.

9. Many of the returns were completed by guess work. Only three questions dealt specifically with female employment. PP 1842, XVI, p.166. The Earl of Crawford's agent, Peace, felt that filling in the forms would involve too much time and trouble so did not bother to do so. Haigh Collieries and Estate Papers 25/7/749, 18 May 1842, The John Rylands University Library, Manchester.
10. PP 1842, XV, p.38.
11. PP 1842, XVII, p.11, no.125, p.647, no.48, p.513, no.313, p.552; XVI, no.116, p.458, no.361, p.501. For comparative ages in other industries see *Edinburgh Review*, 79 (1844), pp.134-44.
12. PP 1842, XVII, no.116, p.458; no.75, p.450; no.208, p.275.
13. PP 1842, XV, p.110; no.263, p.484; XVI, no.238, p.481; no.130, p.460.
14. Mrs Tonna (Charlotte Elizabeth), *The Wrongs of Women* (New York, 1849), p.430.
15. PP 1842, XVII, no.436, p.577.
16. Compare the evidence of Dr Favell of Sheffield with that from Edwin Ellis, surgeon at Silkstone. PP 1842, XVI, no.47, p.235, no.99, p.103.
17. Ibid., no.283, p.295.
18. Ibid., no.116, p.458.
19. PP 1842, XVII, no.440, p.577, no.451, p.580. Culm was tiny coal which could not be used on its own but, mixed with water, clay and beach slime was used to heat homes.
20. See O. Jones, *The Early Days of Sirhowy and Tredegar* (Risca, 1975), pp.35, 86. In the 1880s the average daily wages for Belgian women miners was only 1 franc 80 centimes (a Belgian franc was worth about 9½d). *Chambre de Commerce de Verviers*, 24 November 1888.
21. See B.R. Seth, *Labour in the Indian Coal Industry* (Bombay, 1940), pp.131-2 for the twentieth-century employment of women as coal loaders in the Bihar and Bengal regions of India. They received a share (generally 40 per cent) of the coal cutter's income.
22. PP 1842, XVI, p.181.
23. PP 1851, XXIII, p.3.
24. PP 1842, XVI, no.199, p.251; no.231, p.284.
25. *Revue Industrielle de Charleroi*, 1 August 1886.
26. PP 1842, XVII, no.79, p.124; no.9, p.103; P. McNeill, *Blawearie or Mining Life in the Lothians Forty Years Ago* (Edinburgh, 1887), pp.113, 117.
27. PP 1842, XVI, no.25, p.244; no.153, p.265.
28. PP 1842, p.200, XVII, pp.73-4; no.44, p.512.
29. Scriven found Patience Kershaw of Halifax in a state which the 'uncivilised natives of the prairies would be shocked to look upon'. PP 1842, XVI, no.9, p.103. He also referred to 'profaneness and almost mental imbecility', pp.154, 201; XV, p.195.
30. R. Colls, 'Oh Happy English Children. Coal Class and Education in the North-East', *Past and Present*, no.73 (1976); J. Benson, 'The Motives of Nineteenth Century Colliery Owners in promoting Day Schools', *Journal of Educational Administration*, 3, no.1 (1970).
31. PP 1842, XVII, no.36, p.111.
32. J. Leech, 'Capital and Labour', *Punch*, V (1843), pp.48-9.
33. PP 1842, XVI, no.80, p.243; no.119, p.254, pp.201-4; no.85, p.244; XVII, no.436, p.577.
34. E. Zola, *Germinal* (London, 1973 edition), p.54. Ann David (aged 13) hauled skips (tubs) with her sister at Begelly colliery, Pembrokeshire. They worked regularly for eleven or twelve hours daily, pulling about sixty loads. They were paid on piece rates. Ann described the job as 'sad tiring work'. PP 1842, XVII, no.436, p.577.

35. PP 1842, XVI, no.193, p.276.
36. PP 1842, no.130, p.460.
37. PP 1842, XVII, p.308.
38. See R. Johnson, 'Educational Policy and Social Control in Early Victorian England', *Past and Present*, no.49 (1970), p.97.
39. *Union*, no.1 (1 April 1842), no.10 (1 January 1843). I am grateful to Professor J.F.C. Harrison for helping to identify the author. For a discussion of the arguments against women working in factories and Ashley's fears of the 'root and branch destruction' of families and domestic life, see W.C. Lubenow, *The Politics of Government Growth* (Newton Abbot, 1971), Ch.5.
40. PP 1842, XVII, p.75.
41. It was dated 21 April 1842 but the Home Office attempted to delay its publication until a more timely date. The report however fell into the hands of MPs and although the Secretary of State tried to prevent its sale, it was impossible to stop publicity.
42. W. Strange (publisher), *The Condition and Treatment of the Children Employed in the Mines and Collieries of the United Kingdom* (London, 1842), Preface by 'W.C.'.
43. Broadlands MS, SHA/PD/2, Diary 1, 7 May 1842.
44. *Morning Chronicle*, 14 May 1842.
45. *Quarterly Review*, CXXXIX (1842), p.159.
46. *Union*, no.3 (1 June 1842); *Halifax Guardian*, 14 May 1842; *Northern Star*, 21 May 1842.
47. *Penny Chronicle*, no.77 (15 May 1842).
48. *Leeds Mercury*, 21, May 1842.
49. *Union*, no.2 (1 May 1842).
50. *Halifax Guardian*, 21 May 1842.
51. *Union*, no.2 (1 May 1842). Appendix to 7th Report on Public Petitions (1842). Appendix 195, p.90.
52. C.L. Lewes, *Recollections of my Grandfather* (London, 1898), p.73. See C. Fox, 'The Development of Social Reportage in English Periodical Illustration', *Past and Present*, no.74 (1977) for a consideration of the production of mass visual communication and its impact on the public. I am grateful to Celina Fox for discussion of this topic.
53. Franks and Scriven also did some drawings. T.C. Greenwall, 'On the Underground Conveyance of Coal', *Transactions of the Manchester Geological Society*, X (1871), p.59.
54. See Ch.6.
55. Vane, *Letter to Lord Ashley*, p.96. Hansard LXIV, House of Lords, 24 June 1842, p.538; 14 July 1842, p.118.
56. *Illuminated Magazine* (1843), p.45.
57. Compare the original – PP 1842, XVII, p.61 with the *Weekly Chronicle*, no.297, 27 May 1842; *Westminster Review*, 38 (1842), p.104. See also the frontispiece of *Les révoltes logiques*, 3, Autumn 1976, for the reproduction of an even more exaggerated version.
58. *Penny Chronicle*, no.77 (15 May 1842), no.80 (5 June 1842).
59. *Northern Star*, 28 May 1842.
60. Brotherton (MP for Salford) presented a number of petitions. As with the Short Time petitions, they concentrated on the sort of moral points which might be acceptable to Parliament. One from Binney claimed that the system had been perpetuated since parents worked below ground themselves and so had become immune to the evils. Appendix to 7th Report on Public Petitions (1842). Appendix 194, pp.88-90.
61. Hansard LXII, House of Commons, 7 June 1842, p.1328.

62. Broadlands MS, SHA/PD/2, Diary 1, 9 June 1842.
63. Ibid., 8 July 1842.
64. Vane, *Letter to Lord Ashley*, p.28. Hansard LXV, House of Lords,
14 July 1842, p.102; 12 July 1842, p.3.
65. For example, see Ch.6. Compare the motives behind the 1841 factory
legislation in France. *Les révoltes logiques*, p.15.
66. Hansard LXV, House of Lords, 25 July 1842, pp.583, 585.
67. A concession which made the final exclusion date 1 March 1843 instead
of six calendar months from the passing of the act, was not in practice to make
much difference since the delay in the Lords meant that by the time the act was
passed (10 August), the clause as originally worded would only have come into
force three weeks earlier (10 February) than this amended date.
68. Peel Papers Add. MS 40, 483 CCCIII, 2 August 1842, p.78. British Library.
69. Broadlands MS, SHA/PD/2, Diary 1, 8 August 1842.
70. ILO, *Report on the Law and Women's Work* (Geneva, 1939).
71. HO 45/OS/511.2.
72. According to a survey carried out in India in 1939, attempts to prohibit
female pit labour there produced labour shortages and a reduction of output per
head in addition to a worsening of the women's economic position as they
competed for a limited number of alternative jobs. See Appendix II and Seth,
Labour, p.151.
73. Haigh Collieries and Estate Papers, 25/7/779, 23 July 1842, 25/7/778,
20 July 1842.
74. *Women's Suffrage Journal*, 11, no.21 (1 November 1871). *Wigan Observer*,
13 May 1887. See Ch.6 n.140 'Ignotus' (a Cardiff schoolmaster, John H. Philips)
wrote about the unfortunate effects of exclusion in Wales in *The Last Thirty
Years in a Mining District* (London, 1867). I am indebted to Professor I.G. Jones
for identifying the author.
75. *Revue Industrielle de Charleroi*, no.41 (10 October 1886).
76. Appendix to 1st Report on Public Petitions (1843). Appendix 25, p.19.
Some petitions suggest the influence of management more than miners and
stories were told of inducements to sign them at certain colliery offices.
77. HO 45/OS/511.1.
78. One of the eleven petitions presented on 20 February 1843 by Cumming
Bruce. Appendix to 1st Report on Public Petitions (1843). Appendix 66, p.42.
79. Hansard LXIX, House of Commons, 16 May 1843, pp.453-4.
80. PP 1844, XXII, p.3.
81. *Mining Journal*, 28 December 1844; PP 1845, XXVII, p.3.
82. H. Martineau, *History of the Thirty Years' Peace 1815-46*, IV (London,
1878), pp.208-9. Tremenheere Papers, Family Letters 11-19 December 1844 ,
Penzance Library. *The Economist*, 28 September 1844 described the prohibitions
of female pit labour as 'the sickly sentimentality of the drawing room presuming
to regulate the world'.
83. Quoted in C. Collier, *Gatherings from the Pit Heaps* (London, 1861), p.20.
84. *Edinburgh Review*, 79 (1844), p.51.
85. Hansard LXIX, House of Commons, 16 May 1843, pp.430-78. The notion
of paying working-class women was not seriously considered in 1842 or even later
in the century. A letter in 1886 from a Northumberland miner to the press
explained the precedents for compensation but noted that they all related to a
different class of people – slave-owners, publicans, landlords and the clergy. He
pointed out the irony of failing to give pit brow women equal rights at a time
when attempts were being made to raise the position of women. Yet he also
acknowledged the fact that (as in 1842) depressed trade made compensation
impossible. *Wigan Observer*, 1 May 1886.

86. PP 1845, XXVII, p.3.
87. Hansard LXIX, House of Commons, 16 May 1843, pp.453-4.
88. PP 1844, XVII, pp.4, 16. Hansard LXIX, House of Commons, 16 May 1843, pp.474-5.
89. PP 1844, XVII, p.6.
90. Ibid., p.49.
91. HO 45/OS/511.20, 19 February 1844. PP 1844, XVII, p.52.
92. For example, PP 1844, XVII, no.431, p.575, no.440, p.578. One proprietor believed that Pembrokeshire women worked harder than slaves in the West Indies but added that they were unable to get any other work.
93. This had been started to provide employment for the women excluded from the pits. Munby MS, Diary 20, 19 August 1863; Notebook I, 1865, Notebook III, 1866. For the effects of the legislation on Lancashire women see A.V. John, 'Colliery Legislation and its Consequences: 1842 and the Women Miners of Lancashire', *Bulletin* of the John Rylands University Library of Manchester, 61, no.1 (1978).
94. 'Boompin Nell' (1887). Munby MS, 110[11]
95. PP 1851, XXIII, pp.40, 51-2. *Edinburgh Review*, 117 (1863), p.438. See A.P. Donajgrodski, 'Social Police and the Bureaucratic Elite: a Vision of Order in the Age of Reform' in *Social Control in Nineteenth Century Britain* (London, 1977).
96. PP 1851, XXIII, pp.49-53, Appendix C.
97. In Scotland several owners (for example the Duke of Buccleuch) had excluded women before 1842 though, lacking legal sanction, their efforts met with little success. At a few collieries only single women were permitted to work – explicit instructions at Plean Muir colliery Stirlingshire explained that only forty-five single women and girls over the age of twelve (preferably with some education) could be employed. PP 1842, XVI, no.28, p.442; no.283, p.488; Haigh Collieries and Estate Papers, 25/7/749, 18 May 1841; *Wigan Observer*, 3 August 1867.
98. Loch-Egerton Papers, Mertoun, Scotland. For rules of the Walkden Moor Servants' School see PP 1846, XXIV, pp.59-62; 'Girls working in the Colliery', unpublished MS kindly lent by Donald Anderson. For a fuller discussion of the Bridgewater Estates see F.C. Mather *Before the Canal Duke* (Oxford, 1970) and John, 'Colliery Legislation'.
99. R. Strachey, *The Cause* (London, 1978), p.56.
100. Hugh Seymour Tremenheere's appointment was made *after* the Home Secretary had received information from different parts of the country that the act was being very inadequately carried out. His full title was 'The Commissioner appointed under the provisions of the Act 5 and 6 Vict c 99 to Inquire into the operation of that Act and into the State of the Population.' He was to take steps to 'bring to justice those who openly or by stealth violate the law and frustrate the benevolent intentions of the legislature'. HO 45/OS/511. A former revising barrister, Tremenheere had become an Inspector of schools in 1839, a post which gave him experience in commissions of enquiry. After offending the non-conformists in 1842 over a report on the London schools of the British and Foreign School Society, he was offered the post of Mines Commissioner at the end of 1843. R.K. Webb, 'A Whig Inspector', *English Historical Review*, 70 (1955); F.L. and O.P. Edmonds, *I was There: The Memoirs of H.S. Tremenheere* (Windsor, 1969); *idem*, 'H.S. Tremenheere: Pioneer Inspector of Schools' *British Journal of Educational Studies*, XII (1963); *idem*, 'An Account of the founding of H.M. Inspectorate of Mines', *British Journal of Industrial Medicine*, no.20 (1963); Sir A.M. Bryan, 'His Majesty's Inspectors of Mines: A Centenary Address', *Transactions of the Institution of Mining Engineers*, 109 (1949-50), p.24.

PP 1849, III, p.24, qus.195, 196, 261.
101. F. Engels, *The Condition of the Working Class in England in 1844* (London, 1950), p.251.
102. See for example D. Philips, 'The Black Country Magistracy 1835-60; A Changing Local Elite and the Exercise of its Power', *Midland History*, III, no.3 (1976), p.184.
103. E.C. Midwinter, *Social Administration in Lancashire* (Manchester, 1969), pp.158-60. Twenty-seven men shared six posts between 1836-44.
104. There was a popular belief in Scotland that the law could only be enforced against the collier or the person immediately employing the woman, HO 45/OS/511.4.
105. The defective executive clauses of the act are discussed generally in O.O.G.M. MacDonagh, 'Coal Mines Regulation. The First Decade 1842-52' in R. Robson (ed.), *Ideas and Institutions of Victorian Britain* (London, 1967), p.63.
106. Haigh Collieries and Estate Papers 25/7/785, 12 December 1842.
107. For example HO 87/1, 21 January 1848, HO 87/2, 11 March 1848.
108. Munby MS, Notebook IV, 1870; PP 1845, XXVII, p.3; PP 1850, XXIII, p.65.
109. PP 1867, XXI, p.138; HO 95/3; *The Times*, 5 July 1866; *Wigan Observer*, 18 August 1866.
110. PP 1844, XVII, p.48; PP 1845, XXVII, p.3; PP 1847, XVI, p.36. John Johnston, overseer at the Duke of Hamilton's Redding colliery, was still issuing notices prohibiting female employment in March 1845. J.T. Ward, 'Landowners and Mining' in I.T. and R.G. Wilson (eds.), *Land and Industry* (Newton Abbot, 1971), pp.92-3.
111. For the Miners' Association see R. Challinor and B. Ripley, *The Miners' Association – A Trade Union in the Age of the Chartists* (London, 1968); *Northern Star*, 23 October 1843.
112. *Northern Star*, 7 October 1843.
113. *Miners' Advocate*, no.25 (8 February 1845) in Pitman's Strike Collection, Wigan Record Office. HO 45/OS/1490, 31 December 1846; *Northern Star*, 1 September 1849; R. Fynes, *The Miners of Northumberland and Durham. A History of their Political Progress* (Sunderland, 1923), p.142; see also Tremenheere Papers, Memoirs III, pp.121-2; R.K. Webb, *Harriet Martineau* (London, 1960), p.222.
114. HO 45/OS/511, 8 July 1844, 15 August 1844, 26 April 1845, 23, 31 July 1845.
115. Clause III of the Mines and Collieries Act had permitted 'such person or persons to Inspect and be authorised to go below ground' yet Tremenheere's appointment was an interim measure which preceded the creation of the Inspectorate in 1850.
116. *Northern Star*, 4 November 1843; *Miners' Advocate*, no.16 (29 June 1844), no.24 (11 January 1845).
117. R.H. Campbell, *The Carron Company* (London, 1961), p.230.
118. Haigh Collieries and Estate Papers 25/13/195, 16 August 1846; *Manchester Guardian*, 24 April 1844.
119. PP 1844, XVII, pp.3, 30, 48, 49.

Sorting at the Picking Belts, Wigan Coal and Iron Company.
Sketch by Sue Bedwell from a photograph.

PART II: AT THE PIT BROW

Give me thy hand, high-couraged lass but coy —
The hand that now so deftly grasps thy spade:
Perchance 'twill tell me how so sweet a maid
Can find her calling in such rude employ.

Surely thy life, thy work, should be all joy,
And fair as thou art; yet thou hast essay'd
A strong man's labour! Art thou not afraid
Such tasks as these thy beauty will destroy?

'Nay Sir,' she said, 'I care na if they do!
My hands is what I live by, not my face.
I are no lady, nor no man like you,
As maybe thinks it inna woman's place
To choose her work. Take hold then, an' you'll see,
What sort o' hand best suits a wench like me!

'On the Brow', Munby MS 109[30], 22 June 1892.

The Blundells' Costume, 1886. From a photograph by Wragg of Wigan

3 THE DAILY WORK

For throotchin' corves at bank an' broo,
An' work wi' pick an' spaade,
An' lawdin' troocks and climmin' shoots,
All them was Lizzie's traade.

'T' Pointswoman', Munby MS 110[7]

The generic term 'pit brow lass' suggests a far more clearly-defined occupation than actually existed. The women who worked above ground at Victorian coal mines performed a multitude of tasks which differed considerably according to geological factors, the size and productive capacity of pits and degrees of modernisation. The nature of these jobs altered during the nineteenth century as legislation and expansion produced alterations in the potential use of equipment and skills. The changes in the methods of preparing coal for the market had important repercussions on the conditions of work for those engaged in this process. It is impossible to demonstrate the full extent of differentiation and adaptation between areas. Conditions could, and often did, vary even between local pits. It is, however, essential to recognise this situation of constant flux, innovation and variation since critics, frequently blinded by emotions and partisan interests, tended to generalise and simplify accounts.[1] Whereas the exposures of the early 1840s had drawn attention to women's work below ground, critical assessment of their more evident employment on the surface was largely reserved for a later date. With the exception of brief entries in the 1842 reports and the evidence of the Midland Mining Commission (1843), female surface work was not well documented before the mid-century. This was hardly surprising. Not only was work underground deemed the greater evil but female surface work was operating on a very small scale in the 1840s.

Before discussing the methods of coal preparation and the women's contribution, some consideration of the numbers involved and the geographical distribution is needed.[2] It is extremely difficult to provide anything like an accurate assessment of the numbers of females working underground. This is lessened in the case of surface workers though must still remain highly speculative for the first three-quarters of the nineteenth century. It was not until registers of colliery labour forces became compulsory in 1872 and Inspectors started compiling

69

annual returns that female statistics for surface work became at all reliable. The 1841 census had not distinguished between surface and underground work. Surface workers had not been instructed to return themselves as miners and probably only a small proportion of them did so. The Children's Employment Commission did not provide precise figures although over a thousand females were known to be banking coal in South Staffordshire alone in the early 1840s.[3] Job opportunities at the surface were beginning to multiply and some former underground workers were absorbed into pit brow work. The 1851 census returns however show only 2,649 females as coal miners (1,295 of them aged below 20) for England and Wales. This number had officially increased to 3,763 by 1861 though this was probably still well below the actual numbers working at pit heads at busy times.[4] In 1866 at the Shropshire Lilleshall pits alone there were 592 female workers.[5]

From 1874 onwards the Inspectors' yearly reports provided total figures and area breakdown. They also included the women working at Scottish pits. The figures show those engaged at British mines which came under the aegis of the 1872 Mines Act, that is, mines of coal, stratified ironstone, shale and fireclay. A high proportion of the number returned for South Wales (the eastern counties), South Staffordshire and Shropshire were connected with the iron industry as were some Scottish women.[6] In 1874, 6,899 females were returned as surface workers (though the 1871 census had shown only 3,251 English and Welsh coal labourers and 206 others connected with coal). Between this date and the late 1880s numbers declined fairly steadily though in the last decade of the century they rose again to the level of the late 1870s. By 1900 there were 4,808 females – only in 1888, the year after colliery legislation was passed, had the number fallen below 4,000.[7]

During this same period the proportion of surface females to surface males had gradually and consistently declined. Whereas in 1875, 6.25 per cent of the total surface labour force was female, by 1890 this had decreased to 3.95 per cent. There was however less of a gap in West Lancashire. In 1886 for example the national percentage of females in the surface workforce was only 4.29 per cent but in West Lancashire it was 21.58 per cent. The number of male surface workers also declined between 1874 and 1886 – from 103,319 to 91,977 though there was a slight increase in 1880-3. As with female labour, there was a rise in 1887 followed in 1888 by a temporary fall then steady increase from 1889.

Eleven of the Inspectors' districts regularly employed females. In

Table 3.1: Numbers of Surface Females at Coal, Iron, Shale and Clay
Mines in Proportion to the Total Surface Labour Force, 1874-1900

Year	Females	Total surface labour force	Percentage of total
1874	6,899	110,218	6.25
1875	6,504	108,828	5.97
1876	6,055	105,303	5.75
1877	5,378	99,366	5.41
1878	4,956	92,350	5.36
1879	4,842	91,631	5.28
1880	4,640	93,552	4.95
1881	4,715	96,090	4.90
1882	4,652	97,795	4.75
1883	4,479	97,662	4.58
1884	4,458	98,143	4.54
1885	4,303	96,441	4.46
1886	4,131	96,108	4.29
1887	4,183	97,737	4.27
1888	3,935	96,043	4.09
1889	4,027	100,135	4.02
1890	4,206	106,421	3.95
1900	4,808	155,829	3.13

Source: Based on Inspectors' Reports 1875-1901.

1874 it was the South Wales districts which returned the highest
number of females, many of them working at ironstone mines. Yet
by 1890 their numbers had been more than halved — from 1,603 to
732. During the time of the exclusion attempts in the 1880s the
Tredegar Iron and Coal Company still employed 200 females but
elsewhere in Wales there was a marked decline in job opportunities.[8]
The West Wales anthracite pits, traditionally operating on a small scale,
were being worked out. In contrast to the expanding steam coal trade
of Glamorgan (where women had not been encouraged to start
working), the miners in the Daugleddau coalfield in Pembrokeshire
were experiencing serious problems as high degrees of faulting and
other geological difficulties, coupled with a lack of investment, were
forcing many pits to close. In spite of increased demand for anthracite,
Pembrokeshire only provided six per cent of the South Wales output

in 1890. Whereas in 1877 she had 84 female workers, by 1900 a county breakdown of numbers returned only eleven women. Lower Level colliery had employed 25 women in the 1890s but by the beginning of the twentieth century Bonvilles Court colliery was the sole survivor in the Saundersfoot coastal district, the women and indeed all employees of Moreton, Grove and Lower Level losing their work through closures.[9]

It is more difficult to extract information about numbers further east as the district returns did not differentiate between colliery and other forms of employment covered by the act — for example iron piling and limestone breaking. The Children's Employment Commission had revealed some figures — for example at the Nantyglo and Beaufort Iron works 100 had been employed on the mine banks, 14 at the blast furnaces and 10 at the forges and rolling mills. Individual records can help clarify the situation a little.[10] In 1866 for example 781 employees at the Dowlais Iron works were female but of these only 86 were actually engaged in colliery work (fifteen aged between 10 and 13 and thirty-four aged 14 to 18 with thirty-seven over 18).[11] By the end of the century mechanisation had considerably reduced the numbers at ironworks and most of the women so employed were to be found in the brickworks.

Another great ironmaking district, the Black Country, also employed women and in 1874 the Inspectors' district of South Staffordshire and Worcestershire had the highest number of females for a single district. Yet this number (1,343, of which 926 worked at coal mines) was to decline sharply during the next few decades, particularly in the late 1870s. The reduction in the number of pit bank women can be linked to legislative restrictions (in the form of special rules forbidding work at the pit mouth for women at some pits) and was also due to the adverse publicity given to shaft accidents (see Chapter 6).[12] In the main, however, it was a reflection of the wider economic decline. Women were chiefly employed in the southern part of the coalfield. Much of the coal was used in the pig and wrought iron trade which had flourished since the second half of the eighteenth century. Extensive working of the seam led to rapid exhaustion of the coal supply. Deeper seams were worked but the decline in iron and competition from newer areas forced the rapid collapse of the trade, particularly after 1872. Numerous small pits which had employed women now became worked out. Numbers also fell dramatically between 1874 and 1890 in North Staffordshire, Cheshire and Shropshire district where many iron concerns ceased to operate.

In contrast, the one district which never fell below 1,000 females was West Lancashire. She boasted over 1,300 females during the second half of the 1870s and from 1877 had the highest number of female surface workers. By 1886 when the exclusion campaign was in full swing, West Lancashire had 31.97 per cent of the total number of females employed at collieries.[13] Numbers began to increase at the end of the century (and in North East Lancashire on a smaller scale). By 1900 under a reorganised district system, the Liverpool area had 1,423 females over 16 and 185 between 13 and 16, reflecting the fortunes of a Lancashire coal industry which had expanded enormously. In a district in which women worked in mills and had been associated with mining work for centuries, their increased use in screening operations was understandable.

The situation was very different in the north-east where women were not encouraged to work. The Inspector's district of Northumberland, Durham and Cumberland did contain women surface workers but they were chiefly the screen lasses of the Whitehaven-Workington area. In 1875 for example, seven females were employed in South Durham, six in North Durham and none in the Newcastle area but 348 were working in Cumberland. By 1886 there were three Durham pit women and 395 Cumberland screen lasses. Of those areas which returned women employees, the lowest recorded numbers were for Yorkshire. Formerly this region was one of the main employers of female child labour in the pits, but 1842 appears to have been something of a watershed for such work for Yorkshire females, resulting in a virtual taboo on all their colliery employment. By 1890 only two females were recorded as working at Yorkshire pits. Numbers were also low for most of the century at West Scotland pit heads though they increased in the last years and by 1900 the Lanarkshire district had the highest number of Scottish females.[14] Further east, where work below ground had been so common, women continued to work at the surface though as old pits became worked out, they lost their jobs and were not taken on at many of the newer concerns.

The ages of those at work varied considerably, depending on the type of work, the district and the legislative control which was exercised. In 1842 there was one widow of eighty cleaning ironstone on the surface in the Dowlais district of South Wales.[15] The 1851 census returned eleven women aged seventy-five to eighty, the same number aged eighty to eighty-five and five over eighty-five. Eleven girls were recorded between the ages of five and ten.[16] The 1842 act had not laid down a minimum starting age for surface work. A Shropshire

Table 3.2: Number of Surface Females in Different Districts, 1874-90

Date	North Wales	South Wales[a]	West Scotland[b]	East Scotland[b]	Yorks.	North Staffs. Cheshire Shropshire	South Staffs. Worcs.	Northumberland Durham Cumberland	North and East Lancs.	West Lancs.
1874	144	1,603	69	724	29	1,047	1,363	317	148	1,312
1875	109	1,437	75	652	28	946	1,221	351	142	1,372
1876	101	1,395	57	635	24	876	957	335	166	1,343
1877	98	1,160	58	544	16	766	705	315	173	1,364
1878	73	994	36	632	19	681	522	345	128	1,322
1879	76	993	50	631	11	554	486	344	237	1,370
1880	69	1,002	50	565	10	552	354	357	248	1,351
1881	65	1,010	35	591	8	530	430	376	245	1,331
1882	64	992	41	581	4	502	429	386	241	1,316
1883	68	999	45	566	5	473	306	373	251	1,324
1884	74	1,022	38	584	6	424	299	423	237	1,283
1885	65	915	32	574	4	356	270	417	281	1,242
1886	61	835	41	576	5	319	237	398	317	1,321
1887	64	—	40	557	4	278	201	397	316	1,343
1888	40	803	49	516	3	256	—	315	365	1,360
1889	51	809?	71	584	2	206	208	274	391	1,429
1890	61	732	67	584	2	209	238	286	419	1,637

Notes: a. The Welsh figure includes some Welsh women from the south-western district. b. The Scottish figures show only those employed at collieries.

informant told the 1866 Select Committee on Mines that in his district not much attention was paid to age — at stone mines the youngest girls were seven or eight — the main criterion being whether they could carry stone or coal-boxes.[17] The information given to this committee does however suggest that the majority of girls started work at collieries after the age of ten and the diarist Munby found that most girls were in their teens or early twenties.[18] The 1851 census shows 368 English and Welsh girls of ten to fifteen but 916 aged between fifteen and twenty.

Some collieries adopted their own rules about the ages of female workers. The Wigan Coal and Iron Company for example would not engage girls until they were sixteen. The majority of female surface workers were single but attitudes towards married women workers were not uniform — in South Wales and Cumberland it was extremely rare to find married women working (see Chapter 6). The 1872 act (clause 12, pt 1) stipulated that no females under ten could be employed at coal mines. The debates on the bill revealed some of the

Table 3.3: Number of Surface Females of Different Ages in West Lancashire, 1874-90

Year	10-13	13-16	16+
1874	3	143	1,166
1875	—	180	1,192
1876	1	185	1,157
1877	2	154	1,208
1878	—	129	1,193
1879	—	120	1,250
1880	—	125	1,226
1881	—	102	1,229
1882	—	115	1,201
1883	—	118	1,206
1884	—	111	1,272
1885	—	103	1,239
1886	—	131	1,190
1887	2	109	1,234
1888	—	120	1,240
1889	—	181	1,248
1890	—	191	1,446

Source: Inspectors' Reports.

problems of controlling ages of work. There had been attempts since 1869 to extend the provisions of the Workshops Regulation Act of 1867 and to consolidate and amend legislation concerning the Inspectorate. There were three abortive bills in 1869, 1870 and 1871 but the bill which eventually became law was introduced by H.A. Bruce the Home Secretary and received its first reading on 12 February 1872. Conscious of the precedent set by the Brickfields Act of the previous year which had succeeded in legislating against girls under sixteen, female pit work was attacked at the Committee stage. In spite of a compromise proposal that only females over twenty should work, all females over ten were eventually allowed to continue to work. Some control was also exercised from other directions. For example, Sandon's Education Act of 1876 forbade the employment of boys and girls aged between ten and fourteen who had not reached certain specific educational standards (a certificate of proficiency in the 3 'R's or five years attendance at school known as the 'Dunce's pass'). There were, however, loopholes – for example, a child who lived more than two miles from a public elementary school received exemption and the employment of children out of school time was not forbidden. Mundella's Act of 1880 tightened up on the provisions of 1870 and 1876, making school attendance obligatory for all between five and ten but still allowed those under fourteen to work if they could prove proficiency or past attendance. Conditions of exemption continued to vary between districts as did judgements of proficiency. The 1887 Mines Act eventually raised the minimum age of entry to twelve but the Inspectors' figures showed only two females below thirteen. In the early 1900s, however, there were still girls at the pit who were twelve – they worked half time there, spending the rest of the day at school.

Table 3.4: Number of 10-13 Year-olds at the Surface, 1874-87

1874	22	1881	2
1875	10	1882	1
1876	10	1883	1
1877	20	1884	–
1878	31	1885	–
1879	9	1886	1 (Pembs.)
1880	10	1887	2 (West Lancs.)

Source: Inspectors' Reports.

One woman recalled that when she started working at Plank Lane, Wigan at this age, the manager advised her to bring two bricks to stand on so that she could reach the picking belt.[19]

Attempts to intervene by legislation were in fact made at a time when the methods of work were actually beginning to improve. The 1890s saw the extension of mechanical tipplers, improved screening operations and a greater use of picking belts and tables as well as the erection of washeries. Such developments helped to ease the burdens of manual workers and ultimately to threaten the employment of women quite independently of legislation. And it is to these methods of work that we should now turn. In discussing types of coal preparation it is essential to bear in mind the fact that experimentation and the invention of more advanced techniques did not mean that they were uniformly adopted.

This immediately becomes apparent from considering the first tasks after the coal had left the pit bottom — winding and unloading. By the early nineteenth century shallow pits were using endless chain systems of winding but deeper pits had winding engines with hemp ropes (soon to be replaced by both flat and round wire ropes). In Scotland and at a few Pembrokeshire pits, coal was still being carried on the backs of women coal bearers.[20] Miners and coal were frequently drawn up to the surface by hand — the Children's Employment Commission sketch of Ann Ambler and Will Dyson had advertised this.[21] In Shropshire women helped attach baskets to ropes and wind them up and down the shaft by hand. In the Wrexham area of North Wales girls over twelve helped to turn barrels in the early 1840s and in West Wales women helped land coal and operate windlasses both above and below ground.[22] Some windlasses had been adapted to be worked by horses — the cog and rung gin worked on a wheel and pinion basis.[23] The horse-driven whim gin or whimsey had now superseded the cog and rung — a drum was mounted on a vertical shaft away from the pit mouth and its diameter could be increased to provide faster winding. The number of levers and horses could be increased for heavier winds.

In the Black Country women were employed to bank or unload coal at many small gin pits and at those using winding engines (described by the Commissioner Tremenheere as 'engine' pits) and they became the centre of a short-lived scare about the legality of their employment. Clause 8 of the 1842 act had stated that nobody other than a male over fifteen should have charge of any steam engine or other engine, windlass or gin or be in charge of machinery, ropes, chains or other tackle of any engines which conveyed people up and down the shaft. The next clause stipulated that the person under whose direction the driver of the animal acted, should be the person in charge.

In the Wolverhampton area there were about four hundred females employed at gin pits and it was believed that their work must, in the light of these clauses, be illegal. At the beginning of March 1844 a Bilston owner was accused in court of allowing a pit bank girl to have charge of a mining gin. She landed tubs and gave instructions to a boy who drove the horse gin. The owner Shale was convicted and his appeal failed.[24] As a result all the females employed to land tubs at gin pits in the area were suddenly dismissed.[25] Although several proprietors claimed that the use of women in this work was not contrary to the law, they were in a difficult position since clause 9 implied that the women were in charge illegally. Moreover contravention of this clause meant a fine of at least £20. What however made the situation far more serious was the subsequent dismissal of a large number of the further six hundred employed at the 'engine' pits. Two or more women were employed in banking at each shaft of these pits. Not only was there the prospect of distress for women suddenly deprived of their livelihood but there would also be difficulties for the butty miners or chartermasters who employed them. Within a short time just under a thousand females within seven miles of Bilston had lost their jobs.[26] Several contractors discharged all female surface workers regardless of their particular work. It was debatable whether these pits should fall into the same category as gin pits — minerals were after all drawn up by a steam engine and the women acted under the supervision of the engineer so were not technically in control. Nevertheless fear of prosecution (and detection was obviously far easier than in cases of employment below ground) led to a temporary panic. A number of court cases ensued and Peter Brophy, secretary of the Miners' Association worked hard to procure information against chartermasters. The Home Office learnt that he 'itinerates through mining districts and ferments discord'.[27] Since the real intention had been to prevent boys under fifteen driving machines, Tremenheere was not satisfied and sought legal advice.[28] It was decided that the employment of women at gin and windlass pits was illegal but not their banking at 'engine' pits. Between six and seven hundred women were therefore reinstated in their former employment.[29]

Munby observed the mid-century banking methods in the Midlands. As the cage reached the top of the shaft women helped to push a slide underneath and unloaded the wains (skips, tubs) and pushed them along the pit bank:

She foremost, from the great pit cage
Would hurry with her load
And drive it swiftest o'er the stage
And down the iron road.[30]

They also helped to 'run them in' which meant pushing the empty
wains back into the cage. It was arduous work, generally performed
by the strongest women. According to the manager of the Lilleshall
pits in Shropshire, only about 20 per cent of the 592 female employees
did this kind of work.[31] Munby also emphasised their strength:

Bah Goom! thought the Gaffer,
Hoo's cliver and strong —
Hoo's a rare un, as iver Ah'd seed!
Soom un else 'ull be catching her oop affor long,
For hoo's gan of a better most breed.

Ah'll have her, Ah'll keep her, Ah'll gie her full waage
Hoo's wuth it, Ah'll tell th'Overseer
An Ah'll set her te rawk yon big corves oht o' th' caage,
For hoo's stooter till ony a'ts theer.[32]

Generally a banksman supervised, though at one Shropshire pit Munby
met a female overseer who had been banking for eighteen years and
'acted cicerone in a way I never saw a woman of her class do before'.[33]

In South Wales balance pits were replacing horse gins. Full trams
were raised by lowering empties containing water and thereby acting as
a balance. They were introduced in the Tredegar area in 1829. Ty Trist
was started as a balance pit in 1834, changing to steam winding in the
1860s. The *Morning Chronicle* commented on the workings of a
Merthyr balance pit. Four girls helped to unload, two pushing the full
tram away from the pit's mouth whilst the other two released the
water at the pit bottom by a pulley mechanism and prepared for the
next landing.[34] More advanced winding methods continued to employ
females. At the pit mouth of Garswood Park Colliery, Lancashire in
the 1870s two women and a man helped unload the boxes of coal (as
they were called locally) from the cage while two others replaced them
with empties. They all pushed the tubs along the rails to a point on
the platform where younger girls took over, pushing them on to a pier
and underneath an endless chain. As many as 3,500 full box-loads were
sent up the four shafts in one day.[35] At a few Lancashire pits women

worked in the chutes below but were excluded from work on the
actual brow — Munby found this at one of the Ince Hall pits in 1860,
'an absurd innovation'![36] Women also unloaded tubs at Belgian pits as
drawings by Renard and other *liégeois* artists show.[37]

Before the advent of screening plants, coal would be tipped and
piled into a heap to be loaded into waggons. In Lancashire and
Yorkshire the miners would have given it a primary riddling or sieving
underground. In Pembrokeshire this job had been done by women. It
would also be sorted by riddling at the surface, using hand-riddles or
a large stationary riddle.[38] In the mid-1860s Munby found that besides
thrutching or pushing tubs of coal at the pit mouth and, in some cases
making preliminary examinations of tubs, the women's work mainly
consisted of hand-riddling (contemporary photographs show these large
sieves) and shovelling coal with large spades into wagons.[39] An Ince
miner told the Select Committee on Mines in 1866 that the women's
tasks were mainly riddling and wheeling tubs to wagons or barges for
transportation.[40]

Before the miners were allowed to appoint their own checkweigher
in 1860, the management was free to calculate a miner's payment by
measure. His work was identified by a tin tally and only the tallies
which came up on full tubs of coal were counted, the miner therefore
having no say in whether a tub was full or what constituted good coal.
At many pits a girl used to shout out when a tub had some dirt and
thereby enabled the banksman to know whether to penalise the miner.
The appointment of the miners' own checkweighman and the system
of payment by weight also involved the use of females. After the full
tub had been run to the landing, they helped place it on to a swivel or
turntable where it would be weighed and then run along rails or landing
plates to the tippler. In 1873 Munby noticed the huts for the new
tally-takers (known as tally-snatchers in the Wigan area). These girls
shouted out the miner's tally number and collected the tallies.[41]

Women also helped to operate the tipplers which teemed or tipped
the coal on to the screen. The 'kickup' type (Wain's patent tippler) was
popular in the 1870s. It was shaped like an iron cradle and when the
full tub of coal ran into this cradle, its weight caused it to overbalance
and tip out the coal. It automatically righted itself and the tub was
returned to the shaft. A trap door at the bottom of the chutes
prevented the coal from sliding on to the screen until it was needed.
At some pits a woman regulated this door by pulling a handle, though
occasionally the doors flew open by themselves. Each tub had to be
withdrawn the same way as it entered and wait until the assistant had

removed it. To improve the situation a revolving side tippler was devised. It was power driven through a clutch and operated on a rotary principle. The tub was placed in a cage which revolved about a horizontal axis parallelled to the length of a tub. It was tipped upside down and emptied during a complete revolution of the frame. The frame stopped automatically when the upright position was reached again. The empty tub would be nudged out at the opposite end by the entrance of a full tub. Unloading was facilitated when this tippler came into use in the late 1880s. A number of tubs could now pass through quickly and coal was emptied more gradually and uniformly.[42]

Tipping also became progressively easier for women with the introduction of new tipplers. At the Wigan Coal and Iron Company's Victoria pit in the 1880s the women worked with four-way tubs — automatic tipplers operated by gravity and controlled by a hand-brake through a lever or foot-pedal.[43] The weight of the full tub placed in the tippler made it revolve downwards until the coal was tipped on to the screen. At the same time it brought an empty tub level with the pit bank. This was pushed out of the tippler by another full tub being run in.

At some pits women were not allowed to operate tipplers and were solely employed at the screens. Their work here was actually at the picking belts situated at the foot of the screens. Before the industrial revolution the products of the mine had been sold as one class of fuel.[44] As demand and consumption increased, so did the need for sizing this fuel. The exhaustion of better seams led to the mining of those of inferior quality. Demand dictated that different sizes of coal were produced irrespective of quality so coal from the best seams (such as the famous Arley mine of Wigan) was separated into different sizes along with that of poorer seams. Where house coal and steam coal were produced from the same seam it was impossible to separate the qualities in the loading of the tubs. Hand-riddling had become laborious and increasingly inadequate. From about 1760 collieries in the north-east of England began sorting by using fixed screens on the surface. This gradually spread to other coalfields. The early screens consisted of wooden bars set at a fixed distance from each other. Duck or small coal which passed between the bars would pass into a wagon. Round coal would slide down the screen itself and into another wagon. If more than two sizes were required, coal would pass between two sets of bars with the distance between them being varied in each screen. Cheap small coal which previously had chiefly been used for firing colliery boilers or for the saltmaking industry, now acquired a new importance.[45]

Wooden screens did not last long and since some parts got worn more quickly than others there was a likelihood of imperfect sizing. Iron bars were therefore introduced, one or more of a series of cast or wrought iron bars being arranged in rows and supported by cross pieces known as combs. Women raked the coal in the chutes and had to be very careful not to break tender house coals. Sometimes slack still got amongst the round coal and could be carried with it. The spaces between the bars also got blocked. Screens were expensive – each one required a separate kickup and they also took up a lot of space. The solution was movable bar screens. Pioneered on the Continent – the most famous was invented by Briart in Belgium in 1877 – they consisted of two series of bars, one fixed and one movable, which alternated with one another. Each set was connected to an eccentric of its own – one eccentric being placed at an angle of 180° from the other. They were fixed on the same shaft and as the shaft revolved, the bars were raised and depressed in turn. Although the initial cost was high, they provided much more efficient screening and could be placed either horizontally or at an angle. Jigging screens were introduced towards the end of the century. Based on the old hand-riddles and woven like them, the shakers (as they were called in Lancashire) consisted of screen bars or perforated plates fixed in a frame suspended by rods or wooden hangers. The screen oscillated like a pendulum. Small coal carried along by the larger pieces could now be dislodged as the screen jigged backwards and forwards. In spite of the noise and vibration, it was efficient and fast – quadrupling the amount of coal which fixed bars had been able to handle.

Although the mining of inferior seams did widen opportunities, it presented fresh problems. In addition to sizing, sorting became imperative to remove any impurities. The amount of dirt could vary considerably, some seams being much cleaner than others. Not only might there be dirt from the pit floor but some seams had bands of dirt interstratified with coal. The collier was expected to load only clean coal into the tubs but it could be difficult where the band was thick and pieces of coal large and he would be hindered by poor light. Yet coal not cleaned properly was coal wasted. In the 1890s South Wales owners were reminded of the necessity of improving their screening and cleaning since foreign buyers were complaining of dirt and excessive small mixed with the larger coal.[46] Some examination of the coal was therefore necessary to rid it of stone, shale, fireclay or iron pyrites.

Therefore at the foot of the screens (or placed at right angles to them) travelling bands or belts were erected. Here stood the majority of the pit women, generally about five or ten on each side of the belt, manually checking the coal and removing dirt. By the late nineteenth century mines might be discharging several thousands of tons a week and every bit would have to be inspected. The women might be handling a ton of dirt a day per person. Different sizes of coal went to different picking belts there generally being a different belt for every size of coal other than slack. Large coal usually had its own belt but cobbles or nuts from two or more screens might be placed together on a belt. The coal would be distributed in a thin layer so that it could be properly exposed to view for effective sorting. Picking belts also enabled a further sizing – at the long picking belts in the Midlands for example, manual sizing accompanied mechanical sizing, the larger coal which carried the highest price being lifted out. The main purpose of picking belts was however to separate the dross (dirt) from the coal as it passed in front of the sorters. Cleaning belts might be up to 70 feet long – the dirtier the coal, the longer the belt needed to be. The width would be determined by the distance the sorters could reach.

Belts would be constructed in different ways. Perhaps the most effective type consisted of unperforated steel or wrought iron plates riveted to two long link chains and supported on cast iron rollers about nine feet apart. The belt would usually be driven by hexagonal wheels – two positioned at each end. It moved slowly, perhaps doing thirty to forty revolutions per minute. In Lancashire strong-woven wire-netting belts supported on round cross bars were popular. The early belts used in the 1870s were sometimes made of new flat hemp ropes banded together or old winding ropes. One woman generally stood very close to the shoot with an iron rake ready to spread the coal out as it was tipped down. The others stood along each side of the belt, picking out dirt with both hands. It was essential to concentrate and work swiftly. If the tip wagons contained much dirt, orders would be cancelled. At some pits women were fined if they let any dirt go in the wagons – Bamfurlong colliery near Wigan stopped a penny from wages. There were usually men in charge, some of whom were very strict about thorough cleaning and constant attention. At the Blundells' pits it was a case of 'once you got your heads down over belt you hadn't to lift them up again unless the belt stopped'. If the overseer noticed a single piece of dirt 'he'd be picking it out and bringing it to you if you'd missed that'. Restless workers might have boxes put around their legs.[47]

Girls generally started on the nut belt picking out the dirt from the small coal then progressed to cobbles and eventually moved to the coal belt. The latter was more difficult work as there were often huge lumps of coal. Sometimes the women had to get on to the belt in order to remove them for breaking. They would have to be broken with a chipper or hammer but coal could not be chipped on the belt as it would make slack so it had to be put on one side. The iron chippers were usually light single-pointed hand picks. At Brinsop Hall colliery, Wigan, chipping was done on two planks which ran the entire length of the belts. The pit brow women of the Meadow pit at nearby Aspull would take it in turns to have what they called a 'chipping day' at the end of the shift. All the dirt would have to be removed from the big lumps.[48] Sometimes a considerable amount of copperas would be attached to the coal. At Duxbury Park colliery, Lancashire it was thrown into a box and eventually melted down, a shilling per ton being paid to the seven pit women every three months.[49]

The dirt was disposed of in several ways. Some belts had a partition in the middle which formed a trough into which it could be deposited and then carried along separately from the coal and discharged down a chute. Alternatively it might be thrown on to a parallel belt which would convey it to a bunker from which it could be drawn off into wagons. It might have to be thrown into little tin bins and then when the belt stopped, the woman in charge could knock the iron ring on the wall to alert the men and enable the women to 'shoo' or shovel the dirt on to the belt so that it could pass into a special dirt wagon. Frequently dirt might be simply thrown on the floor and at the end of the day, the women would have to fill barrows and wheel them up planks then tip them over or simply shovel the dirt back on the belt. It might take another hour before the dirt wagon was filled but the work had to be done and the duff or dust which had gathered under the shakers would have to be cleared up. At Victoria pit, Wigan, an old woman spent all day cleaning out the area under the screens.[50] Meanwhile the cleaned coal would have dropped down a chute into a large wagon in the rail road below. Attached to some belts would be a small fixed screen which received the cleaned coal and got rid of any small which had been made during the screening process. Women worked in the wagons with big spades, helping to control the flow of coal in the chutes.[51] They would also trim or level down the coal in the wagons.

At some pits sorting was done at raised picking tables (about 12 to 15 feet in diameter) which consisted of plates revolving around a vertical axis. The women stood around the inner and outer circumference of the tables. Coal entered on one side by a chute and was carried slowly around whilst dirt was picked off and then swept into a loading chute by a scraper. Although coal tended to arrive in a heap, this method at least allowed dirty coal to be carried round a second time by merely raising the scraper. The initial cost was low and they were hard wearing, providing a firm support for the women to chip off any rubbish. They also allowed the same number of pickers as belts but filled less space. A number of Lancashire pits were using them by the late nineteenth century – one example was Abram colliery near Wigan.[52]

Women sorters were not however confined to Lancashire. At Lower Level colliery, Kilgetty, Pembrokeshire, females took drams[53] from the top of the pit and tripped (the local word) them down the screen. Ten of the twenty-five female workers at the straps (belts) sorted slag from coal 'picking as quick as lightning'. The slag went into small boxes and the cleaned coal was heaped up to await shipping. In Scotland women pit head workers were 'picking brasses' at the screens as were young lads. In the Black Country, Shropshire and in Cumberland sorters also worked at the screens. In districts where female labour was not used, old or disabled miners or boys did all this work – in the United States they were known as breaker boys and featured in the interpretative photography of Lewis Hine.[54]

Although by the end of the century the majority of British pit women worked at screening or sorting coal, there were other jobs which they continued to do. Wales had its 'tip girls' who helped to remove cinders from furnaces, unload at the tips and chip bits of iron ore with small picks.[55] Just as the term 'pit brow lass' became extended to cover all forms of female surface work, so too did 'tip girl' become synonymous with female employment at South Wales collieries and ironworks. Women and girls had worked in the Dowlais area since the 1780s, helping prepare mine (iron ore) and pick bits of iron from the furnace cinders. In the nineteenth century they performed many jobs – poll girls took iron ore from trams, sorted out stone and shale, cleaned the ore and piled it ready for the furnaces. Coke girls stacked coal ready for coking and others broke limestone with hammers ready for smelting. Pilers worked in the puddling mills stacking and weighing the heavy iron bars which had been cut to be made into rails.[56] Munby visited South Wales in the 1860s and described women lifting large lumps of coke at Nantyglo, unloading and loading coal and ironstone around Blaenavon and loading bricks at Dowlais.[57] Making refractory bricks for lining furnaces was considered a woman's job at the vast Dowlais Iron Company. Methods were primitive – cold water would be poured on to heated floors in small sheds and the clay had to be worked to an even consistency by treading it with bare feet. Thirty-five pound lumps of clay were also moulded in hot moulding sheds and furnaces which were stoked by women.[58]

The American writer Edgar L. Wakeman who visited the Wigan area in 1891 described how unsaleable slack was transformed into coke.[59] He watched the women wielding long-handled shovels and scooping small coal into the arched doors of coke ovens and was impressed by their deftness and dexterity. Once the oven was charged they built up the doorway with bricks and later split the coke into cobbles which they loaded into trucks. At Staffordshire and Shropshire iron works women helped empty skips and pick out dirt from ironstone, kneeling on the mounds to separate and riddle the smaller bits. The Midland Mining Commission of 1843 condemned the work of the girls unloading and sorting ironstone in the Wolverhampton area, viewing it as an unpleasant reminder of women's work below ground.[60] Yet in South East Wales women were working in conditions which bore a closer resemblance to the subterranean toil. In addition to working at the pit top tipping and screening, they filled, pushed and pulled trams of coal at the patches — opencast workings on the hillsides. They wore leather straps around their waists and these were attached to the trams, the sole surviving example of the girdle system which had in the past harnessed female drawers to their tubs.[61]

There were also women hauliers at Welsh pits.[62] In Cumberland they were called carters and the best known was Sal Madge of Whitehaven.[63] She spent about sixty years in pit work having assisted wagoners since the age of eight. She was praised as a 'capital driver whom no one could have excelled'. Women's jobs also included helping to grease the wheels of tubs — on his travels Munby encountered a number of oilers and greasers, also pointswomen working at railway sidings.[64] Women's jobs also included cleaning coal from the railway lines and filling huge coal wagons, and until 1887, lowering and moving them (see Chapter 6). Contemporaries did not always appreciate the difference between the tubs of coal unloaded from the pit and pushed along the brow to the tippler, and the heavy railway trucks or eight-ton wagons below the belts. Munby saw many women moving wagons along the line — using a lever fixed under the iron wheels. Moving and coupling wagons required skill, strength and experience and even trimming was not easy. One pit brow woman explained how she did this:

> I got on the wagon bumper; as the wagons kept moving down the line, I was trimming them, making room for other wagons, to be

shunted under the screens.[65]

When working in bone coal wagons this same woman would be operating the iron lever of the tippler one minute then jumping into the coal wagon the next whilst it was in motion and handing large cobs of coal to the engine driver.

Although girls and women might be primarily engaged to work at the screens, they might find themselves doing all kinds of jobs. Ellen Grounds who worked at the Arley mine pit belonging to Pearson and Knowles of Wigan, explained to Munby 'Ah works at screening and digs coal theer; but when they shoots "Dirt" then we gaw oop te t'broo, and helps te keck the wagons over.'[66] In 1866 a twelve-year-old girl Ellen Hampson was killed on her first day of work at Moss House colliery, Wigan, after attempting to lower a wagon.[67] When the overlooker was asked at her inquest what work at the screens involved, he replied 'cleaning the coal and such like'. When pressed further and asked whether this included moving railway trucks, he replied in the affirmative. The nature of the work might differ considerably depending on management policy but it would also be dictated by demand. In the summer reduced pressure on supplying coal might mean that women could spend much of their time filling wagons rather than screening.[68] Other jobs included chipping mortar off old bricks and stacking them in barrows. Those who worked near canals might help load coal into barges. Sometimes they might have to fill in for absent workers — Kate Leigh the heroine of *A Pit Brow Lassie*, a story written by an ex-miner of Wigan, was normally a tally-taker but when a screen worker was away she replaced her.[69] At some pits the job might be fairly clearly defined — Blundells' women (and there were about eighty at the Pemberton pits by the turn of the century) only worked at the belts. Yet at a number of concerns women would be expected to perform a variety of tasks. They included filling small-wheeled carts (called bogies in Whitehaven) with chock timber and even helping to saw and stack the timber. Such work was usually done when there was no more coal to come up the shaft. At Lower Level they collected studs for pit props first thing in the morning. Some women began their day by cleaning out the offices and would spend part of Saturday in the engine house, washing floors and walls and cleaning the brass.[70] After the 1872 act a number of female datalers (day wage labourers) also helped carry messages and account books. Munby conveyed the sense of constant variety in 'Daatal Polly':

'Delve deep' says the gaffer 'thy barrow is big
And t'muck is a solid good change;
Ram it down wi' thy spaade, lass, an' then it'll lig
While thoo kecks it reet into yon barge

Thoo mun level this heap — it's a big un, thoo knows
An' wheel it an' teem it away:
An' then, Ah've another good job for thy paws,
At'll tak thee best part of a day.'

'Bah Goom!' Cried the maiden, and looked at him hard,
'It's as plaan as this sweat o' mah faace,
At yo winna for nowt lossen me fro oo'r yard
For te put a fresh mon i' mah plaace.'[71]

The rapid proliferation of colliery work in the nineteenth century meant further jobs with the sinking of new shafts and erection of brows. Munby found three girls at the new Douglas Bank colliery, Wigan in 1865. They were helping to 'make the brow' — unloading trucks full of slate and dirt, carrying rails for the tram roads and logs for props.[72]

A new job was slack washing. Here Lancashire led the way. Hand picking was fine for large coal but with excessively dirty coal or anything below about two inches, it was not adequate. Now that the value of clean small coal for coke making was recognised it was in enormous demand. The solution was a coal washing plant. Early wet washing used sieves placed in troughs of water where coal and dirt could be agitated by attendants using rakes. As early as 1858 a washery was erected at Pemberton to receive slack for the coke ovens.[73] A trough washery was installed in 1875 for the new pits and up to eight hundred tons a day passed through it. Nuts and slack were washed separately, the slack being floated by water to the bottom of a trough while the heavier stones and brasses remained behind vertical stops. The washed slack was then raised by a gauze belt to crushers. After crushing a bucket elevator conveyed it to a hopper ready for taking it to the coke ovens. It was worked by two engines and dirty water could be recycled through pipes aided by a pump which raised it to the troughs. Improvements at the end of the century included moving stops or scrapers which travelled against the flow of water and coal and carried dirt to the top end of the trough.[74] Coking coal could now be purified by the removal of mixed particles of stone, shale and iron pyrites and reducing the ash and sulphur in the coke made it more valuable for iron smelting. By the beginning of the twentieth century

Baum of Westphalia had made further improvements in his jig washer. The women who worked at washeries considered themselves privileged — this job was clean, paid comparatively well for nineteenth-century female pit work, involved a degree of privacy and afforded protection from the weather. One of Munby's favourite pit lasses, Ellen Fairhurst, was a slack washer at Ince Hall, Wigan. Here the slack was carried by a stream of water along open troughs which ran on a high gallery. The two slackwashers had their own wooden hut approached by a ladder. They raked the slack up and down as it flowed past them.[75]

At many pits innovation was slow. Although engineers such as John Wood and Sons of Wigan produced sophisticated plant arrangements, the nineteenth century was not to witness their widespread adoption. A *Manchester Guardian* reporter explained in the mid-1880s that at Fletcher and Burrows' Atherton pits, screening had been 'reduced to a science' but he had to admit that what he saw there was 'somewhat different from any which I had previously seen'.[76] Elsewhere there were still many large stationary riddles in use and even hand-riddles. The Wigan journal *Science and the Art of Mining* explained in the mid-1890s that this situation was gradually changing as customers became more particular and the market value for coal which was well screened and hand-picked increased.[77] Nevertheless screens were costly to erect — the pit brows and screen buildings at the King and Queen pits at Pemberton (three fixed bar screens on each side of the shaft) had cost £6,760 in 1870.[78] In the mid-1880s coal was frequently heaped up in a large heap and riddled in wagons by girls and women. Returning to Wigan in 1887 after an absence of several years Munby commented on the moving belts at number two pit, Aspull Moor (three belts with nine girls at each) as a 'new way' of sorting.[79]

Conditions therefore varied dramatically during the second half of the century. In the 1880s when the pit brow controversy reached its height, the kind of work performed by a woman could assume a number of forms. The very fact that it was a time when new methods were being introduced helps explain why attention was being directed to such employment. Ammunition existed for both attackers and defenders of the work since both modern and antiquated systems co-existed. One feature which does however appear to have been common to all types of surface work was its rapid pace. There was constant activity above ground. Admittedly there were occasional lulls — Munby sketched one Pembrokeshire woman knitting between the arrival of coal loads, engaged in the perpetually hopeless task of

trying to keep her wool clean as she sat beneath the chutes.[80] Generally
however the pace was extremely fast. If the boat was in, these women
had their work cut out getting the coal ready to catch the tide.
Newspapers described pit women 'raking away for dear life'.[81] Tubs
might arrive at the pit mouth every minute or so. Pressure to work
quickly and to act as a team was particularly marked during war time
when there was urgent demand for steam coal for ships. At Duxbury
Park colliery during the Boer War no time was wasted:

> We could not afford to lose a second, and the miners, browmen,
> lassies worked very hard. Whilst it lasted we had not time to spit
> out.[82]

Productivity rates always had to be sustained. When new orders came
in and sample wagons of house coal had to be filled

> not until that wagon was full, dare we look up. While picking out
> Dirt, Copperous and even Shale, while our fingers bled at the end.
> We had it to do, forsake of us losing fresh orders.

Munby's descriptions capture the spirit of incessant activity. For
example he found at the Douglas Bank pits in 1878

> girls thrutching full corves from the shaft, along the iron plates and
> the tramways, or kecking them at the screens: girls with their spades
> standing in the holds of the barges or jumping. . .off and on to the
> full corves, as they ran by their own weight down the tramways, and
> jumping off again just in time to stop them at the waters' edge; girls
> standing in the railway trucks under the shoots, arranging the coals
> with their hands, as each load came thundering down, and when the
> truck was full, climbing down over the side and moving it on with a
> lever between the spokes of the iron wheels; girls climbing the ladders,
> and swinging themselves to and fro, from one level to another, and
> crouching or crawling in the coal-shoots, hid in the clouds of black
> dust.[83]

The day was undoubtedly a long one. One woman who told *True
Story of a Lancashire Pit Brow Lass*, Mrs Holden of Duxbury Park colliery,
recounted how her day began at 4 a.m.[84] She helped her mother do
odd jobs about the house before setting off on a three mile walk in the
dark which always frightened her. Work began at 6 a.m. Yet by the

time Mrs Holden was working in the 1890s the hours of women's work at pits had already been partially controlled. In spite of the fact that coalmining had become the most highly regulated of all British industries, the eight hour day was not won for its workers in the nineteenth century. Following the Third Report of the Children's Employment Commission, the 1872 act had however restricted the hours that female pit workers might be employed. The Commission had claimed that the work of girls about furnaces at night was 'attended with evils of a moral character'.[85] The act forbade all work for women between 9 p.m. and 5 a.m., only allowing the morning and afternoon (fore and back) shifts or turns. Such a measure was not welcomed without some reservations because of the monetary loss. When Bailey had forbidden women fillers to work at night at his Brynmawr Ironworks in 1870, they had been disappointed — their weekly wages of between eight and eleven shillings being reduced to about six shillings.[86] Work after 2 p.m. on Saturdays and all day on Sundays was also made illegal. The Saturday afternoon clause provided additional time for cleaning homes though it did cause some ill feeling between the women and the male miners. With the women leaving work at 2 p.m., the men found that for the last two or three hours there was nobody to deal with the coal they had produced. They also felt aggrieved since at some pits the women's wages had just been raised and the men felt that they had gained more than themselves. In the preface to his poem *Dorothy* Munby commented how

A paternal legislature, ever anxious in its sentimental way to keep women cribbed and coddled and ranked with children, has decreed that all female pit-workers shall leave their work at 2 o'clock on Saturday afternoons, thus spoiling the task of the male workers (as these have often told me).[87]

In response to the Commission's report Menelaus, the General Manager at the Dowlais Iron Company had submitted a detailed memorandum defending night and Sunday employment for females and young persons.[88] In 1866, 781 females were employed at the farms, quarries, mine works and collieries at Dowlais and Menelaus insisted that certain jobs such as piling must be done at night. He stressed that the alternative to night work could only be to cease such employment altogether. Females at Dowlais were employed in two sets, succeeding each other day and night. Lady Charlotte Guest had objected to this and night work had ceased for a time. It had however been resumed and

Menelaus emphasised that the lack of alternative labour made the women dependent on such work. He was also careful to explain that by employing these women the parish was saved the expense, and the severe problem of a scarcity of male labour was at least kept under control. He even appealed to national pride by pointing out that the Belgians were now overtaking the British in iron production. Any interference with the supply of labour must result in the Welsh iron trade being 'seriously crippled'.

However, it was Henry Austin Bruce, a senior trustee of the Dowlais works who as Home Secretary introduced proposals for restrictions on the hours of women's work in 1870. The act two years later extended the regulations for boys of between ten and twelve to all boys and girls under thirteen working on the surface. They were not to work more than a six day week or over six hours a day if employed for more than five days in a week nor were they to work over ten hours in any one day.[89] For females over thirteen the regulations for males over sixteen were to apply – they were not to work for more than fifty-four hours in a week or for more than ten hours in one day. Since some women and girls had previously been employed continuously for well over twelve hours, this was a distinct improvement.[90]

Some controversy arose over the provision for meal breaks. According to the 1872 act those working over eight hours continuously were entitled to a total of one and a half hours for meals. In South Wales the men worked nine hours and took half an hour out of that for dinner. Conforming to the new regulations would mean that the men would have to remain at work for an hour longer than they were accustomed to stay. Some girls therefore found that they were replaced by men or boys. The *Examiner* commented:

> It might be good for the men that they should take a longer rest in the middle of their work but they or their employers do not see it and the result of this benevolent attempt to protect the women has been to drive them into situations where they have more work and less play.[91]

In fact the clause was frequently ignored and women often had only a couple of twenty minute breaks for 'bait'. There were a number of complaints and some legal action was taken. In May 1887 for example eight summonses were brought against Wigan Junction colliery and its manager for not allowing sufficient meal times for two women and making them work for eleven and a half hours. In spite of an attempt to claim that a breakdown in machinery had provided sufficient rest, eight fines of £1 each were imposed.[92] The 1887 act made it clear that meal times could not be included as part of the work time. The wording of the 1872 act had been equivocal on this matter.[93] In West Lancashire it had been interpreted in practice to allow the inclusion of meal times. Now that this was no longer to be permitted, many women found that they were having to work a longer day as a result of the 1887 legislation. These might appear to be small details but they could affect the length of an already demanding day. The lack of explicit directives on such issues also emphasises the extent to which the women's work was considered to be of only marginal importance.

This account of the women's work experience can now be placed alongside their social experience. The women's social life and position within the local community will be examined by looking at one area in greater depth.

Notes

1. In 1886 William Wogan, a Lancashire miner and trades unionist, claimed that the descriptions of pit brow work given by the miners' leader Thomas Burt were at least ten years out of date. *St. Helens Newspaper*, 26 April 1886.

2. Examples of surface arrangements at individual pits will be limited to those which employed women. All females over ten are described as women since girls and adult females all saw themselves as women workers.

3. See p.78.

4. PP 1852-3, LXXXVIII, p.CXXII; PP 1863, LIII.1, p.LXIV. 1,828 under 20 and 1,935 over 20.

5. PP 1866, XIV, p.451, qu.13037.

6. East Scotland had 82 females at ironworks in 1875 but 652 at coal and fireclay mines. The census divisions were 1) Mining, 2) Coal, 3) Stone/Clay, 4) Earthenware. The inspectors' figures would have included some of 1 and 3 but most of these would have been counted under the Metalliferous Mines Act of 1872. This distinction explains the higher figures which are sometimes quoted. For example, Strachey mentioned nearly 12,000 women and girls working in 1874 but they were not all 'shifting and grading *coal* and loading trucks'. See R. Strachey, *The Cause* (London, 1978), p.236. The inspectors' reports did not include slack wasters or those employed at private branch railways.

7. The following account is based on the inspectors' reports for 1875-1901. Over the whole period these included 17 working at Irish mines. Since the figures for 1873 were based on estimates, they have not been provided for the different areas — 6,204 was the figure given for the total number in that year.

8. Article on South Wales in *Wigan Observer*, 7 May 1886.

9. A report on Pembrokeshire collieries in 1806 had claimed that the Moreton collieries 'do not really deserve to be distinguished by that name'. Gogerddau Papers. NLW. See R. Howells, *Old Saundersfoot* (Llandyssul, 1977), p.5, for a photograph of Bonvilles' Court colliery in the 1900s which shows women at

work. See also G. Edwards, 'The Coal Industry in Pembrokeshire', *Field Studies*, 1, no.5 (1963), p.28.

10. PP 1842, XVII, no.7, p.619.

11. Memorandum by Menelaus on the Employment of Women and Children in the Iron Works of South Wales, May 1866. Dowlais Papers. Glamorgan Record Office, Cardiff 2/DG Section, Box 5.

12. Munby MS, Diary 20, 13 August 1863. PP 1854, XIX, pp.13-14.

T.J. Raybould, *The Economic Emergence of the Black Country* (Newton Abbot, 1973). In mid-century 75 per cent of the labour force of the brickmaking industry of South Staffordshire (which serviced the collieries and ironworks) were women and girls.

13. See Ch.4 for details about the Wigan coalfield. In 1899 the county of Lancashire had 2,145 females out of a total for England of 2,969. PP 1900, CII, p.55.

14. PP 1866, XIV, p.206, qus. 6835-6; PP 1892, IV, p.186.

15. PP 1842, XVII, no.162, p.656.

16. PP 1852-3, LXXXVIII, p.CXLVII.

17. PP 1866, XIV, p.175, qu.5775.

18. See Ch.4.

19. Interviewed 24 August 1978.

20. See Ch.1.

21. See Ch.2.

22. In the 1850s the inspector Mackworth described small Pembrokeshire pits which utilised members of the family, the women winding and unloading coal whilst men worked below ground. PP 1854, XV, pp.184-5; PP 1842, XVII, no.199, p.316; *Morning Chronicle*, 3 January 1850.

23. See for example Paul Sandby's painting of a pit head with a horse gin. National Museum of Wales. F. Klingender, *Art and the Industrial Revolution* (London, 1968), illustration 9.

24. HO 45/OS/511, 6, 13 May 1844; 7, 18 April 1844; *Birmingham Gazette*, 27 May 1844.

25. PP 1844, XVI. 1, p.55.

26. Hansard LXXIV, House of Commons, 7 May 1844, p.833; HO 45/OS/511, 21, 11 May 1844.

27. HO 45/OS/511, 21, 22, 11 May 1844.

28. HO 0711, 3 May 1844.

29. HO 87/1, 22 May 1844.

30. 'Heaving Day' in Jones Brown (Munby's pseudonym), *Vulgar Verses* (London, 1891), p.185.

31. PP 1866, XIV, p.451, qus. 13011-2.

32. 'Daatal Polly', Munby MS 109[35].

33. Ibid., Diary 20, 14 August 1865.

34. O. Jones, *The Early Days of Sirhowy and Tredegar* (Risca, 1975), p.50; *Morning Chronicle*, 21 March 1850.

35. *Wigan Observer*, 2 August 1873.

36. Munby MS, Diary 6, 29 September 1860.

37. For a sketch by Renard of a 'rachaneuse' unloading a tub from the pit mouth, see C. Lemonnier, *Le Borinage* (Brussels, 1902), p.88.

38. PP 1842, XVII, p.162 shows the process.

39. Munby MS, Notebook 11, 1865.

40. PP 1866, XIV, p.37, qu.1332.

41. Munby MS, Diary 41, 12 September 1873. See 'On the Pit Brow Weighing the Coals' by J. Nash, *The Graphic*, no.460 (21 September 1878). Although the 1872 act stipulated that all coal must be weighed at the pit head, some owners

delayed, claiming that weighing machines were not immediately available. See B. Lewis, *Coal Mining in the Eighteenth and Nineteenth Centuries* (London, 1971), p.64.

42. See W.S. Boulton (ed.), *Practical Coal Mining*, 3 (London, n.d.), pp.292-9 for details of tipping.

43. *Wigan Observer*, 17 February 1886.

44. F. Atkinson, *The Great Northern Coalfield 1700-1900* (London, 1968), pp.37-8; R.A. Mott, 'Developments in the Preparation of Coal for the Market', *Colliery Guardian*, commemorative number (1935), p.100. See also 'An Order for the Pit' (n.d.), MMP 13/12 Wigan Record Office; C.M. Percy, *Mechanical Equipment of Collieries* (Manchester, 1905); G.L. Kerr, *Practical Coal Mining* (London, 1905).

45. Nut coal is about 2 inches in diameter whereas cobbles are about twice that size. Beans and peas are smaller than nuts and were mostly used for boiler feeding.

46. H.T. Wales, 'Screening and Cleaning Coal', *South Wales Institute of Engineers*, XVIII (1892-3), p.252.

47. Interviewed 25 August 1978.

48. Interviewed 24 August 1978.

49. Mrs Holden, *True Story of a Lancashire Pit Brow Lass* (n.d.). Autobio - graphical MS account of a young Lancashire pit brow woman, Chorley Public Library.

50. Interviewed 24 and 25 August 1978.

51. See an illustration of this in *Pictorial World*, 11 April 1874.

52. H.W. Hughes, *A Text Book of Coal Mining* (London, 1917), pp.405, 408.

53. Tramming and dramming are interchangeable words most probably arising from the Welsh mutation rules.

54. One example is L. Hine, 'Breaker boys in Coal Shute', South Pittston 1914. The Rev. Cobb's collection of photographs of the Nottingham coalfield includes a picture of the screens at Brinsley showing old men and boys sorting lumps of coal. Cobb collection. From Pit to Fireplace, NCB, A120.

55. Oral testimony from the late Mrs Martha Jane Richards (née Waters). Interviewed by Richard Keen on 8 June 1970.

56. *Morning Chronicle*, 21 March 1850; *Ladies*, 1, no.25 (14 September 1873), *Illustrated London News*, LXII, 18 January 1873.

57. T.A. Owen, *The History of the Dowlais Iron Works* (Risca, 1977), pp.65-6, 111-19. Welsh women were also employed at tin works as dusters, rubbers and plate openers and wheeled ore at copper works. See transcripts of taped interviews. Coalfield History Project. South Wales Miners' Library, University College, Swansea.

58. Munby MS, Diary 33, 22 September 1865.

59. *Wigan Observer*, 12 September 1891.

60. PP 1843, XIII, P.XXIX.

61. Munby MS, Notebook 11, 1869. Belgian women wore harnesses below ground until the law prevented this in 1883. Munby MS, Diary 51, 27 August 1883. In Japan harnesses continued to be worn in this century.

62. See for example the photograph of women hauliers at Abergorki colliery c.1880 in C. Batstone, *Old Rhondda in Photographs* (Barry, 1974), photograph 6; Munby MS, Notebook 11, 1869; PP 1842, XVII, no.179, p.659.

63. *Cumberland Pacquet*, 13 April 1899; *Woman's Life*, VI, no.68 (27 March 1899).

64. For example Munby MS, Notebook 11, 1869.

65. Holden, *True Story*.

66. Munby MS, Notebook 111, 1866.

67. See Ch.6.

68. Changes in jobs were sometimes resisted. Munby's friend Becky opposed an attempt to make two girls carry slack at Woodhouse colliery, Shropshire, since this job was supposed to be done by all of them in turn. Yet they were told that failure to comply would result in a fortnight's notice. Munby MS Visits to Hannah, 8, 24 April 1887.

69. *Comet*, no.9 (4 May 1889).

70. Interviewed 25 August 1978.

71. 'Daatal Polly', Munby MS 109[35]

72. Ibid., Notebook 11, 1865.

73. D. Anderson, 'Blundells' Collieries; Technical Developments 1776-1966', *Transactions of the Historic Society of Lancashire and Cheshire*, 119 (1967), pp.173-4. F. Kohn, *Iron and Steel Manufacture* (London, 1873), p.21. Another early washery was at the Wigan Coal and Iron Company's Marsh House colliery where a Béraud continuous jigger was introduced by James Morrison in 1868.

74. H.E. Clegg, 'Some Historic Notes on the Wigan Coalfield', *Colliery Guardian*, 14 November 1957. The washery at the King pit Pemberton for the Wigan 4' slack used travelling trays instead of stops.

75. Munby MS, Notebook IV, 1870; VII, 1878; VIII, 1883.

76. *Manchester Guardian*, 17 February 1886.

77. *Science and the Art of Mining*, V, no.11, 1894-5, p.244.

78. Anderson, 'Blundells', p.175.

79. Ibid., p.171. Munby MS, Diary 9, 29 September 1887; *Lancet*, 30 July 1887. Photographs in the 1880s still showed girls carrying hand-riddles though they were probably studio props rather than implements constantly in use.

80. See Ch.6.

81. *Wigan Observer*, 1 May 1886. The second article in a series commissioned by the *Manchester Guardian* also reprinted in the Wigan Observer.

82. Holden, *True Story*.

83. Munby MS, Notebook VII, 1878.

84. Holden, *True Story*.

85. PP 1864, XXII, p.14. This gave evidence of night work at the Dowlais, Plymouth and Cyfarthfa works in South Wales.

86. Munby MS, Diary 38, 4 October 1870.

87. Munby MS, *Dorothy* (London, 1880), Preface.

88. Menelaus memorandum.

89. They had to be allowed an interval of 12 hours between two consecutive periods of employment although 8 hours were considered sufficient between Friday and Saturday mornings.

90. M.L. Peace, *The Coal Mines Regulation Act of 1872* (London, 1872).

91. *Examiner*, 26 September 1874. The law came into force on 1 September 1874. The 1886 Royal Commission on the Depression of Trade and Industry was told by a director of the Wigan Coal and Iron Company that the 1872 act was extremely difficult to enforce – it was 'bristling with pains and penalties in every possible direction and it cannot be carried out without very considerable cost'. PP 1886, XXIII, p.200, qus. 12, 150.

92. *Wigan Observer*, 20 May 1887. The Orrell Coal and Cannel Company faced 15 summonses several months later, tried the same argument about machinery failure and claimed that the women wanted to work through their dinner hour in order to get away earlier at night.

93. Hansard CCCXXXIII, House of Commons, 2 March 1888, p.33; 12 February 1889, p.22; PP 1887, XXII, p.194; PP 1888, XXIX, p.16.

4 THE HEADQUARTERS

I am an Aspull collier, I like a bit of fun,
To have a go at football or in the sports to run;
So good-bye old companions, adieu to jollity,
For I have found a sweetheart, and she's all the world to me.

Could you but see my Nancy, among the tubs of coal,
In tucked up skirt and breeches, she looks exceedingly droll;
Her face besmear'd with coal dust, as black as black can be
She is a pit-brow lassie, but she's all the world to me.

Orpheus, 'A Pit Brow Wench for Me', v.1 and 2,
Comet, no.2 (26 January 1889)

A.J. Munby once referred to Wigan as 'the picturesque headquarters of rough female labour'.[1] For years he returned to his mecca, devoting page after page of his writings to the pit brow women and girls working in the Wigan coalfield. Wigan was primarily a town of coalminers but combined with the coal industry was cotton. Unlike the monolithic mining communities of many areas, for example the South Wales valleys, it also differed from the great cotton towns of Lancashire. Certainly there were other examples of multi-occupational towns — Burnley was a cotton town which also had coalmining, Oldham had its cotton, coal and engineering. What however marked out Wigan from the other towns was the overwhelming predominance of females in the cotton industry. The majority of the town's male labour force was employed in mining. In 1866 a writer on the cotton famine explained that

> It very commonly happens that whilst the male portion of a family work at the colliery, the females who are of working age are employed in the mill or weaving shed.[2]

It was in fact the daughters who worked at the mill — Wigan's female working population was comparatively young as miners' wives did not usually work.

Cutting across this pattern were the pit brow lasses — over 1,300 of them worked in the Wigan-St. Helens area by the 1880s. By studying a district where pit women and mill workers were employed side by side and where the male miners dominated politics and social activities,

97

some of the problems of acceptance by both fellow pit workers and by other female workers become apparent. Critics claimed that a marked social ostracism operated, the pit lasses not being integrated with other workers. In an attempt to unravel some of the complexities of the pit brow lasses' position within the local community, several types of sources have been used. Criticism from outsiders has been chiefly gleaned from journals and newspapers, and local papers have also been useful in determining social relations. A limited use has been made of census material for 1861 and 1871. Fourteen women who worked at Wigan pits at the turn of the century have provided oral testimony. The principal source has, however, been the voluminous account of the contemporary Munby.[3] There are his detailed diaries spanning twenty-eight years, nine colliery notebooks, sketches, photographs and poetry. In addition his work has the advantage of having been conducted over a considerable length of time. Yet although this is a unique and invaluable contribution it must be treated with caution as the subject was inevitably influenced by Munby's own background and predilections. So too would the pit lasses' responses to Munby have been affected by this intriguing incursion into their world by a persistent middle-class lawyer. Through Munby's writings we can perhaps get closer to the pit women than through any other contemporary source yet at the same time we are always still several stages removed. The fact that their responses are refracted through Munby's conversations and written interpretation must be constantly borne in mind. In order to see how his perceptions may have shaped the evidence, some explanation of the nature of his interest and involvement is required.

A disillusioned barrister in retreat from the essentially male legal world, Arthur Joseph Munby (1828-1910) did not find his alternative employment as a clerk for the Ecclesiastical Commission very fulfilling or remunerative. It did however provide him with one important luxury, the time he needed to pursue his real interests. One of these was teaching part-time as a voluntary tutor at both the Working Men's college and at the Working Women's college. Munby was also a poet of fairly modest fame. Although several volumes of his poetry were published, it was only his long narrative poem *Dorothy* which received much serious acclaim from critics. Robert Browning praised it highly and a review of his work in the *Gentleman's Magazine* of 1904 called it 'the foremost of English elegiac poems' and a 'picturesque delineation of the ideal working woman'.[4] This poem in fact hinted at the core of Munby's concern but details of this were to be carefully hidden from most of his contemporaries. Realisation of his enforced subterfuge and the intricacies of his behaviour have been left to a later generation to question. Recently Derek Hudson has produced an admirable biographical account of Munby based upon his diaries, which explores his personal dilemmas. At the time of Munby's death in 1910, *The Times* obituary had simply paid tribute to his literary talents. An entry in the *Dictionary of National Biography* did however add that he had been secretly married to his servant, a fact which during his lifetime was unknown to his family and all but three of his friends.[5] His will made the situation clearer and he was accorded a certain posthumous notoriety. Furthermore the *Dictionary*'s account had added that Munby had devoted himself to the 'glorification of the working woman with especial insistence on the dignity of manual labour'. This was the central focus of his life but, like his marriage, he had kept it a closely guarded secret.

Munby was continually fascinated by the vagaries of human behaviour. His passion for investigation enabled him to record his findings in minute detail and, with the care of a specialist collector, to classify his specimens. The prime motivation for his involvement has never been unravelled and his diary did not begin until a number of years after his interest had been awakened. He certainly found working-class women far more accessible and frank as subjects of investigation than the ladies of his own class. Though he worked as little as possible at his job, he none the less extolled hard work by others. He also proved to be far more diligent in his adopted vocation than in his official work. Many of his observations were made amongst working girls, female clerks and prostitutes. Such encounters appear to have been confined to long conversations and detailed entries in his diaries. Deliberately avoiding a practical indulgence in the sexual excesses of so many of the 'other Victorians', he did however find, like a number of his contemporaries, that current notions of propriety and numerous constraints forced him to act out his interests, creative ideas and problems in a furtive manner to avoid endangering his social position.[6] Even his eventual marriage to the Shropshire servant Hannah can be viewed as the most daring of a series of experiments running parallel to, but not conflicting with, his other world. And as Leonore Davidoff has shown, it was an experiment which revolved around the theme of class and gender differences, prompting Munby's perceptive question — 'What in the Equation of Life, is the respective value of the terms sex and station?'[7]

In seeking the answers to such problems, Munby removed himself from London society and it was amongst the collier women of Wigan that he found his escape. He spent as much time as possible with them and awarded them the accolade — even among pit women — 'for good hard sweating at muscular work and for energy of toil'. His first visit to the Wigan district was probably made in 1853 or 1854 although his first recorded trip was not until 1859 (see Appendix I). This and numerous subsequent excursions provided a tonic from the 'gnawing worms of city life'.[8] He praised the 'artless meekness', innocence and lack of guile which he discerned there and which were missing in his tarnished metropolitan life. On taking one pit brow girl to be photographed he commented, 'What is sadder than her is our introverted sensibility'.[9] For the Romantic poet, artist and friend of the Pre-Raphaelites, the statuesque dignity and lack of conscious posing were a delight. He was constantly disparaging about the sophistication and superficiality of Victorian ladies of his own class and the pit women were to a certain extent used to emphasise the extremities of behaviour. This found its fullest expression in his sketches and poetry. The former constantly compared elegant ladies of fashion with black, sturdy pit women whilst his poems provided him with a vehicle by which he could challenge the premiss that a robust woman must necessarily be coarse and vulgar. At the same time he could indulge in what he called 'delicious contrasts'. Yet his drawings were, to say the least, paradoxical. On the one hand there was his insistence on the innate dignity of physical labour yet on the other hand this was directly challenged by his own delineation of the physical appearance of the women as vulgar, coarse and barely human.[10] His poetry continued the contrasts. An unpublished narrative poem 'Leonard and Elizabeth' concentrated on the disfigurement of a woman who worked in the pit. Comparing her with other women he declared that

> Women who dwell amid the froth and foam
> Of Surface life, contented but to be
> The Aphrodites of a summer sea,
> Had surely fainted or had died outright
> In such a place of horror and of fright.[11]

Yet Munby's conception of working-class women was one which viewed them as a race apart, people to be accorded a form of respect but none the less not to be judged by the same standards of humanity as his equals. In a poem based on his relationship with Hannah (though named after one of his Wigan pit acquaintances), he explained how Ann

Morgan was 'too obscure to be base, too simple to be vulgar'.[12] He saw
the lives of working women as less complicated than those of 'civilised
society' and he envied their apparent simplicity, making a naïve
equation of manual labour and happiness. His sentiments not
infrequently degenerated into a dubious reverence for a glorified
concept of the noble savage. In spite of an idealisation of rough working
women he saw no inconsistency in continuing to uphold the principles
of the society which perpetuated the exploitation of this class. He never
let deference disappear — even in his poetry the girls respectfully
address him as 'Sir'.

Continually fascinated by the relationship between sex and class,
Munby was interested in all those who for some reason or other did not
conform to the accepted mores and patterns of behaviour as defined by
the society of which he was a part. He felt a vicarious pleasure when
passengers in passing trains saw him with pit girls as he felt sure that
they would mistake the whole group for men. This reinforced his
masculinity, he being the only *real* man amongst them. But it also
stressed that it was not just role reversal that fascinated him. He
believed that external appearances could be deceptive and that a
muscular pit girl might be no less feminine than a fashionable London
lady. At a time when contemporaries were obsessed by the 'sanitary
image' (which was clearly expressed in Kingsley's *Water Babies*) Munby
was able to contrast external dirt with purity within. In *Susan: A Poem
of Degrees* he explained that the woman

> Who spends her days in household drudgery,
> Or toils afield or in the swarthy mine,
> Or at the forge, may still be feminine
> And noble and most lovable and pure,
>   the while robustness to endure
> The charge of wifehood and of motherhood.[13]

Kathryn Dickson of Fidlers' pit was described as 'far more feminine
really than any flirting butterfly of the drawing room'.[14] The pit
women could offer a glimmer of hope for a future which he saw in
terms of physical and moral degeneracy. In a poem called
'Kerenhappuch — a fragment' he compared the stout pit brow lass with
her consumptive brother and his 'puny sweetheart'. She was a
sempstress and together they made

>   a precious pair
> To breed new dwarfs for England's dwarfish days! [15]

Munby's visits to the coalfield served as an anodyne, temporarily relieving him of what he perceived as the problems of modern society and the constant need for emulation. In many respects he saw himself as a failure. Quite apart from the strain of a secret marriage (after five years Hannah moved back to Shropshire though Munby spent a considerable time there) and a job that was not sufficiently demanding, he never received the esteem accorded to his friends. Amongst the pit lasses however, he could not only escape from one lifestyle, but could be accorded the importance he coveted and subscribe to very different notions of women and work from those held by friends such as Ruskin. He deliberately inverted values — on returning to London he declared defiantly that he now felt shabby whereas before he had felt resplendent. In Wigan nobody seemed surprised to see a filthy pit girl in trousers but they did gaze at Munby:

> No one in the crowd was at all surprised to see a grimy mother, with arms like a navvy's walking through the town in this strange medley of breeches and shawl, suckling her baby as she went: but everybody turned round (civilly though) to gaze at me'.[16]

Although he was somewhat pathetically trying to make himself more like an ordinary working man, he was also savouring the respect and recognition which he failed to find amongst his more illustrious society friends. His analysis of pit work was imbued with a sense of personal release and was a form of therapy to help resolve his anomalous position. He was careful to confine his attention almost entirely to pit women and girls. His comments about the few men he encountered at the pit were generally disparaging. At Birket Bank he enquired whether the girls had finished working —

> The man, who looked limp and sheepish answered nothing; but the girl standing firm with feet apart, erect, square-shouldered, soldierly and altogether a taller and more striking figure than her mate, looked me full in the face and said in a loud but not unfeminine voice 'Yah pit's doon'.[17]

In the cabin at Blundells' Venture pit in 1865 he found a 'black trio of brawny maidens' and a pale, slim young man on crutches — 'it was a triumph for the weaker sex!'[18]

On approaching colliery offices Munby would explain how his soul would shudder to see a dapper young clerk whilst all around were 'girls,

begrimed and laborious and sweating among the coals'.[19] The blatant
lack of interest in the men (except as a means of contrasting the
sybaritic male with the powerful female) leaves an unfortunate gap. It
would be extremely valuable to know more about the views of the men
with whom the women worked.

Munby was remarkably lucky that he was accepted so easily. The
only rudeness he encountered at a pit was from Sammy Stocks, a
coalowner of Selney Green.[20] Yet, not only did he talk to the women,
sketch them, accompany them to the photographers and home, but he
also censured them with a paternal concern if he did not approve of
their moral behaviour. He was continually fascinated by hands, the
outward and inescapable manifestation of a worker — 'the mute
credentials of her ambassage' — and would even cut dead skin from
their hands.[21] Viewed by the pit girls as a distinctly eccentric but none
the less friendly and generous visitor, he was nicknamed 'T' inspector'.
It is only possible to speculate how they might have viewed Munby
amongst themselves. His very serious approach to what must have
seemed trivial, everyday matters would no doubt have caused some
amusement, as would his efforts to 'act Lancashire', as he put it. Not
only must it have been extremely tempting to take advantage of his
readiness to distribute money in return for conversation — especially
since daily wages averaged only 1/8d to 1/10d — but in other ways he
would have been a perfect target for a bit of mischievous fun.[22] In 1860
he was chatting to a group of friends when Jane Mercer 'the wit of the
party' began 'teasing me about getting a missus' and made a 'curious
examination of my clothes and watch'.[23]

Munby's frequent presence at the pit must have mystified many and
possibly provided the basis for the tale *A Pit Brow Lassie* written by a
former miner, J.M. Foster.[24] Foster may well have seen Munby talking
to the women and woven a story around this enigmatic character. One
of the major characters Arthur not only had Munby's Christian name
but had started legal training and given it up. Like Munby he had a
relative who was a solicitor with a practice in Manchester. The heroine
lived at Pendleton, the home of Munby's brother. Munby did visit
Wigan in 1878, the year in which the story is set, and even mentioned in
his diary that he went to the actual spot where one of the key events
takes place — the canal bank by Brittania Bridge. The meeting there is
described in terms highly evocative of Munby — Arthur 'shook hands
with her great brown palm'. Arthur spent some time on the brow,
walking about and pretending to take notes and sketch. He claimed to
be a London reporter trying to find out about local habits and the girls

called him 'that theer rahtin chap'.

Whether or not Munby was made the subject of a story, his presence cannot have been missed. It must have been difficult for him to understand local pit talk and dialect (though he was a member of the dialect society and helped R.D. Blackmore with the dialect for his story *Mary Anerley*).[25] In an anonymous letter to the *Manchester Examiner* he claimed that the women saw in him 'simply a person speaking their own dialect and not unlike themselves'.[26] Yet this very claim betrays his failure to understand the situation. Like Orwell he could never really belong. In his anxiety to ingratiate himself, he gave away money he could ill afford.[27] And ultimately he had to come to terms with the fact that he did not want to abandon wholly the world he had left behind and in fact could not do so. Though over time he was able to build up a certain confidence, he was bound to remain at a considerable disadvantage being an outsider, a male and socially distanced from the women. His attitudes towards their work were in many respects remarkably progressive yet his code of behaviour remained firmly entrenched within the limits of a middle-class morality. He glossed over the harsher realities of life — the full extent of the privation caused by the cotton famine seems to have been ignored by him and his picture of Wigan is distorted by his virtual dismissal of the mill girls who constituted the overwhelming majority of Wigan's female work force. In spite of visiting their homes he always resided in the comfort of the Victoria Hotel.[28] Munby also came to Wigan with his mind made up:

> That which I want is, liberty for any woman who has the strength and the mind for it, to turn her hand to any manual employment whatsoever.

His accounts convey a sense of triumph in proving his particular beliefs.[29]

Yet while this can be problematical, it can also be seen as a strength. Munby did not have the usual axe to grind. His obsession may have been all-pervasive but it provides a refreshing corrective to the interpretations of critics bent on exposing the evils of women's work to the world. For example, his insistence that dress had nothing to do with decency was in marked contrast to general opinion as the Wigan photographer Mrs Little explained:

> Some considers it's a shame for women to wear breeches and some takes it for a joke like.[30]

Furthermore, Munby was not the agent of miner or master or commissioned by the government to unearth social problems. He was working for himself without the knowledge that his results must be published. His investigations, like Mayhew's, were based on detailed personal surveys though, unlike the latter's, his work remained unknown (with the exception of the poetic use of a fraction of his material) and was the product of a personal and sustained interest which exceeded the desire for publicity or pecuniary gain.[31] His independence would have enabled him to get closer to the pit brow girls than official investigators or members of the press, and thus compute in detail some of the idiosyncrasies and exceptions to the rule which did not have a place elsewhere and might otherwise have passed unrecorded. He shows, for example, that occasionally women might do extra work for which they would be paid on a piece rate. Mary Ann Rigson (whose three children were looked after by her mother) was doing overtime filling barges with two other women at the Rosebridge pits in 1866. Since he preferred to speak to the women when the men were not there, he was at an advantage compared with government enquirers who were generally accompanied by colliery officials. The visits to homes were particularly useful. As Munby explained:

> I have sat with them at dinner time; I have walked home with them often and sat down and had tea or 'baggin' and sat by sick beds (though I am neither parson nor doctor) and looked in on Saturdays and heard of and shared in the family joys and sorrows; and I have done this at no infrequent intervals during the lifetime of a whole generation.[32]

In addition Munby possessed a unique collection of photographs which included 250 pictures of pit girls, and his sketches (mostly pencilled on the spot), though often crude and exaggerated, could at times be quite perceptive and informative. They are all the more important since Britain lacked artists with an interest in peasant naturalism such as Millet demonstrated or with the particular perception of a Van Gogh or Meunier. Munby also visited European coalfields and watched women miners at work in Belgium. Indeed his qualifications were far greater than contemporaries ever appreciated. In a letter to the press in 1886 he explained (without admitting his identity),

> For reasons of my own I have for more than thirty years studied the subject of female labour, not merely in books and at second hand,

but with my own eyes and on the spot. I have explored for instance, not once only, but often, all the districts in Britain where pit women are employed and not a few districts in foreign countries also.[33]

Thus in spite of Munby's idealisation his vivid and extensive findings constitute a valuable source. By placing his account alongside other contemporary evidence, a more balanced view of the women's work and its relevance to Wigan and nineteenth-century society may be obtained.

Unlike those who saw Wigan as a sorry product of the industrial revolution, Munby valued it as a picturesque medieval town. It had been an important Roman military station and had been a borough since 1246. Until the late eighteenth century it had boasted a woollen and linen industry specialising in bedding but from 1812, when the power loom was introduced to the town, a new phase had developed though handlooms continued to be used for some time. By 1835 there were twenty-one cotton mills employing over 4,500 people. The self-acting mule was in use by the late 1840s but Wigan also specialised in throstle-spinning. This was replaced by ring-spinning in the 1880s. Wigan was once again untypical of the Lancashire cotton towns. The cotton trade had tended to become polarised with spinning predominating in towns to the east of Manchester and weaving also being concentrated in specific towns, notably Blackburn, Burnley and Preston. Yet though spinning tended to predominate in Wigan, the typical firm combined basic spinning and weaving processes and not infrequently included the ownership of a coal mine. The trade in the spinning of coarse cotton yarn meant that the town was particularly badly affected in the 1860s when America, the supplier of cheap raw cotton, was embroiled in civil war. However, recovery and expansion followed in the next decade and by 1891 over 5,000 were employed in cotton.

The borough of Wigan witnessed a six-fold increase in population during the nineteenth century and the number of females consistently outnumbered the males — by 1851 there were 803 more females than males in the borough of Wigan (the municipal and parliamentary borough was co-extensive with the township of Wigan).[34] The birth rate was high as was the immigration rate — by now Wigan had the greatest concentration of Irish-born inhabitants in England, large numbers being employed in the less skilled spinning processes.[35] If the neighbouring sub-districts in the Wigan Union (Ashton, Aspull, Hindley, Pemberton, Standish and Upholland) are also included, the total population of the Wigan registration district was 139,918 by 1881

Table 4.1: Wigan County Borough Population

Year	Total	Females
1801	10,989	5,921
1841	25,517	13,203
1851	31,941	16,372
1861	37,658	19,195
1871	39,110	20,139
1881	48,194	24,686
1891	55,013	27,928

(with 69,458 females) and 166,762 ten years later (82,259 females). It was in fact these communities which were showing the impact of colliery expansion and migration from other coalfields in the second half of the century. In 1851 for example, the civil parish of Aspull had 3,278 inhabitants but 8,952 by 1891 and in Ince the increase was even more dramatic – from 3,670 at mid-century to 19,255 by 1891.[36]

The coalmining industry was based on a coalfield within a five mile radius of the town. This coalfield was heavily faulted, the main faults running parallel to the Pennines, the boundaries being the Great Upholland fault in the west, the Scot Lane fault in the east, an outcrop of mountain seams in the north and the Bickershaw Lane and Aqueduct faults in the south.[37] Mining was chiefly concentrated in the middle coal measures, especially the rich arley or Orrell 4' coal which outcropped at Orrell, Wrightington, Worthington, Haigh and Blackrod and produced good domestic coal. There was also the Haigh Yard, the Wigan 4', Pemberton 4' and cannel seams. The valuable seam of cannel coal with its high illuminating power was over six feet thick at Abram colliery. It outcropped at Haigh, Aspull, Blackrod, Pemberton, Winstanley and Shevington and was chiefly used for gas-making.

Coal production in Wigan was old-established – the first recorded mention of coal in the area dates back to 1350 – and it commanded a flourishing trade by the nineteenth century. It was conveniently situated and making the River Douglas navigable from Wigan to the Ribble had aided development as had the construction of the Leeds and Liverpool canal. Railway development facilitated communications still further. In the first half of the century mining was concentrated in Aspull and Orrell where the cannel and arley seams were nearest the surface and coal was still mined at Haigh. By the mid-century there was greater mining of the middle coal measures in Wigan, Pemberton, Ince and Hindley, the balance of the coal supply gradually moving southwards. There was also a trend towards larger firms. In 1851, 103 collieries (201 pits in all) were recorded in a *History of Collieries round Haigh*.[38] Though the total yearly output was 3.6 million tons, many of these collieries were small, 58 per cent of them each yielding under 100 tons a day. In the next twenty years, however, the industry became monopolised by a few major concerns, the opening up of deeper seams requiring a greater investment of capital. By 1863, 55.3 per cent of the whole coalfield's output was produced by five major firms – the Earl of Crawford's collieries, the Kirkless Hall Coal and Iron Company, the Ince Hall Coal and Cannel Company, Pearson and Knowles and Blundell and Sons, all of whom employed a number of women. At the end of 1865 the Wigan Coal and Iron Company was formed. It was an extremely important merger, bringing together the Crawford collieries (the Earl of Crawford held 60 per cent of the shares), the Kirkless Hall Company, the Standish and Shevington Cannel Company and the Broomfield colliery. With John Lancaster as chairman the company leased land in Wigan and in the townships of Haigh, Upholland, Shevington, Aspull, Standish and Orrell as well as further afield in Westhoughton and West Leigh. Its yearly output was 1.1 million tons and its workforce was 7,000 strong.[39] According to the 1861 census the total number of adult Wigan coalminers was only 9,085.[40]

The same census returned 3,700 females over twenty working in cotton, a figure which (as in other years) was higher than that of adult male cotton workers (2,229 in 1861). Females in textiles actually accounted for over 88 per cent of the total number of females in industrial occupation and one-fifth of the total number of adult females in the Wigan registration district.[41] The pit women were therefore very much in the minority. This census (itself a deficient record of the numbers employed at the pit) returned only 281 pit brow women, representing 4.6 per cent of the industrial female workers of Wigan.[42] The three districts of Aspull, Ince and Pemberton accounted for 187 females. Women pit brow workers did, however, represent over 41 per cent of the non-textile female workers.

The census returns cannot reflect the numbers who were employed at varying times for quite short periods and then were replaced. In three days in 1865 Munby did a trip round the Wigan pits and, wandering from the Kirkless Hall pits to Aspull, on to Standish and Shevington then back through Wigan and Ince to Pemberton and the Winstanley pits he counted 212 pit brow lasses, and time had prevented him calling at a number of pits.[43] Although some of the smaller

Principal Collieries in the Wigan Area Which Employed Women in 1865

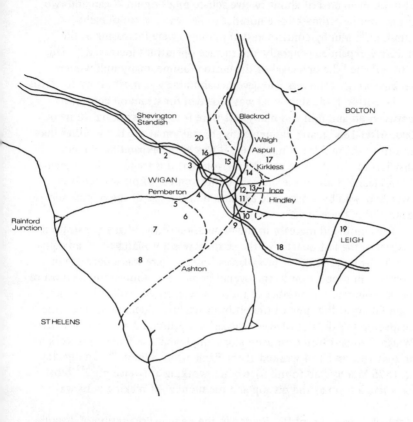

KEY TO COLLIERIES

1 Walthew House	11 Springs, Hindley and Barleybrook
2 Norley	12 Ince Hall
3 Pemberton	13 Moss Hall
4 Worsley Mesnes	14 Rose Bridge
5 Pemberton	15 Birket Bank
6 Winstanley	16 Ince Hall Coal and Iron Works
7 Winstanley	17 Kirkless Hall Coal and Iron Works
8 Blackleyhurst	18 Bickershaw
9 Bryn Moss	19 Atherton
10 Platt Bridge	20 Kirkless Hall Coal and Iron Works

concerns might have had only a handful of women workers, the two Rosebridge pits had 36 and at larger pits 15 to 20 was an average. William Pickard the local miners' agent told the Select Committee on Mines in 1866 that there were between four and five hundred women at work in an area of about twelve square miles round Wigan and two years later he estimated the number to be nearer seven or eight hundred.[44] Munby confirmed that numbers were increasing as the industry expanded generally and surface operations increased.[45] This also reflected the upheaval of the cotton famine, many mill women seeking work at the pits. However, coalmining was itself hit by the crisis in the cotton trade since coal was provided for steam on contract between pit and mill and many pits were forced to work half-time or less. After 1865 many women chose to stay on at the brow rather than return to the mill (see Chapter 6). It was in the expanding colliery districts of Aspull, Ince and Pemberton that this trend could be seen most clearly, though the increase in the number of pit women was overshadowed by a dramatic expansion in the size of the population generally in these areas.

The continued increase in the population of the Wigan registration district in the last quarter of the century was not matched by an equal rise in the number of pit brow lasses. In fact there was a decrease in numbers in proportion to the overall population, though unlike most of of the country, the number of pit brow women was still rising rather than falling at the time of the pit brow exclusion debate. In 1886 the Inspectorate's district of West Lancashire returned 3,421 females. The Wigan Coal and Iron Company alone employed 238 female pit workers in that year and 164 worked at the Pemberton colliery.[46] On one day in 1878 Munby had found 91 women working at twelve pits.[47] Most now had a team at the pit top and the number of picking belts was

Table 4.2: Number of Pit Women in the Female Population of Aspull, Ince and Pemberton, 1861-71[48]

	1861		1871	
	Females of all ages	Pit Lasses[a]	Females of all ages	Pit Lasses
Aspull	4,004	63	5,457	107
Ince	4,005	51	5,864	117
Pemberton	5,254	71	7,266	92

Note: a. Those recorded in the census.

increasing. Aspull Moor No. 2 pit now had 48 women and girls, mostly at the belts, there were 20 at the Alexander pit, Whelley, 30 at Douglas Bank. Meanwhile 50 were cleaning coal for Fletcher and Burrows nearby at Atherton.[49] The late-nineteenth-century photographs of pit girls at work reveal average groups of about twenty. So although the percentage of pit brow lasses in the Wigan area was small in proportion to those working in the cotton trade, the pit brow woman was of some significance in comparison with the national figure for female surface labour.

Anyway, Wigan pit workers stimulated an interest which far outweighed their numbers and the degree of attention which the women received cannot simply be attributed to numerical concentration in this area. The reasons for this interest require examination and can help elucidate not only social relations within the community but also the wider implications of the exclusion campaign of the mid-1880s. Part of the interest no doubt emanated from the fact that it was a Lancashire manufacturer, Ellis Lever, who launched the main attack on the women's work in 1883 and thus prompted hasty investigations of conditions by newspaper reporters (see Chapter 5). Attacks did however pre-date this. Wigan was already known to possess a unique feature – here the pit women wore 'those unmentionable nether garments' – trousers were not even worn at St Helens – and undoubtedly they contributed to the debate about the suitability/unsuitability of such work. By the 1860s the central Ince Hall pits had become so popular that they had to forbid visitors to the pit brow.[50]

The focus on the Wigan pit women in preference to those in the more isolated colliery areas also suggests not just a place which was more accessible for strangers than many other locations, but may be interpreted as part of a wider indictment of industrial and in particular, urban, evils, even though in fact many pit girls lived and worked outside the town itself. There was a morbid fascination – Wigan could epitomise the sordid and potentially destructive forces of man and industry, a Coketown realised. It invited comment long before it was made the target for music hall jokes or became branded by Orwell. Ruskin contributed to this.

Those children rolling on the heaps of black and slimy ground, mixed with brickbats and broken plates and bottles, in the midst of Preston or Wigan, as edified travellers behold them when the station is blocked, and the train stops anywhere outside, – the children themselves, black and in rags evermore and the only water near them either boiling, or gathered in unctuous pools, covered with rancid clots of scum in the lowest holes of the earth heaps, why do you not paint these for pastime? Are they not what your machine gods have produced for you?[51]

Thus Wigan might reinforce certain preconceived notions about the evils of women's work, providing a context and ammunition for the debate on female pit brow labour and at the same time raise wider issues such as the impact of industrialisation on the family and fears of urban degeneration.

The town's bad image was exacerbated by a serious riot in the centre of Wigan in 1853. The cotton famine accorded it further adverse publicity. Wigan was the first place to have a relief committee and its dire state was spelt out by a local man, John Whittaker, whose letters from a 'Lancashire Lad' were published in *The Times* in 1862. Edwin Waugh's accounts in the *Manchester Examiner* in the same year described the 'slutchy streets' and 'sallow tattered women'.[52] The Scholes district with its large Irish population was 'one of those ash tips of human life' where 'the very children seemed joyless at their play'. This was the town at its nadir. Not surprisingly the pit women were viewed as part and parcel of this environment, to be especially pitied as they represented the reverse of the feminine ideal.

In 1863 Emily Faithfull had delivered a paper to the Edinburgh conference of the Social Science Association where she branded pit brow work as one of the 'unfit employments for females'.[53] Influenced by this, John Plummer of Kettering, a staymaker, poet and denouncer of trades unions, visited Wigan. He published his impressions of the town in the journal *Once A Week*. In terms evocative of Richard Ayton (see Chapter 2) he prepared the reader for an encounter with pit women. Describing the tip as a huge black mound to be crossed before the 'sombre and gallow like erection over the pit' could be reached, he explained how he then 'beheld a spectacle utterly repugnant to my feelings and according but ill with the character of the age'. He found women performing work which in some other areas was done entirely by men and he believed that it was totally unsuited to their sex.[54] Munby was particularly horrified by his outburst:

I knew the above must come someday; but now it has come, it annoys me beyond expression. Am I to brave publicity in this matter and try to show the fools that a woman may wear trousers and have coarse hands if she likes? Or must we let this healthy simple labour be ended also, as other good things are daily ended? It is monstrous, the fond philosophy of these shallow philogynists.[55]

Munby had been visiting Wigan for years and by now knew several hundred pit girls personally. Plummer had only been there twice and then very fleetingly and during the extraordinary times of the cotton famine. His distance from the everyday world of coal mining was exemplified by his surprise that, as a pit girl proceeded unabashed through the streets of Wigan, nobody (apart from himself) seemed to regard the degrading sight as being at all unusual or disturbing! He commented that no stranger could have detected that these women were the wives and daughters of English working men.

Unwittingly Plummer had drawn attention here to the ignorance of critics such as himself who were judging something alien to their experience. Were the pit women wives and mothers who were neglecting their families? Was there a significant distinction between the way strangers perceived them and how they were viewed within the community? In order to determine whether they were in fact socially segregated from other workers, an analysis of their patterns of employment is necessary. Munby's evidence used in conjunction with census data can help throw light on their place in Wigan's occupational make-up. The census enumerators' returns for the Wigan sub-districts of Aspull and Pemberton and the township of Ince (part of the sub-district of Hindley) have been used, also Scholes in the township of Wigan. Aspull to the north-east of Wigan, Pemberton in the south-west (later to become the centre of the pressure group organised in defence of the women) and Ince in the south-west were all rapidly expanding colliery areas, whereas Scholes in the centre of the town (with only eight pit women recorded in the census returns of 1861 and nine in 1871) was a working-class district with a large number of mill workers. Taken together the four districts contained a high proportion of the local pit women, 193 females in 1861 − all but 90 of those recorded for the Wigan registration district − and 325 in 1871.[56] Munby visited all four districts many times and his accounts of individual pit brow girls and women and their families can be matched with the details recorded in the census.

The evidence suggests that the pit brow women of the Wigan coalfield were generally young adults. Munby recorded the ages of the girls he met and the majority were under twenty, although there were a significant number in the thirty-five to fifty age range, chiefly widows. He recorded details of the ninety-one women he encountered on one

Table 4.3: Ages of Female Pit Brow Workers in Four Wigan Districts in 1861 and 1871

	Under 15	15-19	20-29	30-39	Over 40	Total
			1861			
Aspull	8	21	21	7	6	63
Ince	5	23	12	9	3	52
Pemberton	18	15	22	12	5	72
Scholes	1	2	2	3	—	8
	32	61	57	31	14	195
			1871			
Aspull	10	43	31	12	11	107
Ince	3	35	47	17	15	117
Pemberton	6	23	44	9	10	92
Scholes	1	1	5	—	2	9
	20	102	127	38	38	325

day in 1878 and estimated that all except for six were aged between sixteen and thirty. Of the sixty-three female pit brow workers recorded in the census for Aspull in 1871 the youngest was a girl of twelve and two others were fourteen. The majority were aged between eighteen and twenty-five.

Employment prospects varied considerably. Quite apart from the cotton famine, the demand for coal fluctuated due to market forces, seasonal variations, strikes, modernisation and other factors. Some women anyway tended to leave the pits at certain times of year when there might be temporary agricultural work available on nearby farms. The evidence given in an 1887 pit-brow deputation suggested that the women generally worked on average for about five years at the pit-brow though Munby's findings indicate that in the Wigan area they frequently worked for longer. They might however move from pit to pit and in the Haigh area they alternated between pit work and the jobs at John Sumner's brewery where single girls were employed and continued to wear trousers.

Munby found some women who had been in pit work for ten years and others who had fifteen or twenty years' experience of the work. Though changes of location and breaks in employment over the years were common, there were some women who worked continuously at the pit — the 1911 deputation heard of one woman aged seventy who had worked for thirty consecutive years.[57] A number of the pit brow lasses in the 1871 census had been doing the same job ten years earlier though changes of name and possibly addresses after marriage, may have camouflaged further examples. Sarah Lygoe had spent twenty-one years at the pit when Munby met her in 1882 and Jane Battersby of Ince boasted twenty-seven years. The daughter of a miner, she and her sister Mary had worked at the Rosebridge pits. She had a grown-up daughter and a crippled son of fourteen and continued to look after him. Another woman, Ellen Meggison (Boompin' Nell in Munby's poetry and sketches) had been at the pit for thirty years and kept her disabled husband for three years before he died. She was still working in 1887 but had moved several times, getting jobs at different pits around Wigan and Aspull. This appears to have been fairly typical — the working-out of old pits, sinking of new shafts nearer to home perhaps, encouraged change. Mobility of labour was anyway a marked feature of the Wigan colliery workforce generally, part of the continued effort to improve pay and working conditions and assert independence. Very few of Munby's friends remained at the same location between the 1860s and 1880s although they might be doing the same sort of work. On the whole there was greater mobility to the pits than from them, particularly during the cotton famine. As John Monk Foster commented, whilst it was rare to find a woman leaving the pit to work in the mills, it was common enough to witness the opposite.[58]

Although Munby did not usually enquire why the women were working at the pits — such employment did not need justifying in his view — the overall impression conveyed by his investigations is that they were working as part of a family tradition and a number of the older women had previously been employed below ground. Where there was a pit brow woman in a family, the head of the household, if a male, would with very few exceptions, be a coalminer. This was also the experience of all the fourteen former pit women who were interviewed. They all had fathers who were miners and at least one other member of the family (generally a brother) who was in mining. Four had mothers who had worked at the belts and two had grandmothers in pit work (one had been employed underground). Munby met a number of girls whose mothers had worked in the pits and eventually transferred to surface work — Mrs Hilton (57) had been a thrutcher from the age of seven until she was turned out. In 1866 Munby found her at the pithead with her three daughters — one aged twenty-seven was a pit brow worker, another was a deaf and dumb child who chipped copperstone with a hammer whilst the youngest was not old enough to work but accompanied her mother. The census shows that in the relatively rare cases where pit girls did not have collier fathers, there would usually be some other connection with the pits, generally an elder brother working there. In Aspull in 1871 there were only four pit brow girls living with their parents who did not have a relative living at home who was connected with mining and Pemberton, Scholes and Ince only had one such family. Sisters frequently worked together — Munby, the census returns and later oral evidence all showing that younger sisters would replace their older sisters as they left pit work. The defenders of the pit brow carefully developed this theme, cultivating the image of a happy family atmosphere. At one suffrage meeting held in defence of the women, a photograph was handed around entitled 'A family of pit brow workers' showing Ann Bradshaw and her four sisters who worked at Pemberton colliery.[59] Most of the women and girls came from local families though some had moved with their families from other mining areas. One woman explained how her father had been persuaded to move to Wigan from Durham since he had seven daughters and could not hope to find work for them all in his native town.[60]

Although pit brow girls had fathers who worked at the pits, it did not follow that miners' daughters necessarily became pit brow girls. As has been shown, Wigan's employment prospects for females lay chiefly in mill work. In Scholes for example there were fifty-four families headed by miners in 1861 where one or more of the daughters were working in some branch of the cotton trade, many as spinners. A typical family pattern was for a pit girl to have a father who was a miner, a mother who did not work, an elder brother who was a miner and younger brothers working in the pit as drawers. She would probably have at least one sister working at the mill (many younger daughters worked there, the smaller ones as piecers).

The majority of pit brow girls appear to have been daughters living at home. There were however a number of lodgers and boarders who were pit girls. Areas such as Ince and Pemberton were expanding so rapidly that they faced severe problems of housing. Lodging was a temporary answer and often a welcome additional financial help for families, particularly for the widows of colliers. One such lodger was Mary Ann Morgan ('Welsh Nan') who had originally been a tip girl in Merthyr until her parents died and then after a brief spell in service at Birkenhead had come to Hindley where she lodged with several mill girls and paid 3/6d rent fortnightly. In 1871 there were sixteen pit brow girls lodging in Aspull, twenty-three in Ince, six in Pemberton and two in Scholes. Most of the heads of these households were miners or widows.[61] A number of the latter worked at the pit, their employment sometimes being the only way to continue living in a colliery house. Some of these widows were quite young, their husbands having been killed at the pit. There were women in their twenties and thirties who had young children to support. Helen Pardy (32) worked at the same pit as her twelve-year-old son and was having to provide for three daughters and a son all aged below eight years. One-parent families faced considerable difficulties. Some women had been deserted by their husbands, others were unmarried but had children to raise and so worked at the pit. Hannah Rothwell was thirty-three, single and had a daughter of four at school and another of one month, yet had to return to the pit very quickly to earn the money she so badly needed. Some grandparents helped by looking after a child or children while the mother worked.[62] Munby found that the mothers of illegitimate children generally eventually married the fathers. And as William Pickard explained, ninety-nine per cent of the pit brow women's marriages were to miners.[63]

Miners' wives did not work themselves if their husband was in employment. At some pits (for example at Pemberton colliery) married women were not allowed to work. Some women worked for a short time after marriage but generally ceased employment when their first child was born. In the areas considered for 1861, the census shows that out of 195 pit women, there were only 13 who were wives and 47 out of 325 in 1871. The increase in the ten years would have reflected the difficulties facing Wigan but even at the later date, only fourteen per cent of the pit women were married and living with their husbands. It is quite likely that some of those women simply recorded as 'miners' wives' did in fact work though Tilly and Scott have shown how increasingly in nineteenth-century industrial areas contributions from married women workers were expected only if the wages of other working members of the family were insufficient for household requirements.[64] The productive activity of wives was becoming 'a kind of reserve, a last resort'. In mining families this was particularly marked and was linked to the strong assertion of authority by the male miner as the head of the household. Admittedly there was a high risk of losing the male breadwinner and therefore forcing the colliery widow to earn a wage but on the whole, unless this happened, miners' wives did not work. Alice Yates of Barley Brook told Munby in 1863 that she had recently married and that if she wanted to stay at home her 'felly' would keep her. When he saw her a year later this had happened. Union opposition no doubt contributed to this tendency whilst the possibility of continuing work inevitably hinged around the birth of children, the number of children, family size and order, a child's sex and age and the amount of money coming into the home.

Those mothers who worked tended not to be married to colliers and the latters' opposition to their wives working (whether at the mine or mill) needs to be seen in the context of the domestic demands made on miners' wives. Those who worked in the Wigan districts that have been studied appear to have done so for two major reasons — either because they had no children to keep them at home or because they were at a particular stage in the family cycle where children were young and there were no other breadwinners in the family to boost the family income. For example Ann Rayner (32) of Aspull had a daughter of eight and a son of six. With no other source of income in addition to her husband's wages yet with children who were not so young that they required her presence at home, she had returned to pit work. Of the thirty families containing pit brow females and headed by male miners in Aspull in 1861, the wife did not work in all but six cases. In those cases where she was employed, either the family was childless or else there were small children to be fed and no older ones to help supplement the income — only two families did not conform to this pattern. Ten years later, twenty-seven out of thirty-five similar families did not have working wives and half of the families where they did work consisted of childless couples. If a mother did work she was generally replaced by her daughter or son once they were old enough to be employed. Mary Heyes of New Springs was forty in 1861 and working at the pit. She had one daughter at a mill but a son of eight to support as well. Ten years later her daughter had replaced her — her son was now eighteen and a drawer. With two incomes coming in she was now able to stay at home and since her unmarried daughter had a child, she could look after him during the day.

The evidence about Wigan pit women seems to reinforce the belief that mining families were close-knit and lends credence to John Benson's claim that 'the nineteenth century mining family was stronger, more resilient and altogether more responsible than it is ever given credit for'.[65] There appears to have been a concept of familial support which went beyond a reciprocation of duties and services or occasional help in times of crisis. Pit girls helped to look after the home and younger sisters and brothers and received support from their parents. According to Munby the pit girls usually married in their early twenties and either continued to live in the wife's family home or, in many instances, set up home nearby and maintained close links with their family of origin. Since they usually married miners, the patterns of their lives remained tuned to the pit even though they would probably no longer be working there themselves.

It would seem therefore that, unlike the impressions conveyed by outside critics, the Wigan pit brow lasses were, in the main, young, single girls. For the minority with children, familial support was strong. Certainly Munby found examples of good, indifferent and bad homes but these homes were usually looked after by the non-working mothers of pit girls. Perhaps the critics' perception of social relations between the pit lasses and other workers was also distorted? The *Manchester Examiner* claimed a rigid distinction, arguing that relations between the mill girls and pit girls were so bad that

> between the two sorts of girls there is an undying enmity. The mill people look down on the collier lasses with contempt and the collier lasses, to do them justice, return the compliment with all earnestness. What the result would be if they met in battalions is fearful to contemplate.[66]

Once again it would seem that critics were indulging in a certain poetic licence (which no doubt produced an interesting story for readers) and ignored some basic facts. As has been shown, many pit brow women started work at the mill and later moved to the pit (and usually did not move back). Although the catastrophic experience of the cotton famine produced competition for jobs, it did mean greater mobility between the mill and pit and helped to blur distinctions between the groups of workers. By June 1862 eighteen mills had ceased production, putting 6,800 out of work. Five others were on short-time and only 380 mill workers were employed full-time.[67]

Not only might pit women have sisters who worked at the mill but their mothers would most probably have been pit or mill workers in their youth. Moreover pit women were an accepted part of Wigan and its history and as the Lancastrian Edwin Waugh explained in *Lancashire and its Factory Folk*, though the 'singular appearance of these women has puzzled many a southern stranger', these 'dusky damsels' were 'to the manner born, and as they walk about the streets, thoughtless of singularity, the Wigan people let them go unheeded by'.[68] A bookseller in the Scholes bridge area (a predominantly mill-employing area) was not conscious of antipathy between mill and pit girls and declared that he had never heard anything bad of the pit girls who constantly came

into his shop.[69] Munby too was guilty of hyperbole. Blinded by
partisan emotions he seems to have exaggerated the gulf between the
two by virtually dismissing the mill workers in a few strokes of the pen.
In *Dorothy* he described their

> ugly hats, their tawdry ribbons and sham flowers
> their ill-made impudent frocks, limp and white-faced
> weaklings, they were potential mothers of disease.[70]

The centre of Wigan was less interesting for him than the colliery
districts because here one was within range of 'factory temptations'.
He described the mill women 'drinking gin besottedly' while pit brow
women were apparently abstemious! At times though he was forced to
admit that the latter did try to persuade him to buy them gin. He heard
one girl urging her friend to tell him 'we're dry' but 'I did not take the
hint'![71] Probably the two groups were not as set apart as Munby liked
to think.

    However, a closer look at their lifestyle does show that the pit
women were treated as an identifiable group which could be
distinguished in a number of ways from other workers and from their
sisters at the mill. The pit women tended to spend much of their free
time together. Although the social life of the male miner has been well
documented, emphasising aggressive and frequently violent sports such
as dog and cock fighting and in Wigan, purring or kicking with sharp
pointed clogs, the recreational activities of colliery women have not
been considered (excepting the involvement of miners' wives in the
social life of the chapel in some parts of the country). Perhaps in the
case of the pit brow lasses social life was non-existent given the long
day and need to help with domestic chores. When the miners' day
ended, the second phase of the women's day was starting. In the words
of one pit woman, the hours outside the pit were the ones when you
had to 'muckle in with mother', helping to clean and bake in small
cottages inhabited by large families.[72] Stone floors had to be scrubbed,
steps whitened, grates cleaned out and fires laid. Some women might
have children, disabled or aged dependants to tend. Some were luckier
than others. One twenty-four-year-old pit girl told Munby that if her
'felly' got back from work before her he would make the tea.[73] Many
others must have had to spend much of their time helping to cook for
hungry miners coming off shift. The prohibition of night work for
women and in particular, the granting of the Saturday afternoon break
in 1872, must have helped.

Otherwise, barring the Monday 'playing' following the fortnightly 'reckoning' day, there was little free time or formal entertainment though Wigan did have fairs on Maundy Thursday and 28 October as did Scholes in June and October. There was also the Upholland pleasure fair in July. Munby frequently met the pit girls at the market on Monday and Friday evenings and on Saturday afternoons. Local entertainment included pastry feasts which were especially popular in the Blackrod and Orrell areas. Courting couples would be judged for their good looks – the prettiest girl receiving a pint of rum and a 6d pastry whilst the booby prize for the ugliest was a black pudding![74] The pit lasses also told Munby that they enjoyed tea parties and dancing though it was not until the 1900s that annual 'pit broo stirs' were organised.[75] They sang at work and, according to a local bookseller, enjoyed buying songs as well as penny romances. Yet in 1863 Munby commented that not one girl in five in the coalfield could read at all.[76] Some owners had set up schools – at Haigh, Haydock, Highfield, Park Lane and Worsley girls could receive some education but on the whole literacy rates were low.[77] The mines inspector, Higson lamented the fact that there were 'hundreds of untaught girls daily employed in outdoor labour with their education almost totally ignored'.[78] A survey of educational attainment at the Ince Hall pits in 1863 showed that of the forty-nine females employed there, only twelve could read and one sign her name.[79] Others were learning – Ja:·e Brown was being taught to read at the 'Methody'.[80]

Claims of separation between the mill girls and pit girls were extended to religious practice. One reporter declared that pit girls as a class kept away from both church and Sunday school. He argued that at Aspull Moor mill girls attended services regularly but pit girls, rather than be snubbed by them, stayed at home.[81] Such a claim fitted in with the image of the irreligious mining community – the religious census revealed that under thirty per cent of Wigan's population attended a religious service on the census day of 30 March 1851. However, the reporter's comment sounds rather sweeping since not only would pit girls have been more than able to defend themselves in a mining area like Aspull but other evidence suggests that they did attend church. Munby used to see them dressed in their Sunday clothes on their way to and from church and J.M. Foster stressed in his stories how the girls regularly attended church and chapel.[82] In the mid-1880s clergy eagerly claimed them as members of their congregations. The Rev. Canon Fergie of Ince told of one of the most 'gentle and godly girls I ever knew', a pit brow girl who had not been absent from his

Bible class for seven years. The Rev. Siddall of Ashton knew pit girls
who had been attending Sunday school for up to fifteen years and the
Rev. T.J.O'Fenton had prepared a number for confirmation. Several
were Sunday school teachers.[83] It was local clergy who helped to
mobilise support for the pit women when their work was threatened
in 1887 and later in 1911. However, the clergy knew the bad press that
their profession had received at the time of the Children's Employment
Commission and did not want to be accused of ignorance of their
parishioners again so many well have deliberately emphasised their
concern for pit girls. Anyway they still tended to treat them as a
distinct group – the wife of the Rector of Wigan explained in 1886
that some special classes were held for girls who worked at the pit.[84]

The separate nature of pit women's lives was reinforced in other
ways. The organisation of their day necessarily imposed a particular
pattern. Not only were many following in an old-established family
tradition but they were *outdoor* workers, a category which was always
kept very distinct from indoor work and which was particularly stressed
in the 1800s. They were usually seen when dirty and wore a distinctive
uniform. They operated as a team (a tendency increased by the
adoption of picking belts and tables) in an industry already renowned
for its clannishness. They seem to have deliberately stressed their
exclusiveness – one Aspull woman explained 'we were a happy lot, we
were, different to what the others were anyway'.[85] Being a small group
at the pit they were in a sense a privileged section of the workforce and
sometimes had their own cabin. Unlike the situation in the female-
dominated mills, the pit brow lasses were working in surroundings
which were overwhelmingly dominated by males.

Conditions in the mill were hardly more healthy, wages were low
compared with other Lancashire towns but the work was indoors. It
was clean and, unlike some of the pit brow jobs, it was not usually
physically demanding. In contrast to the image of strong, rather
masculine pit women (Munby even claimed that pit girls could be
picked out by their stronger frames), the factory girl had acquired a
rather different reputation which reinforced the distinction between
the indoor and outdoor worker. Fond of finery and independence, she
was accused of pretensions as a poem in the *Comet* shows:

Can this be the factory flirt, you say;
You'll not believe? Just so,
But wait for a while, and I'll make you smile,
For the truth on't you shall know

Yes, wait till she's thrown off the scent of the mill,
Till she wanders forth in her gayest dress,
Up Wigan lane to roam.[86]

A further distinction between the two groups lay in the fact that
whereas mill work could lead to something, pit brow work had no
apprenticeship or training stages. Though in practice it required
dexterity, it was not viewed as skilled employment. Mill workers,
however, saw things differently. They prided themselves in the
knowledge that their work involved skill and in this sense saw
themselves as learning a trade. As one weaver explained:

You've a trade in your hands, a wonderful trade, a weaver.
A trade in your hands if you learned to weave.[87]

Not so for the pit brow woman. One pit lass summarised her work by
saying:

Oh we had to fill dirt on belt and then tip it into a wagon
[a dirt wagon would go on at end of shift]. Oh, I was used to it
you know. . .there was no trade in it, no trade in it.[88]

They were conscious that the mill girls saw themselves as higher up the
occupational ladder. Another pit brow woman explained the mill
workers' attitudes:

Some think they're above you but they're going to the same place. . .
they looked down really – because you worked at the pit you were
nothing, but we were as good as them – we can come up to them
any day.[89]

And the sheer weight of numbers helped ensure the hegemony of the
female mill worker. Yet though the mill girl appears to have looked
down on pit work it is interesting to note that what she may have
turned to as a last resort during the cotton famine was not always
relinquished when opportunities at the mills began to expand again at
the end of the 1860s. Nevertheless, there was some suspicion of the
work and it was a suspicion reinforced by the current ideology of
woman and the home. A dialect story 'A day at Blackpool with pit
brow women' told how three pit brow lasses 'carried on' when visiting
Blackpool on a colliery day trip – 'but then, they were nowt but pit

broo wenches'.[90] The *Lancet* argued that 'they have little or no social status to maintain. Among the working classes they are contemptuously called *canacks*, and rarely marry other than collier lads'.[91]

Yet in spite of the fact that the pit women's status within the community was low, they were not treated with overt hostility as puzzled outsiders believed. There was greater interaction between the mill and pit in occupational and household terms than critics appear to have realised. Nevertheless the pit women's low status was reinforced because even within the coal industry they were not fully accepted. Here the solidarity of the male peer group was evident. The coalminers formed an aristocracy of labour in Wigan but the pit women were outside this. Excluded from the highly-skilled, dangerous and intimate world below ground, as well as from the traditional recreations outside the pit, they were denounced by some of the most powerful miners' leaders, including William Pickard.

Throughout the nineteenth century the women remained outside any miners' union. An examination of their activity reveals, however, that at times they did demonstrate solidarity, pit brow lasses and non-working miners' wives combining to resist threats to the entire colliery workforce. In the 1868 and 1881 strikes the women attended meetings and demonstrations and helped repel blacklegs. At one meeting in 1881 held at Amberswood Common, the home of local protest, support was pledged from the men and women of Hindley, Ince and Wigan.[92] The meeting was chaired by a woman who had been involved in two previous strikes. Her husband had been out for a month but she would not let him return to work. About forty women hurled abuse at the 'Knobsticks' attempting to work at Knowles' Wheatsheaf pit and three women were arrested as ringleaders.[93] One pit brow woman who helped to lead meetings addressed a large open air gathering at West Leigh heath and was described by the local press as 'one of the pluckiest women we have ever seen'.[94] Pit brow women also travelled around the coalfield collecting money for the strikes.[95]

Yet no encouragement was given for them to come under the aegis of the union nor were they set much of an example by the local cotton trade where workers were much slower to organise themselves than in other Lancashire mill towns. It was not until the mid-1890s that Helen Silcock, the daughter of a miner, began working for the Women's Trade Union League to raise the level of the Wigan weavers' list.[96] One miner complained that 'there is scarcely a town in the kingdom where the cotton operatives are in such a state of disunity as they are in Wigan: hence their miserable earnings'.[97] The pit women did however attempt to improve their own situation and to reduce the discrepancy of wage rates between the pits. Munby described 'the wenches invariably thronging to serve some master who gave 2d more than others, till the whole level of pay was raised'. One woman, Ellen Grounds, who worked for Pearson and Knowles explained her course of action. When her wages had stood for some time at 1/10d

> me and soom oother yoong women went to th' overseer an' t'men was getting moor, an' 'waat'd him for two shillin'. Well, he'd see aboot it, he said: an't next Saturday, 't reckonin' was maad aht for t' wenches to ha' two shillin'.[98]

They were also concerned about regularity of payment. In 1855 the Countess of Fllesmere received a deputation of women from Middle Hulton. They urged her to persuade the Bridgewater Trustees to return to the former system of fortnightly pay on a regular day instead of paying wages on the 8th and 15th days of the month.[99] This was awkward since in some months there might be as many as sixteen or seventeen days between pay and on these occasions they were 'well-nigh clemmed'. A Winstanley agent wrote to the manager at Pemberton in 1867 complaining that the colliery women had gone on strike since he had changed the method of paying their wages. He added,

> I am told that one Elizabeth Hitchen has got on at Blundells', if such should be the case please send her back to at least serve a proper notice.[100]

During the cotton famine Munby was told that some of the younger girls were eager to go on strike over the low wages — 'if t'men would join'.[101] Yet lacking union backing they were not likely to be able to exert sustained pressure at any time, a factor which the management clearly recognised. Miners' leaders chose to endorse the exclusion of the women from their work. At a time when they were placed in a vulnerable position themselves, they could see no value in supporting claims which might later be used against them (see Chapter 6).

Some women were not prepared to support strikes — Munby found them still working at the Welch Whittle pit at Coppull in 1863 although the men were out on strike and they were also doing odd jobs at Douglas Bank.[102] The problems of balancing household budgets did however lead colliery women into a different kind of involvement, that of combining to resist high food prices. This was something which outside critics did not comment upon and it illustrates the fact that in spite of the exclusiveness of the pit women, a working-class solidarity could and did operate within the community. Miners' wives led the Anti-Beef agitation of 1872 and received support from pit and mill workers, protesting against the exorbitant price of butchers' meat.[103] This was the continuation of an old custom of asserting community pressure and was spurred on by the fact that similar collective action had forced a reduction of prices in Newcastle-upon-Tyne. At one Scholes meeting women publicly repeated their refusal to eat any meat (except bacon) until beef and mutton prices had been reduced from 10d and 11d a lb to 6d and 7d. It was resolved that any woman who spent more than 7d should forfeit her husband's wages for a week. Further meetings were held at Hindley, Ince, Aspull, Chorley and Golborne. The butchers found themselves fighting a losing battle and those who traded at Wigan market were forced to reduce prices. Public community sanctions were enforced against offenders in the 'rough music' tradition.[104] A watch was kept on the shops to detect those who bought meat 'on the sly'. Nocturnal visits were made to the homes of offenders and the national anthem sung loudly outside, tin pans and tambourines beaten and whistles blown. At an Aspull meeting it was decided that those who violated the community's decisions should be burned in effigy and at a meeting held at a disused Bolton coal pit the same tactics were adopted — effigies would be carried through the streets then burned at the offenders' front doors.[105] Anti-Beef associations sent letters to Parliament and discussed both the idea of buying cattle on a co-operative basis and the policy of exclusive dealing — using just one butcher of their choice. The women's determination was immortalised in the 'Women's Song of Little Lever' which they composed for the *Bolton Chronicle*.[106]

As well as exciting community pressure the women were anxious to resist any attempts to stop them working. A rumour at the Venture pit of a ban on female pit brow work met with an indignant response and expressions of determination to continue.[107] No doubt remembering the practice of former days, one woman at the Bye pit declared that she would come dressed as a man if they tried to stop her.[108] Quite apart from economic need, the women seem to have perceived their work as part of a tradition which should be maintained. Yet in this effort they did not receive the wholehearted support of the male miners. Ironically the campaign to defend their right to work was to a large extent taken up by those far less familiar with the experience of pit work.

The pit brow women of the Wigan coalfield were therefore in an ambivalent and vulnerable position. Intent on tendentious criticism, many outsiders inaccurately portrayed them as social outcasts. It is interesting to note that at the Wigan meetings held to uphold female pit brow work, decency was one of the words most frequently and deliberately urged, as if this were something not normally associated with the women and therefore required special emphasis. They failed to see how deep-rooted women's pit work was or how many families contained both mill girls and pit girls. They saw the miners as resolutely opposed to the work, forgetting that many of the attacks came from non-female-employing areas and that there was some local support among rank-and-file miners who might themselves be the fathers of pit brow girls and who, anyway, as coalmining employees, shared some problems in common with the pit brow women. Some stigma was attached to the pit women's position and they were usually on the defensive. Yet the pit brow debate was to concentrate not so much on these women's reactions as on the implications of their work for women's employment more generally.

Notes

1. Munby MS, Diary 39, 29 September 1871.
2. J. Watts, *The Facts of the Cotton Famine* (London, 1968), p.143.
3. A.J. Munby came from a family of Yorkshire lawyers and was the eldest of seven children. After graduating from Trinity College, Cambridge in 1851, he went to Lincolns Inn and was called to the bar in November 1855. In 1860 he joined the Ecclesiastical Commission. For further biographical details see D. Hudson, *Munby, Man of Two Worlds* (London, 1972).
4. *Gentleman's Magazine*, CCXCVII (1904), pp.503-8.
5. *The Times*, 5 February 1910; *DNB* (1901-11), pp.661-3, written by a friend, Austin Dobson.
6. Ellis Lever (see Chapter 5) challenged 'AJM's' motives in reply to his own letter. See *Wigan Observer*, 8, 23 April 1886. Compare for example the recent evidence about the Rev. Charles Kingsley discussed in S. Chitty, *The Beast and the Monk* (London, 1974).
7. For an analysis of his relationship with Hannah see L. Davidoff, 'Class and Gender in Victorian England, The Diaries of Arthur J. Munby and Hannah Cullwick', *Feminist Studies*, vol.5, no.1 (1979). It is argued that their obsessions 'flowed from their social situation'.
8. Munby MS, Notebook I, 1865.
9. Ibid., Diary 6, 29 September 1860.
10. Ibid.
11. MS poem formerly in the possession of the late Dr A.N.L. Munby.
12. A.J. Munby, *Ann Morgan's Love* (London, 1896).
13. Munby, *Susan, A Poem of Degrees* (London, 1873), p.43.
14. Munby MS, Notebook IV, 1869.

15. Ibid., 109[34].
16. Ibid., Diary 21, 18 August 1863.
17. Ibid., Notebook VIII, 1878.
18. Ibid., Notebook I, 1865.
19. Ibid., Notebook I, 1865. Mary Evans, a banker at the pit mouth, was compared with a young male commercial banker —lolling in his carriage.
20. Ibid. He was once assaulted by seven collier lads who thought he might be Jack the Ripper (Diary 56, 8 October 1888). In Shropshire he was mistaken for an informer checking on the special rules of the 1860 Inspection Act − 'It was cruel; an enthusiast for female labour to be suspected of informing against it.' Diary 20, 13 August 1863.
21. Munby, *Ann Morgan's Love*. Failing to recognise both Munby's actual knowledge and his use of symbolism, one critic of *Dorothy* declared that Munby insisted too much on the roughness and hardness of hands. L. Hearn, *Appreciation of Poetry* (London, 1916), p.38.
22. See Ch.6 for a discussion of wages. On reading the report of the Royal Commission on Agriculture (1867) he commented 'would that I had been one of those Commissioners'. He did make enquiries about the post of Factory Inspector in 1866 but since the job only paid £300 p.a., he did not pursue the idea. Notebook IV, 1870; Diary 34, 12 July 1866.
23. Munby MS, Diary 6, 29 September 1860.
24. *Comet*, nos. 9-18 (1889-90). J.M. Foster, *With Pick and Pen* (n.d.), Wigan Public Library. John Monk Foster (1858-1930) came from Scholes and worked in the pits from the age of nine. His work was cut short in 1885 as a result of criticisms of the Inspectorate which, by coincidence, were published in the same week as the Clifton Hall colliery disaster occurred. In 1888 he began writing professionally for a literary syndicate based at Bolton. He published numerous stories in newspapers and wrote novels. The *Comet* was a fortnightly journal which he started in 1889.
25. *Mary Anerley* was dedicated to Munby. MS letter in the possession of Peter Mendes to whom I am grateful for the reference.
26. In *Wigan Observer*, 30 January 1886, signed 'AJM'.
27. He gave away 8/- on one day alone in 1887. Munby MS, Small Notebook, 22 September 1887.
28. His social survey of Victorian society never progressed to political criticism or suggestions for remedying the *malaise* he detected.
29. Munby MS, Diary 19, 16 May 1843.
30. Ibid., Diary 20, 20 August 1863. Compare this with the disparaging views of trousers discussed in Ch.6.
31. In 1892 he explained to the publisher, George Bentley, that his special interest was 'real hard handed working women. Of these I have many notes and descriptions taken from my own observations; but I have kept back most of them from print, for fear of injuring the women themselves by making them known. Some, however, might appear if you care for such a subject.' MS Letter, 20 January 1892 (Osborn collection, Yale University Library). Most probably Munby's own fears of revelation were as strong as his concern to protect the pit women. His material was never published, though he did write several brief articles on Yorkshire, for example in the *Fifeshire Journal* and *Temple Bar*. He wrote to the Rev. N. Robertson Nicoll in 1882 to explain that he hoped to publish some of this material. This did not happen, neither did he proceed with a plan for arranging the posthumous publication of two volumes of his writings on Hannah. Munby Papers formerly in the possession of the late Dr A.N.L. Munby, Letters of 17 and 20 November 1882.
32. In *Wigan Observer*, 30 January 1886.

33. Ibid. For Munby's photographs see M. Hiley *Victorian Working Women, Portraits from Life* (London, 1979).

34. PP 1852-3, LXXXVI, p.64.

35. Munby found quite an influx of Irish pit girls in 1860. Munby MS, Diary 6, 29 September 1860.

36. PP 1883, LXXIX, p.45; PP 1893-4, CIV, p.173. The 1861 and 1871 census reports attributed the growth of Ince, Pemberton and Aspull to the expansion of mining and manufacturing, influx of miners and the operation of building clubs. PP 1862, L.1, p.549; PP 1872, LXVI, pt.II, pp.397-8.

37. H.E. Clegg, 'Some Historic Notes on the Wigan Coalfield', *Colliery Guardian*, 14 November 1957.

38. A.J. Taylor, 'The Wigan Coalfield in 1851', *Transactions of the Historic Society of Lancashire and Cheshire*, no.106 (1954), p.118. Although this did not include the Haigh pits, it extended as far as Billinge and Shevington in the west, north to parts of Chorley, to Westhoughton and Leigh to the east and south to Ashton. In 1884 the inspector Dickinson listed fifty-four collieries around Wigan and a total of 363 for the coalfield. PP 1854, XIX, pp.80-1.

39. D.H. Turner, 'Wigan Coal and Iron Company 1865-85', unpublished BA diss., University of Strathclyde.

40. PP 1863, LIII.2, p.646. There were also two female coal dealers.

41. In class V of the census (factory workers and artisans). See K. Tiller, 'Working Class Attitudes and Organisation in Three Industrial Towns 1850-75', unpublished PhD thesis, University of Birmingham, 1975, p.11.

42. PP 1863, LVIII, p.632.

43. Munby MS, Notebook I, 1865.

44. PP 1866, XIV, p.49, qu.1730; PP 1868, XXIX, p.14, qus. 16, pp.89-90.

45. A fact confirmed by Thomas Knowles, proprietor of the Ince Hall Colliery Company. PP 1866, XIV, p.392, qu.1536.

46. *Wigan Observer*, 19 February, 27 March 1886. Women also worked further north around Chorley and south in the Garswood, Haydock, St Helens and Prescot districts.

47. Munby MS, Notebook VII, 1878.

48. Home Office Population Census. Schedules for Wigan RG 9 1861 2769, 2780-1, 2782-3; RG 10 1871 3882-3, 3894-6, 3891-3; PP 1862, L.1, p.569; PP 1872, LXVI, pt.II, pp.397-8.

Number of Females in	Aspull	Ince	Pemberton
1881	6,591	7,808	9,354
1891	6,894	9,461	12,042

PP 1883, LXXIX, p.45; PP 1893-4, CIV, p.173.

49. Ibid., Diary 55, 22 September 1887; Notebook IX, 1887; *Wigan Observer*, 17 February 1886.

50. The *Manchester Guardian* claimed that many factory girls knew that their occupation would be fatal yet continued to work in mills until their health broke down rather than wear trousers! In *Wigan Observer*, 17 February 1886; Munby MS, Diary 21, 20 August 1863.

51. J. Ruskin, *Fors Clavigera* (London, 1896), letter XIV, p.290.

52. E. Waugh, *Lancashire and its Factory Folk* (Manchester, 1881), pp.143,151.

53. E. Faithfull, 'Unfit employments in which women are engaged', *Transactions of the National Association for the Promotion of Social Science* (1863), p.767. She later changed her mind and pledged support for the women.

54. J. Plummer, *Once A Week*, XI (1864), p.279.

55. Munby MS, Diary 28, 22 September 1864.

56. These formed the main areas of female colliery employment — in 1861 all but 90 of the female pit workers recorded in the census were living in one of these

four districts. The women were variously described as 'pit brow lasses', coal fillers', 'coal labourers', 'coal pickers', 'coal pit brow labourers', 'colliery labourers' etc. Occasionally more specific descriptions were given — for example, 'oiling railway waggons'. Except where stated, the following analysis is based on RG 9 1861 and RG 10 1871 for these four areas, Munby's diaries and notebooks and oral interviews with former pit brow women from the Wigan coalfield. For evidence on occupational patterns in another Lancashire town in the nineteenth century see J. O. Foster's discussion of Oldham in his 'Nineteenth Century towns: A Class dimension' in M.W. Flinn and T.C. Smout (eds.), *Essays in Social History* (London, 1974).

57. *Wigan Observer* 1, 5 August 1911.

58. *Comet*, no.9 (4 May 1889). See Ch.6.

59. Arncliffe Sennett collection, Add. MS C121, British Library.

60. Interviewed 24 August 1978.

61. *Globe*, 3 July 1896 explained that preference was given to widows.

62. See M. Anderson, *Family Structure in Nineteenth Century Lancashire* (Cambridge, 1971) for an examination of kinship relations in Preston.

63. See Chapter 6; PP 1873, XI, p.151, qu.202.

64. L. Tilly and J. Scott, *Women, Work and Family* (London, 1978), pp.129-30, 135. See also their discussion of the mining area of Anzin, France, p.134.

65. J. Benson, *British Coalminers in the Nineteenth Century: A Social History* (Dublin, forthcoming).

66. In *Wigan Observer*, 17 February 1886.

67. Watts, *Cotton Famine. Wigan Observer*, 13 September, 6 December 1862.

68. Waugh, *Lancashire*, p.112.

69. Munby MS, Notebook I, 1865.

70. Munby, *Dorothy* (London, 1880), p.25.

71. Munby MS, Diary 6, 29 September 1860; Diary 33, 30 September 1866.

72. Interviewed 24 August 1978.

73. Munby MS, Notebook I, 16 August 1873.

74. *Wigan Observer*, 16 August 1873.

75. Interviewed 24 August 1978. The *Manchester Guardian* referred to their 'extraordinary liking for tea parties'. According to the Rector's wife 'their craving for this light form of dissipation was generally met'. In *Wigan Observer*, 17 February 1886.

76. Munby MS, Diary 20, 15 August 1863.

77. See J. Dickinson, 'Statistics of the Collieries of Lancashire, Cheshire and North Wales', *Memoirs of the Literary and Philosophical Society of Manchester*, 2nd series, XII (1855), pp.76-9.

78. PP 1869, XIV, p.407.

79. Tiller, 'Working Class Attitudes', p.141.

80. Munby MS, Notebook I, 1865.

81. In *Wigan Observer*, 17 February 1886.

82. For example, J.M. Foster, *That Wench O'Ballin's. A Mining Sketch of Lancashire Christmastide* (n.d.), Wigan Public Library.

83. *Wigan Observer*, 17 February, 17 April 1886; *Manchester Guardian*, 10 May 1886. Welsh tip girls were praised for their strong religious and moral temperament. The Vicar of St Andrews at Bordesley, Staffordshire praised pit bank women for their attendance at services, lectures, Bible classes, tea parties and Sunday school.

84. *Wigan Observer*, 17 February 1886.

85. Interviewed 24 August 1978.

86. *Comet*, no.2 (26 January 1889), V2.

87. Quoted in J. Liddington and J. Norris, *One Hand Tied Behind Us* (London, 1978), p.57.

88. Interviewed 25 August 1978.

89. *Idem.*

90. *Comet*, no.74 (31 October 1891).

91. *Lancet*, 30 July 1887.

92. *Wigan Observer*, 24 April 1868, 16, 17 February 1881; *Manchester Examiner*, 14 February 1881.

93. *Wigan Observer*, 16 February 1881. There was a tradition of female resistance to blacklegs – this had been evident for example in the 1844 strike at St Helens.

94. Quoted in *Wigan Observer*, 3 February 1886. See the comments on family solidarity and strike support from miners' wives in P.N. Stearns, 'Working Class Women in Britain 1890-1914' in Vicinus (ed.), *Suffer and Be Still. Women in the Victorian Age* (Bloomington, 1973), p.107.

95. Lancashire and Cheshire Joint District Committee, 'Arbitration on the Scale of Minimum Wages for Females' (NUM Bolton, 1919), p.9.

96. Liddington and Norris, *One Hand*, pp.97-8.

97. *Comet*, no.13 (29 June 1889).

98. Munby MS, Notebook III, 1866.

99. Loch-Egerton Papers 2/V/19n, 2 September 1855.

100. J.M. Bankes, 'A Nineteenth Century Colliery Railway', *Transactions of the Historic Society of Lancashire and Cheshire*, 114 (1966), p.173.

101. Munby MS, Diary 20, 19 August 1863.

102. Ibid., Notebook III, 1866; Notebook IV, 1869.

103. Prices had been raised by a restriction on the importation of foreign cattle. See PP 1842, XVII, no.24, p.507 for the use of this tactic at Merthyr Tydfil. *Northern Star*, 15 July 1843; *Wigan Observer*, 20 July 1872. Butchers in turn began boycotting cattle markets.

104. See E.P. Thompson, 'Rough Music. Le Charivari anglais', *Annales*, 27 (1972), pp.304-8.

105. *Wigan Observer*, 20, 27 July 1872, 3 August 1872.

106. *Bolton Chronicle*, 3 August 1872, verse 3:

> Then o my! is all the cry
> No beef for dinner or tea,
> The butcher wants 11d per pound
> But the wives will let them see.

107. Munby MS, Notebook III, 1866.

108. Ibid., Notebook I, 1865.

PART III: THE TEST CASE

It is the test case in which in all human probability the right of women to perform rough manual labour for wages and out of doors will for a long period be decided.

> The *Spectator* on the attempt to remove women from the pit brow, 27 March 1886.

Munby's Interpretations. From His 66 Rough Sketchs of Colliery Girls, Munby MS, Trinity College Cambridge.

5 THE CONFLUENCE OF OPINION

'Tis out of women's sphere, they say
To bear the burdens of the day
In out-door, manual labour;
And that a woman should be strong
And like such work, is very wrong
Well, to her weaker neighbour.

But work does not degrade the mind,
And purer morals oft we find
'Mong field-girls and pit wenches
Than in the salons of the rich,
With culture at its highest pitch
So high, it feeling quenches.

Thomas Hutchinson, *Hard Hands in Woman*,
30 July 1891, in Munby, *Vulgar Verses*

The second half of the nineteenth century was punctuated by attacks on the work of the pit brow women. Many were simply minor criticisms devoid of any systematic scheme to remove them. In the 1880s however they coalesced to form a more sustained and calculated challenge to the women's right to work. The consequences of the colliery legislation of 1842 had initially served to sharpen opinion and establish an official union standpoint. In 1859 the secretary to the Miners' Amalgamated Council had appealed for information about grievances at work and had suggested female pit labour as one possible topic.[1] Opposition was expressed at the conference of the National Association of Coal, Lime and Ironstone Miners of Great Britain held at Leeds in 1863. This was consolidated in the evidence given by miners to the Select Committee on Mines of 1865-6 which provided an unprecedented opportunity for publicity and a collective condemnation of the work. Not surprisingly, Munby was interested in such proceedings — he made at least eight visits to the House of Commons and met and corresponded with the chairman and several members. He found the 'prospect of another false and foolish measure against the women. . .simply distracting'.

Yet the pit women survived the Select Committee with little difficulty. It was a body predisposed towards the continuation of the work and its members had made up their minds before they ever

finished their questions about the women's work.[3] The chairman
Neate admitted this to Munby but, though the latter was relieved, he
was nevertheless disturbed by the unsympathetic and despotic attitude
of Neate and his all-male committee. At the same time as John Stuart
Mill was presenting the first suffrage bill to Parliament, Munby was
saddened to find that Neate, a professor of political economy who
called himself an 'advanced Liberal', could not recognise that the
women had any claims to rights of their own. Such stubbornness led
Munby to conclude:

> I see no one who will deal with the thing on principle, and in that
> great bustling strife of business men I grow saddened and maddened
> to think that the strength and purity of womanhood which I have
> seen at the pit mouth in Lancashire and Wales may be about to
> vanish for ever.[4]

His feelings may have been somewhat premature but they were not
ill-founded. Although the 1872 Mines Act did not really threaten the
women's livelihood, by the 1880s the demands for exclusion had
become much more vociferous. Yet ironically, whereas the work of the
sixties and seventies could be seen as appropriate for males — landing
tubs, shovelling coal, moving wagons etc. — the later trends in surface
work, especially sorting at picking belts and tables, were less demanding
physically and not so easy to attack in terms of suitability. Nevertheless,
improvements were much more marked at some pits than others, a fact
which intensified the opportunity for debate.

Central to an understanding of this debate is an analysis of the ideas
which informed it and the forces which made such a situation possible.
Why was it that discontent which had been brewing over a number of
years should come to a head at this time? In the mid-1880s there were
nearly 3,000 less pit brow women than there had been ten years earlier.
Why, anyway, should a group of women who always remained under
seven per cent of the total surface workforce become such an issue?
The desire to complete the process of female prohibition at mines must
be placed in the context of the belief in the efficacy of state regulation
of female labour, already witnessed in the Factory and Workshops Acts
of 1874 and 1878 which had reduced women's work from sixty to
fifty-four hours weekly. Concern about restricting hours and types of
work through 'protective' legislation was spreading, segmenting the
labour force and posing wider issues about women's work in the future.

In 1883 the stonemason-MP Henry Broadhurst sought a ban on girls

working in the nail-making industry.[5] During the course of the debate
Sir Charles Dilke revealed that only nine girls would actually be
affected by these proposals and Broadhurst's efforts failed to produce
any change in the law. Encouraged however by the Commons discussion
of female work in such a trade, a wealthy coal contractor Ellis Lever of
Bowden, Cheshire had published a letter in *The Times* (16 May 1883).[6]
Here he enunciated his disgust at the work of the pit brow women. In
his opinion, anybody unfamiliar with the facts would have difficulty in
recognising that the 'creatures in hideous costume, all coal-begrimed
were of the female sex, so little do they resemble women'. He
emphasised the dangers of adolescence – the mere association of the
sexes in such work must brutalise the nature of men and women. The
consequence was that men shirked responsibility. Since there was a
need for domestic servants, women should be going into service rather
than working at the pits. The main thrust of his argument was the
degradation and debasement of women due to the work. Lever felt
himself to be particularly well qualified to air such pejorative views
since he had long been connected with coalmining in Lancashire and
Wales.

Lever was a constant and persistent advocate of reforms.[7] He
frequently wrote to the press and his most constructive schemes were
related to safety in coalmining. Having viewed the superior conditions
in Belgian mines, he had presented the miners' union with five hundred
pounds to be paid to the inventor of a safety lamp. Concern about
colliery conditions prompted him to send resolutions to the 1885 TUC
conference at Southport. His failure to give the statutory two weeks'
notice meant that his proposals were not discussed (though they were
printed by the Parliamentary Committee). Lever therefore supplied the
readers of *The Times* with their contents. His provocative statements
included a challenge on a national basis. His first proposal made explicit
his views on female labour:

There are employed within a few miles of Southport at collieries in
the Wigan and St. Helens district, thousands of women and girls who
are dressed wholly or partially in male attire and whose duties are
those of 'banksman' and loaders and screeners of coal, together with
other work certainly unsuited for females. In Durham, Northumberland and other important mining counties this evil is
prohibited or discontinued greatly to the moral, social and physical
advantage of both sexes. Although nearly half a century has elapsed
since the employment of female labour in the mines was prohibited

by the legislature, Lancashire and a few other districts are still disgraced by the continuance of this pernicious custom of employing women and girls on the pit bank. The only reform possible in this matter is the absolute discontinuance of the practice.[8]

The statement produced a polemical debate in the press. Newspapers sent reporters to the colliery districts (chiefly West Lancashire) and produced accounts of the work and its effects.[9] Dozens of individuals sent letters to the press (some wrote several times) and there were elaborate pseudonyms such as 'A Lancashire Witch', 'An English Matron' and 'Pro Bono Publico'. Lever clung to his opinions despite accusations of psychopathic behaviour. Prohibition of female pit work would, he claimed, still be necessary were there only several hundred women at work.[10] Some Lancashire contributors (including a number of miners) reacted indignantly to the claim that miners' behaviour was superior in districts where women did not work — such a comment demonstrated the 'execrable taste of a Lancashire coal merchant maligning the men who provide his trade'.[11] Several visits to the Wigan pits, depression in the coal trade and continual pressure from opponents did persuade Lever to concede that there had been some improvements in the work demands in recent years and in 1886 he modified his proposals by suggesting that a ten-year period elapse before the women be totally prevented from doing colliery work.[12] In the meantime, however, his plea had been a signal for a more concerted attack on the women. Opposition was intensified in January 1886 with the acceptance by the miners' Birmingham conference of Thomas Burt's resolution that 'All female labour shall be entirely prohibited at coal pits.'[13]

The opportunity for more direct intervention came with the Coal Mines Regulation Act (1872) Amendment Bill (108) introduced by Gladstone's new Liberal government in February 1886. This was a direct result of the reports from the Royal Commission of 1879-85 on Accidents in Coal Mines and Means for their Prevention. The question of women's work was raised during the third reading by John Wilson MP for Houghton-le-Springs, Durham.[14] A pit worker himself from the age of thirteen, and a committed Methodist from a non-female-employing area, he now sought the total exclusion of women from any kind of pit work. He argued that it was only fit for strong muscular men and that it was 'a woman's place to do much more delicate work than that'. However, no exclusion clause was actually put forward. On 17 May the Home Secretary Childers announced his intention to introduce another safety measure. As no statement had been made to the contrary, anti-exclusionists prematurely concluded that a clause forbidding women's work would form part of this new bill. In fact the bill failed to get beyond its first reading and the government fell at the end of the month.[15]

It is interesting to note the degree to which the mere *possibility* of legislation against the women caused panic among their supporters. They had begun to organise themselves in anticipation of an attack *before* the abortive bill was even introduced. Lever's concentration on the Wigan-St Helens area and the earlier attention paid to this region helped ensure that it would be further exposed to attention and viewed (somewhat erroneously) as a microcosm of the national situation.

The first meeting in defence of the pit brow lasses was held near Wigan at the schoolroom of St Pauls Church, Goose Green, where the Vicar of the nearby St Johns Church, Pemberton set in motion what proved to be a very effective pressure group. The Rev. Harry Mitchell had been at Pemberton for five years though at the end of 1886 he was chosen by King's College, Cambridge as the new incumbent for the nearby living of Prescot.[16] There he also became involved in local concerns — opposing threats to deprive women of work, supporting the revival of the Prescot watch trade and aiding the formation of a Lancashire watch company which included workmen as partners. His support for the pit brow women in 1886 and 1887 was a product of his desire to be active in the community. It was also related to his other interests, notably his involvement in educational developments. He was chairman of Prescot Grammar, Church and Council schools from 1887-1919 and in his first four years at Pemberton, Mitchell had undertaken an extensive scheme designed to improve the parish schools' accommodation.[17] By October 1887 seven day schools and eight Sunday schools had been started and Sunday school attendance at Pemberton was increased by thirty per cent. Behind this activity lay a fervent desire to prevent the establishment of a Board school. Church schools at Pemberton and Orrell were started for this reason and at the opening of the latter in 1882, the coalowner Colonel Blundell spoke against the idea of a Board on grounds of economy as well as religion and expressed his gratitude to Mitchell.[18] Such independence was however expensive and in this work Mitchell was ably assisted by local gentry, chiefly coalowners who employed females. They included the Bridgewater Trustees, the Walthew and Norley Coal Companies and the Orrell Coal and Cannel Company. The opening of a school at Lamberhead Green in 1884 had been aided by a three-day sale of work at which it was hoped that money would be raised for the erection of a Vicarage for Mitchell. He had already been promised land by 'a generous benefactress' and the Blundell and Egerton families were contributors, their employees helping to raise some of the money. So although Mitchell disclaimed personal knowledge of coalowners' views about pit women, his connections with these local owners were clearly rather more than tenuous.

Mitchell became the local leader of the pit women's campaign to continue working. He was chairman at the Pemberton meeting of 13 February which coincided with an annual tea party. Over two hundred attended and he pledged his support for the pit brow cause, declaring that he intended to 'take it up pretty strongly'.[19] The first general meeting in defence of the women was held just over a month later at the new school at Lamberhead Green. Its purpose was to protest against Wilson's proposals. About 120 of the 400-strong audience were pit women. They included some from the Crawford pit, Aspull, from the Garswood collieries, Brinsop Hall colliery and from the pits belonging to Lamb and Moore and the Bankes family. About twenty came from the Orrell Coal and Cannel Company and six Blundells' women had pride of place on the platform. The meeting was chaired by the Mayoress of Wigan, Margaret Park and a petition supporting their work was signed. Like Mitchell, Mrs Park was a seasoned intervener in local affairs.[20] The *Sunday Chronicle* interviewed her in 1886 and commented on her local reputation as the leader of movements to help the poor. Her husband had been Mayor since 1881 and she complemented his long term in office by her active and beneficient public role. She involved herself in issues of social purity and was a local leader of the White Cross Army for the protection of young girls, a district visitor and played a prominent part in organising a day nursery for the children of Wigan mill workers. Like Mitchell, Mrs Park (whose husband was an iron merchant) was at pains to emphasise her altruistic concern for the women and detachment from the coal industry.[21] At the meeting she first mooted the idea of raising funds to take four or five hundred women to London to prove that they were not the 'degraded, unsexed health-injured creatures' depicted by their detractors.[22]

Mitchell compared the impact of the Pemberton meeting to that of fired gunpowder.[23] Though the Liberal Home Secretary was adverse to the idea of receiving a deputation, local organisation rapidly gathered momentum. For the next few months large and enthusiastic meetings were held in the Lancashire colliery districts. One meeting held at West

Leigh in April (convened by the Rev. T.A. Knowles and chaired by James Thorp, a cotton manufacturer and chairman of the local Board of Health) was told by Mrs Amelia Hughes of Aspull that if the exclusionists could find her and her fellow pit women work, all would be fine. If not they would find themselves in the workhouse.[24] Further meetings were held at St Helens (one was chaired by the Mayor) and all received support from local councillors, doctors and clergymen, including the Bishop of Liverpool.[25]

Organisation was not confined to Lancashire. At the end of April 1886 a large meeting was held at Tredegar to support the women.[26] In this area the Tredegar Iron and Coal Company alone employed over two hundred women. In the same month a meeting was convened at Whitehaven market hall for the same purpose and 125 of the 150 local screen women were estimated to be present. The Rev. J. Anderson moved

> That this public meeting of the screen girls of the Whitehaven colliery and the people of Whitehaven protests most earnestly against the proposed prohibition of female labour above ground at collieries, and calls upon the borough and county members to assist in defeating such an unjust and tyrannical measure.[27]

The sense of urgency was modified somewhat after April. From August the Conservatives led by Lord Salisbury were in power with Henry Matthews as the new Home Secretary.[28] The fact that local meetings were restricted to the first four months of the year suggests that the barometer of reaction can chiefly be measured by a Parliamentary rather than an economic timetable. Nevertheless current economic difficulties were making the situation appear more urgent and Parliamentary bills provided a convenient platform for airing grievances on this score. The need for safety legislation made it inevitable that the question would be revived before long. The bill which eventually proved to be the greatest threat to the women was brought in by the Conservatives. It was a new Coal Mines Regulation Act Amendment Bill and received it first reading on 31 January 1887 (Bill 130). It was designed to amend and consolidate the 1872 and 1886 acts and to incorporate the report of 1886 based on the Royal Commission on Accidents in Mines.

Party competition for achieving success in mines legislation and the more careful surveillance of mining conditions generally by the 1880s help account for the extension of interest in the women's work. It is

necessary however to consider more closely the particular combination
of circumstances which made possible not only the climax of the pit
brow question but translated it into wider terms, enabling it to be
viewed as the start of a campaign to save outdoor work and according
it the status of a test case which mobilised support within and beyond
the mining localities and Parliament.

The issue must be viewed against the disillusionment of the 1880s
and the concern about Britain's role in the world economy. There was
a prolonged cyclical depression in 1884-7, with a particularly severe
winter in 1885-6. And to economic gloom was added political fear,
fear generated by the rediscovery of poverty. If the swelling residuum
of society were not restrained there might even be revolution, and the
growing sense of unease was redoubled by the influence of Hyndman's
Social Democratic Federation and the London rioting of February
1886.[29] Liberal policies now sought to win and harness the support of
the trades unions and the respectable working class and to distance
them effectively from the chronic casual residuum for whom traditional
laissez faire policies were clearly no longer sufficient.

Whilst the pit women could hardly be equated with the casual
residuum of the East End of London now being eagerly investigated by
social explorers, it was none the less true that colliery communities had
never been readily associated with the respectable working class. And
though the higher echelons of the male miners' union had achieved a
certain status, colliery women were once again being discovered. These
pit brow women could be seen as a moral threat, a challenge to the cult
of motherhood and another forceful image of darkest England.

Misgivings about their employment had already been voiced by Lever
who spearheaded the attack. The women were subjected to minute
scrutiny by the local and national press. The nature of the enquiries
followed a familiar pattern. They were not being defined as a 'problem'
for the first time and as with earlier enquiries their investigation had its
roots in traditional fears and ignorance about coalmining.[30] But there
was an intensification of interest in their work which assumed novel
implications in the context of the position of women in the 1880s. One
aspect of this was demographic. Whereas in 1851 the country had over
300,000 excess females, by 1881 this had risen to over a million and
the issue of the 'redundant' woman was attracting considerable
attention and might indeed be conveniently urged to the disadvantage
of the working woman. In addition there were new openings for women
which were expanding rapidly and were believed to be more appropriate
for the female sex than rough outdoor work. Between 1881 and 1891,

for example, the number of women clerks and secretaries rose from 5,989 to 17,859.[31]

The wisdom of advocating female surface exclusion as the natural corollary to women's prohibition from work below ground was reinforced by the publicity given to the Belgian coal strike of 1886.[32] Over 4,000 women still worked in the pits of Belgium and British newspapers noted the absence of violence in areas such as Ghent where females did not work underground. They contrasted this with the Liège-Charleroi district where they did still work and where scenes of 'anarchy and discontent' were common.[33] The publication of Zola's *Germinal* in England in 1885, demonstrating 'the very extremity of intensity', provided further fuel for the opponents of female labour who were prepared to draw upon European fact and fiction to prove their point.[34] A.J. Mundella warned that England might well have witnessed the riotous scenes that Belgium experienced had she not forbidden work in the pits in 1842. He went on to argue that total exclusion must be the most advisable policy.[35] Meanwhile further attention was drawn to pit women by the work of socialist realist artists, notably Constantin Meunier, and his followers in the *liégeois* school of artists. Meunier's bronzes include statuettes of defiant *hiercheuses* (drawers). He also produced a number of sketches and paintings (in watercolour and oils) of women miners between 1882 and 1888. His 'Intérieur de Charbonnage' showed women pushing tubs while his sketches depicted young girls leaning against tubs of coal, their trousers (which only reached mid-calf) and confrontational stance leaving the viewer in no doubt that they were of the female sex.[36] His work was taken up by others such as Rassenfosse and Douard who continued to sketch and paint pit women.

At the same time as the pit brow issue was being debated in England, arguments were being marshalled in Belgium for and against female work in the pit. The British press followed the findings of the *Commission du Travail* set up in April 1886.[37] In the summer it sat at different centres interviewing a number of witnesses. There were some interesting parallels with earlier British conditions and attitudes. Although further advanced in safety techniques, Belgium's concern for human labour was minimal and evidence of physical, moral and economic exploitation was much stronger than it had been in Britain in 1842. For those unfamiliar with pit work some of the shocking tales of poverty and moral temptation could, however, blur the distinctions between such harsh and exacting work for women below ground and the conditions of surface work at British collieries.

Within the coalmining industry there was no such danger of confusion. But though the miners understood the differences in conditions of work, they did not appreciate the continuation of female colliery employment and linked it to wider grievances. Lever's attack had pinpointed contentious issues which had been dogging the miners' unions for years. Now there was an opportunity for the labour movement to test its strength. In 1872 there had been no miners in Parliament but two years later Thomas Burt and Alexander MacDonald were returned as the first two members 'in the working men's interest'. Both had mining backgrounds and were experienced in trades union leadership. MacDonald's National Association had opposed the women's work at the Leeds conference in 1863. This attempt to integrate the federations of district unions meant that it was, in effect, a revived rather than a new union though it became known as the National Miners' Union.[38] It did, however, operate very differently from the Miners' Association of the 1840s. The Inspection Act of 1860 had given miners a valuable weapon at the local level, the checkweighman, a permanent official for the pit lodge. The same act also demonstrated the extent to which safety grievances had not been met. Such a problem was made painfully clear in the amendment to the act forced by the 1862 Hartley colliery disaster. New and more sophisticated trades union tactics were necessary and under the leadership of MacDonald there was a change in direction. Aware of insecurity through a failure to influence conditions effectively through strike action, the NMU decided (unlike its more militant rival the Amalgamated Association of Miners) that political action via legislation might be a more realistic means of effecting change and forcing improvement than striking.[39] Opposition to female employment fitted in with this policy. It could be urged as part of a scheme for the general betterment of the miners' situation and an extension of a principle which had been accepted in 1842. Worries too about a labour surplus were heightened by the Lancashire cotton famine and it is no coincidence that the miners' first concerted opposition to women's surface work came in 1863 at the height of the cotton crisis. The issue was being forced to a head locally in Lancashire. John Lancaster, no doubt influenced by the Wigan miners' leader William Pickard, responded by reducing the number of female workers at his pits. Munby was told by one girl that the intention was to 'knock off t'wenches and put pit men i'wer plaaces and wer leaven'.[40] MacDonald spoke in opposition to female pit work at a number of meetings in the mid-sixties. In 1865, for example, he addressed a public meeting of Wigan miners on this issue and also denounced the work at the national conference at Newcastle.[41]

After MacDonald's death in 1881 Burt took over the leadership of the union, supporting female pit exclusion both in and out of Parliament. He made emotional appeals at the local level – at a Haydock demonstration in 1883 he drew upon Elizabeth Barrett Browning's poem 'The Cry of the Children' written forty years earlier and concerning work *in* mines.[42] He also spoke at a number of conferences, continually urging the need for a legal ban on women's surface work.

Union officials had therefore been maximising opportunities for airing such grievances for some time. Lever's timely outburst, set against a background of depression in the coal trade, provoked an acceleration of pressure from the miners. The adoption of Burt's resolution against female employment at the Birmingham conference in January 1886 was followed on 18 March by a deputation of miners' delegates to the Home Secretary.[43] A number of grievances were discussed and Burt claimed that the miners were practically unanimous about the necessity of female exclusion. Although this proved to be an exaggeration, it was a view which appeared popular since there were no MPs in the Commons representing female employing districts in 1886 or 1887 and therefore these areas could not have the opinions of their miners expressed. West Lancashire, staunchly Conservative, did not even have any members with trades union sympathies (see Chapter 6).

The coalowners retaliated by also visiting the Home Secretary and this was countered in February 1887 by a second miners' deputation.[44] Once again Burt led an attack on the women's work. He outlined his hope that the government would fix a time after which no more females would be engaged at pit work. More positive action followed. On 6 May an amendment in Committee sought that from the passing of the act 'No female shall be employed at a mine on any work involving the getting, processing or preparation of coal unless she was in the employment of the mine on that date.' This was defeated by twenty-one to fourteen votes. Burt put forward a similar amendment whilst the Liberal lawyer Atherley Jones went further, proposing the exclusion of all females rather than the prohibition of newcomers.[45]

Walter McLaren, MP for Crewe, a colliery director and the first Liberal to support the women actively, wrote to *The Times* expressing a desire for help for their cause.[46] He followed this with a request in the Commons for the Home Secretary to receive a deputation of those opposed to the amendments. This was taking up a challenge issued by

Henry Matthews on meeting the miners:

> All I can say is that I should like to receive a deputation from the
> women. (Loud laughter.) I should like to know what they think.[47]

The request was duly granted and McLaren contacted Mrs Park who in
turn called a meeting of the colliery proprietors.[48] Meanwhile a second
meeting was held in Whitehaven where screen women elected three
representatives.[49] Eventually in May (the same month that Charles
Booth outlined to the Royal Statistical Society details of his first year's
work on his survey of poverty in London) they and twenty Lancashire
women came to London, the trip being arranged by Mitchell, Mrs Park
and McLaren. Munby was at Euston station to greet them, finding this
an ideal way to further one of his most important causes and a unique
opportunity to blend his two worlds without embarrassing
repercussions.[50] The women spent several days in London being shown
the sights — including the underground railway, the American
exhibition complete with Buffalo Bill's Wild West Show and Madame
Tussauds. They also visited the House of Commons and met
sympathetic MPs. For the visit to the Home Office on 17 May they
wore their best clothes, though the Blundells' girls wore their pit
costume. They formed a procession with Munby at the head
(accompanying Elizabeth Halliwell of Pemberton) and they marched
in twos to their appointment.

A vast and motley crowd had assembled to hear their defence.[51]
McLaren acted as the chief spokesman, explaining that nine different
towns and villages were present to defend their work and in particular
to oppose Burt and Jones's amendments. Mitchell and Mrs Park both
spoke as did some miners who supported the cause. The Conservative
MP for Whitehaven, Cavendish Bentinck, delivered a speech on behalf
of the screen lasses and Archibald Hood, the managing director of
Glamorgan Coal Company and former President of the South Wales
Coalowners' Association, defended the work of the Welsh women.
Some coalowners' wives, for example Lady Crawford and Mrs Burrows,
also spoke. The pit women's contribution was however significantly
shorter — emphasising the extent to which they were being carefully
exhibited rather than encouraged to put forward their ideas. The
situation was similar in 1911 when there was a second deputation. A
Blundells' pit brow woman who attended then has recalled how the
two-hour interview with the Secretary of State was dominated by the
men who did almost all the talking. In 1887 one woman did briefly

outline her preference for the work and the lack of danger whilst Elizabeth Halliwell, the only other woman reported as contributing, interrupted Matthews and, much to the amusement of the press, regaled him with a tale of her brief and unhappy time as a domestic servant.[52]

Matthews appears to have been impressed by the visit and explained that he was now convinced of the right of the Lancashire people to determine their own fate. At the miners' deputation he had commented on the work as hard and unwomanly but here he concentrated on the sense and decency of the 'rather Bulgarian dress' and stressed that the evidence did not support the arguments that the work was detrimental to morals or health. He hoped that no more would be heard of 'an attempt to interfere with an honest and praiseworthy industry'. He suggested that he had wanted to oppose intervention since the first drafting of the bill and was now convinced that this was the right course of action.[53] No doubt he was influenced by the fact that the pit women's defence was being uttered by some of the loyal Conservative party members, men who played a key part in furthering the party's fortunes in their localities. The pit brow agitation was anyway set against a background of intense debate over the Home Rule question. With party feeling running high, both Liberals and Tories were anxious to prevent each other stealing a victory by engineering a successful mines bill. Yet the Liberal bills of 1886 had not really tackled the question of female labour despite growing concern within a section of the party. The Conservatives lost no time in pointing out the Liberals' failure to do anything about the women themselves when they were in power.

The question was not, however, fought purely on party lines. An analysis of the thirty MPs who actually spoke on the subject of female exclusion in the Committee debates in June shows that the only really certain criterion for supporting the women was to be a Conservative coalowner representing a colliery district. Loyalty to localities also made a difference and the issue could be used as a local vote-catcher. Not only did Colonel Blundell, Conservative member for Ince and F.S. Powell, Wigan's Tory MP, support the women in and out of Parliament, but Blundell's defeated opponent C.M. Percy, a Liberal and defender of miners' rights, also opposed the 'prattle about the morality of the women'. J.P. Thomasson, former MP for Bolton and a suffrage supporter, spoke at a Liberal ward meeting in April 1886 and expressed disappointment at Burt's views and hoped that a petition could be drawn up to oppose Parliamentary interference with the women's work. The MP for West Glamorgan, Yeo, was a Liberal colliery owner (a partner in Cory, Yeo and Company) but supported the pit lasses. Similarly Colonel N. Wood, a Conservative colliery owner, could oppose the women because he represented a Durham constituency where no female pit workers were employed.[54] If the issue threatened to oppose local interest it could lead to a reversal of opinion — Seton Karr, Conservative MP for St Helens, made a hasty diplomatic move towards supporting the women once he realised that his attack on their work had not been in accordance with the feelings of his constituents! Karr (who supported votes for women) even went so far as to despatch a written representation to the Home Office on behalf of the women.[55]

The polarisation of the pit brow agitation in the mid-1880s was partly brought about by the involvement of the early suffrage movement which couched the pit brow argument in absolute and uncompromising terms. Mitchell's claim that they were 'fighting a battle for the women of England generally' may have sounded like impassioned rhetoric but behind it lay important questions about the rights of adult women, their relationship to their fellow workers and employers and the responsibility of the state towards them as women, as workers and as individuals.[56] The greatest support for the deputation came from women and the existence of a counter-argument to theories which deified the home and the implications of protective legislation, meant that the level of debate and potential strength of the defenders of the work was significantly different from the days of 1842 when legislative control of women's work had initially developed as a lateral extension of concern about children's employment. Over a third of the ninety-nine people known to have accompanied the women at the Home Office were involved in feminist issues of some sort. Suffrage leaders such as Lydia Becker, Mrs Bright Lucas and Mrs Fawcett were present. The latter also escorted the Cradley Heath women chainmakers on their deputation to resist the attempt to fix by law the weight of the hammers they used. Eleanor Whyte, secretary of the women bookbinders was there, Josephine Butler and Isabella M. Tod, Mrs T.H. Wells and Madame Venturi of the Ladies' National Association. Ada Heather Biggs, Caroline Ashurst Biggs, Clementina Black and Helen Blackburn were also present. Through the *Englishwoman's Review* and the *Women's Suffrage Journal* they had already propagated the pit women's right to work.[57] The Central Committee for Women's Suffrage had also sent a memorial to the Home Secretary claiming that it was 'unjust for a Parliament, in the election of which women have no votes to interfere with the right of women to work'.[58]

Not surprisingly opponents objected to the intervention of 'fine fingured ladies'.[59] It was not difficult to prove that they knew little about the actual conditions of employment. It has been argued that the women's movement was born 'not in the factory or mine but in the Victorian drawing room' and this was to a certain extent true.[60] Munby was saddened by the 'cold and cruel crowd of doctrinaires' he encountered at Aubrey House and other fashionable London meeting places for women.[61] In his poem 'Women's Rights' he claimed that they ignored the real heroines, working women:

> We seek the middle classes' good
> Their overflowing womanhood
> Exactly suits our plan:
> Which is to prove the latent might
> Of women, and assert their right
> To work abreast of man.[62]

His judgement was harsh though it was none the less accurate to say that in the early years the movement was largely dominated by middle-class women. This does not, however, mean that they were not interested in the lives of working-class women. Championing the less fortunate was one of the few permissible forms of 'work' open to middle-class women. The problem was not so much their degree of concern but their inevitable lack of familiarity with the everyday lives and problems of working women. A letter from a pit brow man asked:

> What does the Countess of Lathom, Miss Faithfull, Mrs. Bright Lucas or Miss Lucas know about these women? I will venture to say not one of them has ever seen a real live pit brow girl in her working dress much less can they know anything of their work and its effect on them in many ways.[63]

It was also easy to spot condescension. Recalling the events of 1887 in the *Woman's Signal*, the editor Mrs Fenwick Miller explained that she had purchased a photograph of a pit woman at the deputation and kept it in her study 'to remind me of the duty of educated women in defending the right to labour of the poor women'.[64] Unlike the later radical suffragists, the early feminists had nothing to lose by opposing trades unionists. The mid-1880s therefore witnessed constant tension between the women and the unions. The former did however make some attempt to familiarise themselves with the nature of the work. Lydia Becker (for whom Munby did have some respect) was Secretary of the Manchester National Society for Women's Suffrage and visited a Pemberton pit in 1886. She also addressed a Whitehaven meeting of screen girls where she argued that they should be free to follow the occupation of their choice.[65] But the distance of most suffragists from the pit was more than a geographical one. This was only too evident from their romanticised accounts of the work. Mrs Fawcett spoke about the pit women at a Colchester suffrage demonstration in 1886.[66] She explained that she had been told by those who had watched the women at work that it was quite picturesque to see their rosy faces shining through the coal dust. The novelty value persisted. In 1911 a poster announcing a meeting to oppose the abolition threat and demand the franchise announced that twenty pit brow women in their working dress would be on the platform.[67] A further meeting was arranged with fifty women exhibited 'in their homely garb'.[68] Mrs Fawcett wrote to the Secretary of the London Society for Women's Suffrage and asked her if she could get any of the pit brow women for an 'At Home' and explained how the request for the loan of the pit girls might be arranged.[69]

Though some of the later radical suffragists were working women who, as Liddington and Norris have shown, began to campaign within the Lancashire mill towns for better conditions, the early suffrage movement was operating outside such an experience.[70] The women failed to appreciate fully the implications of restrictions on work as they were themselves so far removed from the pit. They doggedly opposed any regulation whatsoever of either factory or mining work for women. Their uncompromising attitude had already been revealed in their reaction to the Factory and Workshops bill — in 1878 the *Women's Suffrage Journal* had complained bitterly about any restriction on adult female employment.[71] But there were dangers in seeing all women bound together by a common oppression. Oppression certainly did exist but working-class women were doubly oppressed and by only recognising sex as the basis of all problems, and ignoring class, it was easy to assume that all the female sex faced the same difficulties.[72] In their desire to oppose a restriction of hours worked by women they ignored some of the practical problems facing working wives or daughters helping to look after large families. Unlike many of their middle-class counterparts the pit women had to look after homes themselves. Extolling the right to work at all costs these suffragists differed from the radical suffragists of ten years later who were able to advocate political reform but nevertheless also recognised the need for reform within work and for a reduction in the ways in which women could be exploited. The way in which the *Women's Suffrage Journal* deplored the proposal to prohibit the moving of wagons betrayed a lack of appreciation of the physical strength required for such work. The journal instead concentrated its argument upon the wider implications inherent in such a move:

> though the practical hardship of the new restriction may be small, or even nil, the evil principle of legislative interference with the liberty of the adult woman will have received fresh legislative sanction, and an evil principle may be trusted sooner or later to bring forth evil fruits.[73]

The demand for the vote had been carefully orchestrated since the formal organisation of suffrage societies in the 1860s. The pit women exemplified the need to stop legislation being controlled by and for men.[74] And the timing was particularly important. Coming in the wake of the third Reform Act which had made it possible for an illiterate male agricultural labourer to vote but not one single woman, the suffragists intensified their campaign. Suffrage bills were introduced at regular intervals between 1884 and 1887 but apart from the carrying of the second reading of one bill in 1885, no favourable majority was gained before 1897. Political organisations of women also upheld the pit brow cause in a number of areas. The Bradford Women's Electoral Association, the Southport Women's Liberal Association and the Hyde Women's Liberal Association all pledged support.[75]

Meanwhile the TUC was slow to recognise the rights of women to work. In 1877 their annual conference had passed a resolution favouring the prohibition of women from work in the chain and nail trades and so encountered opposition from the Women's Protective and Provident League. The nut and bolt makers appealed to congress seven years later to 'stamp out the iniquitous system of female labour'. Whilst discussing the work of young girls in the iron trade, their representative Juggins stressed that they should be 'good wives and daughters, and useful in the sphere for which by nature they were intended'. When Mrs Ellis (Huddersfield and District Power-Loom Weavers) and Miss Wilkinson (Upholstresses Trades Society) tried to reason, Threlfall (Southport and District Trades Council) intervened, hoping that the ladies 'with their fine sense of modesty and their delicacy would let the matter drop'.[76] The scant support provided for the few women delegates significantly came from those industries which could not be directly threatened by female competition. For example, a Cleveland delegate representing the Blastfurnacemen's Association, emphasised that men had no right to drive women out of work. The *Women's Suffrage Journal* feared that unions, already jealous of women's labour in the best-paid branches of manufacturing industries would extend their demands until every trade and occupation which working men considered suitable for themselves would be prohibited to women and the industrial rights of females 'absolutely confiscated'.[77] Agnes Sunley of Leeds (who became the organising agent for the Women's Franchise League) suspected the hidden motives behind the move for female exclusion.

> The intention may be good, but when restrictions on women's labour are so often urged by representatives of trades unions, one cannot but see the cloven hoof peeping from beneath the paternal habilments.[78]

The miners themselves were subjected to accusations of economic self-interest (see Chapter 6). In her Whitehaven speech Lydia Becker had traced the origin of the pit brow agitation to the desire of the trades unions to drive women out of employment.[79] She mentioned other cases — the opposition of Kidderminster men to women weaving carpets and the letter press printers' successful agitation against women.[80]

It was felt that the fate of the pit brow women might affect the aspirations of other women. Though poorly paid they were at least an established part of the labour force and in that respect were in a position which many women coveted. Not only were there serious implications for other outdoor work but any decision to restrict their employment would be retrospective at a time when the female sex should be invading the avenues of employment rather than retreating from them. The *Englishwoman's Review* objected to the 'ill-considered benevolence' which aimed at depriving competent women of their earnings and independence and 'by lessening the openings for the employment of women, chokes to overflowing and starves down those which remain untouched'.[81] The pit women were a particularly impressive example of the potential of female labour. Unlike sempstresses and factory girls cooped up in stuffy atmospheres for long hours, it could be argued that their work was healthy and exhilarating. In contrast to many critics the *Englishwoman's Domestic Magazine* went so far as to describe them as living hammers to knock down all your theories respecting woman's feebleness, all your prejudices against woman's independence, all your jealous fears that freedom for woman may mean what it often does for man — an impunity for sin.[82]

The concern of women's magazines and societies was hardly surprising given the personnel organising the pit brow defence. A network of associations ensured that the two would work together. Mrs McLaren was on the Central Committee of the National Society for Women's Suffrage. At the local level the British Women's Temperance Association provided considerable support. Founded in 1876 the President was Mrs Bright Lucas, the youngest sister of John Bright and a relative of Walter McLaren. A number of branches were established in Lancashire — one founded in Pemberton in 1881 had eighty-eight members within a year. By mid-1884 there were fifty Lancashire branches.[83] Any woman who signed the pledge could join. At first sight it seems incongruous that a society whose aims included 'by every legitimate means to seek the restriction and removal of the causes which lead to intemperance' should endorse the continuation of the women's work. After all critics only too frequently pointed out that the wages earned by the women provided 'pin money' for miners to indulge themselves in local pubs and it was often suggested that the women's absence from home encouraged husbands to seek solace in this way. The BWTA however admitted that it was preferable for women not to do this work but did also recognise that many of the men who went to the pubs would go anyway, regardless of whether or not the wife worked. It also argued that women should take the pledge in order to set an example and restraining influence and thus hopefully convert them. Anyway, it was accepted that most of the pit women were not married and sought to inculcate sober habits on youth. It attracted a hard core of 'do gooders' and Mrs Park was President of the Wigan branch. She and Mrs Lucas were presented at a crowded meeting held in 1886 to revive the branch. Here one speaker referred to the pit brow women as noble women 'doing their duty in the sphere of life in which God had placed them'. The branch included a number of pit women and/or miners' wives.[84]

Within Parliament another member of the Bright family, Jacob Bright, supported the pit women. Like a number of fellow members (for example Bradlaugh and Conybeare) he was an advocate of women's suffrage and viewed the pit issue in the context of the advancement of women's rights. One Conservative MP, Hardcastle who represented the female-employing district of Westhoughton, Lancashire, was so impressed by the *Women's Suffrage Journal*'s arguments about coalmining that he decided to strike a bargain — if the editor was prepared to use her powerful organisation to prevent 'this piece of selfish cruel legislation', he would readily support and promote the suffrage cause in return.[85] The two issues were not, however, necessarily linked. There were MPs such as Abraham, Ellis, Burt and Wallace who were at times prepared to support the principle of women's suffrage but for whom, in this instance, the interests of coalmining far outweighed any belief in women's rights.[86] In 1875 William Pickard had moved the first resolution at a Wigan women's suffrage meeting yet when, several months later, a meeting was held to establish a branch of the National Union of Working Women, he was 'unavoidably absent'![87]

In 1911 when the suffragette campaign was at its height a further attempt to remove the pit women again brought the issues together. A meeting held at the Albert Hall, Manchester, had a dual purpose — to protest against the renewed threat to remove them and to urge the need for the franchise for working women.[88] Speakers included Miss King-May (on the Committee of the National Industrial and Protective Suffrage Society) and Eva Gore-Booth (on the executive of the North of England Society for Women's Suffrage and Co-Secretary of Manchester and Salford Women's Trade Council). They had tried working at the pit brow at Easter. Miss King-May considered it 'almost an ideal occupation' and Eva Gore-Booth boasted that she had managed 'tub shoving' with one hand! She, McLaren and the Mayor and Mayoress of Wigan also attended a London meeting with pit brow women.[89] Both the necessity of their work and the need for gaining the vote were reiterated. On the same day that the deputation of pit women visited the House of Commons, Mrs Pankhurst was forcibly ejected (see Epilogue).

The pit brow campaign of the mid-1880s was also espoused by the supporters of individual liberty for both male and female adults. Here was a case where women should be allowed to judge the situation for themselves. When Roebuck had expressed such ideas in 1843 his arguments had been described as 'long and laboured' and were rapidly dismissed.[90] During the Commons debates of June 1887 a similar claim was challenged but nevertheless found some support. Bradlaugh contended that if legislation could be passed against grown women, it might also be extended to grown men. An all-male Parliament had no right to destroy the self-reliance of the women:

You may take care to sweep away all the unfair and artificial restrictions which prevent them from getting a fair wage for their labour but, short of that it is neither your duty nor your right to constitute yourselves the guardians of how they are to do their work.[91]

Wigan's MP, Powell, claimed perfect freedom for the women to gain their livelihood, though such arguments were combatted by those who questioned where a line might be drawn — women might even become engineers and enlist in the army if control were not exercised![92]

A recognition of the need to 'defend the right of women to labour as they please and when they please' prompted the intervention of groups determined to uphold the individual's right to work.[93] The struggle for saving the pit women is to some extent a comment on the involvement and ramifications of pressure groups concerned about liberty from state interference and propagating social feminism. The deputation proved to be an effective way of fusing not only local and national concern but also, through the personnel common to several societies, a greater cohesion was provided. The possibility of alliance between apparently disparate groups for a common concern at this period has been demonstrated by Brian Harrison. He has examined the concerns of fourteen moral reform societies which were in existence in 1884.[94] A number of members belonged to several societies — Mrs Bright Lucas was a member of six of the fourteen and Jacob Bright of three. These societies could be loosely grouped into six major areas of involvement — Sunday observance, personal liberty, sexual purity, women's rights, animal cruelty and temperance. And although the links between them should not be too tightly drawn, they did indicate certain general traits which included concern (direct or otherwise) about poverty and a fear of the cruder type of popular recreation which they saw as an attack on moral progress. Raising the status of women was a further common interest and all but one of the moral reform societies had direct feminist links. At the same time, upholding the liberty of the individual was also a crucial consideration into which the pit brow issue neatly fitted. Identity was established with this group of poor, adult, female workers in an industry which was already highly regulated, where comparisons with slavery (the anti-slavery campaign had been the model for these organisations) were abundant, but whose overall recruitment was still increasing. Several of these pressure groups — the British Women's Temperance Association, the National Society for Women's Suffrage and the National Vigilance Association —

actively supported the pit brow women as did a number of individuals involved in various aspects of social purity.

The National Association for the Defence of Personal Rights recognised the value of using the pit brow issue to demonstrate its beliefs. In the face of increasing collectivism it defiantly asserted the adult individual's right of choice encouraged by Mitchell's claim that 'Our cry is absolute freedom for women to earn a living within the limits of propriety.'[95] Its origins lay in the 1871 'Vigilance Association for the Defence of Personal Rights and for the Amendment of the Law wherein it is Injurious to Women.' In 1881 it dropped the second part of its title and from 1886 became formally known as the National Association for the Defence of Personal Rights though was generally referred to as the Personal Rights Association. Its policy of anti-statism had already resulted in it voicing opposition to the Contagious Diseases Acts, echoing Josephine Butler's demand for women to be considered as complete human beings. It opposed early closing and compulsory vaccination seeking '. . .perfect equality of all persons before the law in the exercise and enjoyment of their individual freedom and personal rights'.[96] It examined daily all Parliamentary notice papers in order to anticipate threats to personal liberty and propagated its views through the *Personal Rights Journal* which, like the suffragist papers, challenged the idea of prohibiting even the moving of wagons at the pit head by women.[97] The secretary in 1887 was Frederic Charles Banks who had been secretary of the National Society for the repeal of the C-D Acts. He claimed that the women's deputation was the inspiration of his society and wrote to the *Wigan Observer* to stress this.[98] The Association had helped organise affairs in London — McLaren was an active member and was elected to the new executive committee formed soon after the deputation. Before going to the Home Office the pit women had first assembled at the Westminster Palace Hotel at the invitation of the Association and at least thirteen of those known to have accompanied them to the Home Office had been active in the Vigilance Association and/or Personal Rights Association. The pit women were discussed at the society's annual general meeting in May 1887 chaired by the Liberal lawyer Charles Hopwood QC, a Parliamentary spokesman for personal rights and a suffrage supporter. Munby also attended as did three Blundells' girls who had been brought to London especially for the occasion.[99] They too were treated to a tour of the sights.

Similar in name but separate in organisation was the National Vigilance Association. This had been founded in 1885 to oppose the sale of indecent literature and to protect young girls from corruption at a time when the prevalence of child prostitution was being painfully spelt out by the revelations of the 'Maiden Tribute of Modern Babylon' in the *Pall Mall Gazette* and the subsequent trial of its editor W.T. Stead. The society's secretary William Coote organised the pit women's London accommodation, arranging for them to stay and be entertained without cost at the Girls' Club and Home in Greek Street run by the society's President Maud Stanley.[100] The Girls' Friendly Society also pledged its support and the Countess of Lathom who was President of the Liverpool branch spoke publicly in favour of the women.[101] The threat to women in the nail trade had already produced some response from the Society for Promoting the Employment of Women and it now petitioned Parliament in defence of female pit brow work.[102] Its President was the Earl of Fortescue (who attended the deputation) and one of its three Vice-Presidents was the Earl of Wemyss (who became Lord Elcho) who also presided over the Liberty and Property Defence League. This body had been formed in 1882, upheld the ideas of Herbert Spencer and has been described as the first 'thoroughly dogmatic pressure group for extreme *laissez-faire*'.[103] A prosperous organisation, it reacted against interventionist policies and sought the federation of groups constituted for the defence of personal rights.[104] One connection with mining existed in the charter membership of the Iron Trades Employers' Association. Also the Wemyss family had extensive interests in the coal trade. The President had taken part in the 1872 debate on colliery legislation and in the controversy resulting from the 1880 Employers' Liability Act the society had staunchly opposed Burt's bill which was designed to prevent employers contracting out of the legislation.[105] It even went so far as to get the signatures of over a thousand working miners from Burt's own constituency of Morpeth and mobilised action successfully enough to ensure the defeat of the bill in the Commons. Munby had visited the society's Parliamentary committee at their request and had discussed the pit brow question at some length with the President and several members.[106] The society resolved to support action taken by the women. Its attitudes were summed up by one of its members, Constance Plumptre.[107] She was also a member of the Society for the Employment of Women, the Individualist Club and a keen Spencerian rationalist. In an essay on 'The Reasonableness of Personal Direction in Personal Matters' she stressed that individualism must always remain a safer teacher than legislative rule. She emphasised that what was at stake was not whether one worked or did not work in mining but the difference betwèen 'starving on the one side or working in the mines'. This, she argued, was surely for the women to decide rather than the state.

Yet there is little evidence to suggest that the pit women were ever really encouraged to speak for themselves. Although the significance and unprecedented nature of their deputation should not be minimised, in many ways it was no more than an elaborate charade, a gathering of a host of well-known names and causes and a convenient platform for interests such as suffrage, social purity and individualism to further their claims. This is underlined by the newspaper reactions. Several interviews with the women were relayed with sardonic humour and comments on their ingenuous country manner. Speculation on the origins of such a visit produced fairy tale explanations. At the first hint of a deputation the *Birmingham Daily Post* claimed that a wealthy widow of an MP was financing the venture.[108] A former pit girl herself, 'her heart still warms to the linsey-wolsey trousers and the high hob-nailed boots'. Her courage had saved the life of an important visitor who had been pitched into the yawning abyss of the pit. After rescuing him she nursed him back to health. He had then taught her to read and before long they had married! Such a fantastic mixture of truth and fiction characterised the whole debate and can easily camouflage the attitudes and degree of voluntary involvement of the pit brow women themselves.

An examination of the arrangements for the London visit reveals that it was not quite the spontaneous response that was claimed. Such an undertaking required careful management and available cash. The influence of the organisers was such that the railway company even laid on a special carriage so that the party did not need to change at Crewe! Mrs Park explained that the women were chosen by ballot at the colliery though critics suspected that healthy appearances dictated their selection.[109] The *Labour Tribune* called it 'a bogus deputation for the purpose of throwing dust in the eyes of the public'.[110] The procedure adopted for the second London visit in 1911 shows the lack of any real freedom of choice. Former pit women have recalled how this deputation was organised. At Aspull young Ellen Bentham was 'picked out from all th'area around' for her rosy cheeks and general good looks.[111] It was the same story at Pemberton. One of the four Blundells' women selected explained that the management chose them and Colonel Blundell paid.[112]

The women on the 1887 deputation were all (with two exceptions) aged between sixteen and twenty-six. The financing of the trip was provided by the owners and individuals (including Munby).[113] Mrs Park mentioned that repayment was being organised in the form of weekly instalments by the women.[114] Certainly the novelty and excitement of a holiday from work and the sort of treats which were laid on in London were strong inducements to encourage those selected to defend their work. Although they were opposed to a threat to their livelihood, it would be misleading to see the deputation as a reliable indicator of their feelings. The successful mass-lobbying cannot prove the strength of their belief in either their right to work or the virtues of that work (two questions which were frequently and conveniently conflated). Instead, the deputation demonstrates one of the ways in which late-nineteenth-century pressure groups operated and reveals how the pit women might be used to further interests which appeared to have little direct relevance to coalmining. In order to gauge the complexities of the pit brow debate it is necessary to examine the arguments articulated for and against their work in and beyond Parliament and the press. Only by considering the validity of these arguments in the light of the women's experiences can we begin to see the ways in which conditions of work might have helped shape the pit brow women's responses to their employment.

Notes

1. *Wigan Observer*, 3, 9 December 1859.
2. Munby MS, Diary 34, 17 April 1866.
3. This committee had been set up after a request for an enquiry into the Inspectorate from the Leeds conference of miners in 1863. The fifteen-strong committee (all male, as were all the witnesses) began its hearings in June 1865 with A.J. Ayrton in the chair. Their number was increased to seventeen and Charles Neate became chairman in 1866. Witnesses were interviewed in 1866 and 1867. On 14 June 1866 Munby was told that the Committee did not intend to interfere with female labour yet the questioning on this subject had not been completed and continued until 6 July! The formal decision was contained in a statement issued in 1867 which declared that 'compulsory legislation on this subject would be vexatious and in some respects unjust and would therefore be inexpedient'. PP 1867, XIII; PP IV, XXIX. See also Marx, *Capital,* 1 (London, 1976 edition), pp.535, 538-9. For further details of the arguments used by the witnesses see Ch.6.
4. Munby MS, Diary 34, 17 April 1866.
5. Broadhurst's attempt to stop girls under fourteen working at nail-making had received a setback when, in the course of the debate, Sir Charles Dilke had revealed that the proposed measure would in fact affect only nine girls. In 1886 Broadhurst was Under-secretary of State. The Agricultural Gangs Act of 1867 had stated that no females should be employed in the same gang as males and they could not work under a male gangmaster unless a female licensed to act as such was present.

6. *The Times*, 16 May 1883. Ellis Lever (1833-1911) was the youngest son of a miner-farmer from Kearsley, Lancashire. After selling wire ropes to collieries and manufacturing brattice cloth, he became a wealthy supplier of coal and coke for gas works, developing outlets throughout Britain and overseas. During the cotton famine he helped organise relief committees and sewing schools for women. *Manchester Evening News*, 2 May 1911.

7. *The Times*, 14 September 1885. There were twelve other proposals which included the lighting of mines, shot-firing arrangements and the creation of a post of Minister of Mines.

8. *The Times*, 20 October 1885.

9. For example, both the *Manchester Examiner* and *Manchester Guardian* provided a series of articles on the colliery districts in 1886. The *Lancet* set up its own commission of enquiry and local, national, specialist and daily newspapers sent reporters to visit coal mines and the meetings held in defence of the women.

10. *Wigan Observer*, 30 January, 17 April 1886.

11. Ibid., 10 April 1886.

12. *Wigan Examiner*, 27 January 1886.

13. Hansard CCII, House of Commons, 3 March 1886, pp.1856-7. Wilson also raised the subject of the excessive hours worked by Whitehaven screen lasses. Ibid., 3 June 1886, pp.826-7; 7 June 1886, p.1124.

14. A similar bill was introduced by the Conservatives later in the year (bill 15) but was withdrawn at the beginning of September.

15. *Wigan Observer*, 23 April 1886.

16. Canon Harry Mitchell (1847-1933), a graduate of Emmanuel College, Cambridge, had been ordained in 1872. After several years in Derbyshire parishes where he established a reputation for local improvement and began a branch of the Church of England Temperance Society, he moved to Pemberton near Wigan in 1881. Here he carried out extensive alterations to the church fabric. After transferring to Prescot he was made Rural Dean, an honorary canon of Liverpool and in 1919 became a Canon Emeritus. Scrapbook of Vicars of St John the Divine, Pemberton. *Wigan Almanack*, 3 December 1886, 30 January 1887; *Wigan Observer*, 4, 15 December 1886; *Liverpool Post and Mercury*, 5 January 1933; *Liverpool Evening Express*, 5 January 1933; *Liverpool Review*, February 1933, p.73.

17. *Wigan Observer*, 26 May, 19 October 1887.

18. Scrapbook of Vicars; *Wigan Observer*, 24 October 1885, 29 November 1882. 352 girls and infants attended Sunday school at St Johns church. *Manchester Guardian*, 12 May 1886.

19. *Wigan Observer*, 27 March 1886; *St. Helens Newspaper*, 24 March 1886.

20. Mrs Margaret Park (née Richmond) (1835-93) was the second wife of Henry Park, the only Mayor of Wigan to have held his office for five consecutive years. She claimed to have had ten years' personal acquaintance with pit women. She spoke on this subject to the Council of the Liverpool Ladies' Union of workers among women and girls at a conference on women workers in 1891. Manchester Library Archives in 30/S 6/3; *Wigan Observer*, 14 April, 27 October 1886, 23 December 1893. I am grateful to Cyril Park for information about his grandmother. The White Cross Army had been formed by Ellice Hopkins in 1883 after an appeal to the miners of the north-east to help the cause of social purity. See E. Bristow, *Vice and Vigilance* (Dublin, 1977), Ch.5.

21. For example, see *Wigan Observer*, 20 May 1887.

22. Ibid., 27 March 1886.

23. *St. Helens Newspaper*, 8 May 1886.

24. *Wigan Observer*, 17 April 1886.

25. Ibid., 23 April 1886; *St. Helens Newspaper*, 6, 17, 24 April 1886.

26. *Wigan Observer*, 7 May 1886. According to Mitchell there was also some organisation of the Staffordshire pit bank women. Ibid., 17 May 1886.
27. Ibid., 17 April 1886.
28. Henry Matthews QC (later Viscount Llandaff) was the first Conservative member for Birmingham East. His influence with Lord Randolph Churchill led to his appointment as Home Secretary in his first year as an MP. *Pall Mall Gazette Extra*, 29 July 1886, p.23.
29. See G. Stedman Jones, *Outcast London* (London, 1976), especially Introduction and Ch.15.
30. See E.P. Hennock, 'Poverty and Social Theory in England: the Experience of the 1880s', *Social History*, 1 January (1976), which argues that the 1880s represented not so much a watershed in the viewing of social problems as a systematising of past attitudes.
31. R. Strachey, *The Cause* (London, 1978), p.226.
32. The Belgian coalfield formed a strip round Liège, spreading over to Namur, Charleroi and Mons, crossing part of the province of Liège and the whole of the Namur and Hainaut provinces. Although women worked in Namur and Liège, numbers had declined as alternative opportunities developed and most were employed in the Hainaut area. In 1883 there were nearly 7,000 women working underground. Increasingly adverse publicity led to a prohibition of boys under twelve and girls under fourteen in 1884.
33. *Wigan Observer*, 17 April 1869; *Lancet*, 10 April 1886.
34. Notes of intention quoted by Tancock in E. Zola, *Germinal* (London, 1973 edition), Introduction. The employment of women in French pits was forbidden in 1874.
35. Hansard CCCXVI, House of Commons, 23 June 1887, p.789.
36. See for example C. Lemmonier, *Constantin Meunier* (Paris, 1904), pp.8, 36, 49, 65, 70, 76, 86, for Douard; idem, *Le Borinage* (Brussels, 1902), p.13 for Rassenfosse; idem, *L'Ecole Belge de Peinture 1830-1903* (Brussels, 1906), p.12.
37. The Belgian Industrial Labour Commission *(Commission du Travail)* was set up in 1886 and examined the condition of the working population, demonstrating the particularly gruesome conditions and low wages. *Revue Industrielle de Charleroi* (1886), *Chambre de Commerce de Verviers*, 24 November 1888. B.S. Chlepner, *Cent Ans d'Histoire Sociale en Belgique* (Brussels, 1956), pp.215-6. See T.S. Ashton, 'Haydock and Bolton Miners Trades Union Minutes' (1889-90), p.12 for Belgian miners' opposition to women's pit work.
38. R. Challinor, *The Lancashire and Cheshire Miners* (Newcastle, 1972), Chs. 4 and 5; R. Page Arnot, *The Miners* (London, 1949), p.45. Its full title was the National Association of Coal, Lime and Ironstone Miners of Great Britain.
39. The Lancashire based AAM had been founded in 1865 with Thomas Halliday as President. Although opposed to women working (for example, an attack was made on their employment at pit heads at the Manchester conference of September 1871), it does not appear to have placed as much emphasis on this as its rival the NMU. The AAM chose rather to concentrate on centralised control and systematic support for local strikes.
40. Munby MS, Diary 21, 20 August 1863.
41. *Wigan Observer*, 14 January, 3 June, 25 November 1865.
42. *Wigan Observer*, 4 August 1883; T. Burt, *Pitman and Privy Councillor. An Autobiography* (London, 1923), p.50. 'The Cry of the Children' had been published in 1843 in *Blackwood's Magazine* and, like parts of Disraeli's *Sybil* (1845), it was based on the Midland Mining Commission. Elizabeth Barrett Browning corresponded with one of the sub-commissioners, Horne.
43. *Wigan Observer*, 10 April 1886; Hansard CCCXVI, House of Commons,

23 June 1887, p.815.

44. *Wigan Observer*, 19 May 1886, 9 March 1887; *Women's Suffrage Journal*, XVII, no.207 (1 March 1887). A number of MPs (including George Howell, Bradlaugh, Atherley Jones, Conybeare, Paulton and Henry Richard) accompanied the deputation.

45. *Personal Rights Journal*, no.71 (1 June 1887). Atherley Jones was the son of the Chartist Ernest Jones. He represented North West Durham and appeared as counsel at numerous inquests on accidents in mines. L.A. Atherley Jones, *Looking Back. Reminiscences of a Political Career* (London, 1923).

46. He also wrote to the *Pall Mall Gazette* and to the Manchester newspapers. *Manchester Guardian*, 14 May 1887; *Wigan Observer*, 11 May 1887. Walter Stow Bright MacLaren was a nephew of John Bright and a textile manufacturer. He and his wife Eva were active supporters of women's suffrage. He was Secretary of the Parliamentary Committee of the Manchester Society for Women's Suffrage and was on the executive committee of the Personal Rights Association.

47. Hansard CCCXIV, House of Commons, 9 May 1887, p.1268; CCCXV, 16 May 1887, p.226. Petitions were presented on behalf of the women – one was signed by 1,000 women resident in Wigan – *Wigan Observer*, 14 May 1887.

48. *Wigan Observer*, 12 February 1887.

49. *Women's Suffrage Journal*, XVIII, no.210 (1 June 1887); *Manchester Guardian*, 14 May 1887.

50. Munby's name was not included in the press reports (excepting the account in the *Personal Rights Journal*). He may have exaggerated his contribution (and convinced himself that he was providing invaluable help). Matthews was in fact an old acquaintance and Munby treated Mitchell to dinner several times. Munby MS, Diary 54, 14, 20 May 1886; Diary 55, 10, 16 May 1887, 28 January, 26 May 1887.

51. See A.V. John, 'Women Workers in British Coal Mining 1840-90, with special reference to West Lancashire', unpublished PhD thesis, University of Manchester, 1976, Ch.8, Section A, Appendices for lists of the pit women and the names and interests of those who accompanied them.

52. The press reported that the women voiced approval of the proceedings. *Wigan Observer*, 20 May 1887; *Mining Journal*, CVII, no.2700 (21 May 1887); *JUS*, no.21 (25 May 1887).

53. His support was remembered. In February 1892 Mrs E.C.W. Elmy (Elizabeth Wollstenholme) writing about Matthews' intervention in the Shop Hours' bill commented that 'he had not forgotten the Lancashire pit brow women'. Correspondence of Mrs Elmy, Secretary of Women's Franchise League 1, 22 February 1892, p.252. Add. MS 47, 449 British Library.

54. *Wigan Observer*, 17 March, 10, 26 April 1886.

55. *St. Helens Newspaper*, 6, 13, 27 March 1886; *Women's Suffrage Journal*, XVII, no.197 (1 May 1886).

56. *Wigan Observer*, 10 April 1886. See how this theme was later taken up by Parliamentary defenders. Hansard, CCCII, House of Commons, 3 March 1886, pp.1856-67.

57. For example, *Englishwoman's Review*, no. CLIV (15 February 1886). I am grateful to the feminist history group of the Women's Research and Resources Centre, especially Linda Walker, Anna Davin, Jean L'Esperance and Leonore Davidoff for discussion of this subject.

58. Founded in 1872, the Central Committee helped to co-ordinate the efforts of the National Society. This society had brought together the Manchester, Edinburgh, Bristol and Birmingham societies. A split in 1871 over Josephine Butler's campaign had resulted in the London National Society remaining aloof from the rest. The National Society's aim was to obtain the Parliamentary

franchise for women on the same grounds as men by acting as an information centre, producing literature and holding public meetings. *Women's Suffrage Journal*, XVIII, no.215 (1 November 1887).

59. For example, see *Labour Tribune*, 21 May 1887.

60. V. Klein, 'The Emancipation of Women. Its motives and achievements' in H. Grisewood (ed.), *Ideas and Beliefs of the Victorians* (London, 1969), p.262.

61. Munby MS, Diary 39, 22 March 1879.

62. A.J. Munby, *Verses New and Old* (London, 1865). See also Munby's *Dorothy*. In 1859 Munby wrote that 'those who prate of women's rights, if they knew their own meaning, would honour such mighty daughters of the plough as much at least or more than the strongminded females who have neither the shrinking grace of their own sex nor the bold beauty of ours'. Diary 1, 28 January 1859.

63. *Wigan Observer*, 10 April 1886.

64. *Woman's Signal*, VI, no.132 (9 July 1896).

65. *Wigan Observer*, 10, 23 April 1886. Letter from Lydia Becker to *Manchester Examiner and Times*, BR, F324.3B6 Manchester Archives, Manchester Public Library. Lydia Becker was a friend of the geologist Binney and was convinced that underground exclusion had been justifiable.

66. *Women's Suffrage Journal*, XVII, no.197 (1 May 1886). See also her visit to the Bryant and May matchgirls described in M. Ramelson, *The Petticoat Rebellion. A Century of Struggle for Women's Rights* (London, 1972), pp.106-8.

67. Arncliffe Sennett collection, Add. MS C121, British Library.

68. Ibid.

69. Industrial Suffrage File, Fawcett Collection. City Polytechnic, London. I am grateful to Jill Liddington for this reference.

70. J. Liddington and J. Norris, *One Hand Tied Behind Us* (London, 1978).

71. *Women's Suffrage Journal*, IX, no.92, 1 March 1878.

72. See B.A. Carroll (ed.), *Liberating Women's History* (Urbana, 1976), especially Gordon, Buhle and Dye, p.86 and J. Mitchell 'Four Structures in a Complex Unity'.

73. *Women's Suffrage Journal*, XVIII, no.209 (1 May 1887), no.211 (1 July 1887).

74. See *Wigan Observer*, 7 October 1911.

75. *Englishwoman's Review*, no. CLXIX (13 June 1887), CLIV (15 February 1886). *Women's Suffrage Journal*, XVII, no.197 (1 May 1886). In 1898 the annual council meeting of the Women's Liberal Federation carried a resolution against the closing of pit work to women. *Dictionary of Employment Open to Women*, no.1 (London, 1898), HD 6058, TUC Congress House; Appendix to 14th Report on Public Petitions (1887). Appendix 174, p.88.

76. TUC Yearly Reports (Congress House, London, 1884), pp.40-1.

77. *Women's Suffrage Journal*, XVII, no.197 (1 May 1886).

78. *Leeds Mercury*, 12 May 1887.

79. BR F324, 3B6 Manchester Archives, Manchester Public Library.

80. A letter to the press from J. Fielding, General Secretary of the Operative Spinners' Association objected to female labour in the spinning rooms. At the end of this year the Operative Cotton Spinners Association of Bolton resolved that no member should teach the trade of piecer to a girl. *Manchester Guardian*, 17 December 1886.

81. *Englishwoman's Review*, CLXIX (15 June 1887); the President of the United Sisters' Friendly Society supported this argument in a letter to the *Manchester Guardian*, 13 May 1887.

82. *Englishwoman's Domestic Magazine*, 15, no.159 (15 July 1873). See Ada Heather Biggs's defence of the work in which she compared other occupations for

women, *The Times*, 22 October 1885. See Ch.6 for arguments about health.

83. *Wigan Observer*, 23 September 1882.

84. *Wigan Examiner*, 27 February 1886.

85. *Women's Suffrage Journal*, XVII, no.197 (1 May 1886).

86. *Pall Mall Gazette Extra*, 29 July 1886, p.23; Parliamentary Divisions (1887), pp.699-701.

87. *Wigan Observer*, 13 May 1875. For biographical details of Pickard see Ch. 6.

88. Ibid., 7 October 1911.

89. Industrial Suffrage file, Fawcett Collection.

90. Broadlands MS, SHA/PD/2, Diary 1, 16 May 1843.

91. Hansard CCCXVI, House of Commons, 22 June 1887, pp.793-4. In *Dorothy*, Munby (no doubt bearing in mind his meetings with Neate) had questioned how the Liberals could be pleased with the idea of coercion, asking a woman to do just what men said and no more.

92. Hansard CCCXLI, House of Commons, 23 June 1887, pp.788, 814, 820; *Miner and Workman's Advocate*, 13 June 1863.

93. *Shield*, 20 July 1886.

94. Harrison interpreted moral reform as reform of morals, reform for moral reasons or reform which was deemed educationally valuable because its end product was moral change. B. Harrison, 'State Intervention and Moral Reform in Nineteenth Century England' in P. Hollis (ed.), *Pressure from Without in Early Victorian England* (London, 1974).

95. *Wigan Observer*, 10 April 1886.

96. *Personal Rights Journal*, no.171 (1 June 1887).

97. For example, 'The pit brow women may be, and we believe are, able to pass unscathed through this fire; but, in the interests of women generally, we cannot allow the right of men to make them do so a condition of being allowed to choose their own sphere of labour.' Ibid., no.71 (1 June 1887).

98. *Wigan Observer*, 4, 11 November 1887. This prompted a hasty letter of apology from Mrs Park who had neglected to acknowledge the contribution in an earlier letter.

99. *Personal Rights Journal*, no.71 (1 June 1887). Munby had previously discussed the subject with the society at the beginning of May. Munby MS, Notebook IX, 1887; Diary 55, 5 May 1887. *Wigan Observer*, 5 June 1891.

100. *Wigan Examiner*, 4 November 1891.

101. The Girls' Friendly Society, founded in 1874, was a nationwide organisation devised to bring 'respectable' young girls together and save them from temptation by religious and moral training. It viewed itself as a surrogate family. By 1885 there were 121 branches in England and Wales. B. Harrison, 'For Church, Queen and Family: The Girls Friendly Society 1874-1920), *Past and Present*, no.61 (1975), pp.108-38.

102. *Englishwoman's Review*, CCXVI (15 April 1886).

103. E. Bristow, 'The Liberty and Property Defence League and Individualism', *Historical Journal*, XVIII, no.4 (1975), p.776.

104. Ibid., p.761.

105. E. Bristow, 'The Defense of Liberty and Property in Britain 1880-1914', unpublished PhD thesis, Yale University, 1970, pp.128-30, 140. The League claimed to have opposed 386 bills with 'more or less success' by 1891. It received dedicated support from a hard core of backbenchers.

106. Munby MS, Diary 54, 14, 17 April 1886. He also visited on 3 May 1887.

107. C. Plumptre, *Studies in Little Known Subjects* (London, 1898), pp.306-9.

108. In *Wigan Observer*, 1 May 1887. This 'entertaining yarn' amused local

people who claimed that they were the last to hear about it!

109. Hansard CCCXVI, House of Commons, 20 June 1887, pp.646, 747, 787.
110. *Labour Tribune*, 18 June 1887.
111. Interviewed 24 August 1978.
112. Interviewed 5 June 1974 and 25 August 1978. John Knowles helped to finance this venture (six Pearson and Knowles' girls went to London) and the Mayor of Wigan and his wife visited several pits to find suitable representatives. See Epilogue.
113. Hansard CCCXVI, House of Commons, 23 June 1887, pp.821-2, 787.
114. *Manchester Guardian*, 14 May 1887; *Wigan Observer*, 20 May 1887. Munby gave £1 towards the expenses. Munby MS, Diary 55, 26 May 1887.

6 A PIT BROW PROTEST?

Is honour dead, is justice out of date,
That thus your law-amenders tyrannise?
Shall envious greed attired in angel guise
Of morals, decency and health dictate?
No, from the dark pit's brow where quaintly dressed
But not unsexed and free from taint of ill
There toil the sisters of the whirring loom.
Let the brave lads of Lancashire attest
Though hands are hard, yet hearts are gentle still
And maiden blushes mount where roses bloom.

H.D. Rawnsley in *Wigan Observer*, 3 April 1886

The ramifications of the pit brow debate were extensive. The quintessential features of the arguments levied for and against the work can however be broadly subsumed under three categories of physical, moral and economic criticism. Collectively they provided an indictment of past and present attitudes towards women and work and also posed questions about the role of women in outdoor work for the future.

Criticism on physical grounds concentrated on danger to safety and health. It was also argued that because their physical appearance was unprepossessing it constituted an affront to femininity. Looking firstly at the specific allegations that the work was dangerous, it must be pointed out that critics frequently generalised and failed to indicate specific areas or types of danger. Closer examination reveals that certain jobs were considerably more hazardous than others. A survey of 114 known deaths of pit brow women between 1852 and 1890 reveals that over thirty per cent were the result of shaft accidents. Some of these were particularly gruesome.[1] There were piteous examples of women and girls being precipitated down shafts to an instantaneous death. Frequently women were pushing tubs and went down the shaft with them. One such victim was Mary Cannon of Bilston.[2] She was pushing an empty tub to the mouth of the shaft. It suddenly went faster and pulled her in with it. She was one of a number of Staffordshire bankswomen killed in this year. Brough, the district inspector, denounced such a job as unsuitable for women. He cited the case of Rebecca Vincent who was also from the Bilston area. She had simply put out her hand to get hold of a chain, missed and fell down the shaft.

Twenty-one-year-old Mary Swift was working on a dark night in slippery conditions at Monmore Green, Wolverhampton. She stretched out her arms to hang out a horse net on to a hook, missed and fell down the shaft.

A particularly unfortunate death occurred when Priscilla Vincent, a bankswoman of Stourbridge, fell down a shaft whilst pushing her tub.[3] She got hooked on to it and being pregnant was unable to disentangle herself. Staffordshire and East Scotland appear to have been the most dangerous areas for shaft accidents. Bridget Mechan, who fell down a shaft after her tub, was one such example from Airdrie.[4] There were similar instances elsewhere. The balance pits of South Wales involved very precarious work. The *Morning Chronicle* had explained how the girls would step on to the platform and with one foot on the open side of the pit mouth would be 'suspended over the abyss'.[5] Hannah Rees (17), of the Tredegar Iron and Coal Company, fell from the top to the bottom of the deep pit at which she worked — she used to mount the cage in order to get the loaded tram as the cage platform was placed at an awkward angle. Some sort of mistake, perhaps from the signals or a reduction in power, resulted in her being 'dashed to pieces'.[6]

The tragedy of these deaths was that so frequently they could have been avoided. Their cause was not just carelessness, although human judgement obviously played no small part in anticipating and escaping from danger. Only too often accidents occurred because of the lack of effective safety provisions at collieries. Alexander MacDonald told the 1866 Select Committee on Mines about the death of one girl who fell backwards into the shaft because the flooring on the pit top was loose and moved with her weight on one end of it.[7] A serious accident happened at Coalbrookdale where a man and a woman went to tip a loaded tub and when returning rode on an empty wagon down the incline which led into the pit. Due to a defect in laying out the pit bank road, once the wagon picked up speed there was no time to get off so they were both killed.[8]

Many accidents arose from a simpler cause. The lack of covered shafts meant that only too often workers and even passers-by fell down them. Sarah Eden of Blackbrook colliery, St Helens, was pushing wagons when she had a fit and fell down the shaft.[9] A large number of deaths could have been avoided had provisions been made for landing tubs properly from cages and fencing them off at all other times. The inspectors pointed this out frequently but for a long time nothing was done to enforce it. In 1855 Wynne, inspector for North

Staffordshire, Worcestershire and Shropshire complained that

> The unprotected shafts both in work and out of work in my district,
> and by which nineteen persons of both sexes and of all ages, have
> been hurried into eternity, call loudly for legislative enactments of
> the most stringent character, as nothing short of severe penalties
> strictly enforced will ever bring my district into even a creditable
> state as regards unprotected shafts.[10]

The third general rule of the 1855 Inspection Act did require the
fencing of shafts which were not being worked. Yet surface workers
and the general public found that this was generally ignored. The
adoption of a guard to protect against falls at working pits was an easy
remedy yet inspectors continued to lament the fact that they were not
used even though they were cheap and easy to erect. The inspector for
West Scotland complained that most pits in his district did not have
them.[11] A new device had appeared in 1854. It consisted of a strong, square
frame erected around the pit's mouth with two doors connected by
rods and cranks. They simultaneously opened or shut down over the
pit mouth when a lever was pulled. The weights of the door were
counterbalanced by heavy blocks which were secured to the shafts
which carried the cranks.[12]

Gradually the number of shaft accidents was reduced as owners were
forced to adopt safety measures. In North East Lancashire alone there
were twenty-eight separate fatal shaft accidents (both male and female)
in 1854 but by 1860 this had been reduced to eight. The Inspection
Act of 1860 required that working and pumping shafts should always
be fenced and one of the general rules of the 1872 act stipulated that
'the top and all entrances between the top and bottom of every working
or pumping shaft shall be properly fenced'.[13] This however did not
solve the problem completely as fences could be temporarily removed
for repairs and even where they had been erected, fences and gates were
not always used. In 1880 Jane Winning of Southfield no. 1 pit, Stirling,
toppled down the shaft with her tub and three years later Ellen
McPartland (17), of the Rawyard Coal Company was assisting on the
pit head when she fell down the shaft with an empty tub, the gate
having been left open.[14] One case involved a Lancashire girl whose
apron and skirt had got caught in the shaft. Elizabeth Greenough
normally stood in front of the fencing rail and sheet iron protected her
clothing from the revolving shaft.[15] However, she had been removed
from her normal place of work to a spot where there was no sheet iron

and her skirt had blown in the wind and got caught. Fences were particularly necessary in windy, exposed areas.

It cannot be denied that the job of bankswoman, or indeed any job involving proximity to the shaft, was potentially dangerous especially in the years before 1872. The manner of death was extremely brutal. When fourteen-year-old Bridget McHale of Wolverhampton toppled down the shaft with her tub, she fell seventy yards and was mangled 'in a manner far too shocking for description'.[16]

Another killer was the wagon. It accounted for thirty-four per cent of the 114 cases and Lancashire claimed twenty-six of these. Jane Eastham of Hindley Green was passing between the buffers of some wagons at a time when some others were being lowered.[17] They began running too fast because it was wet and the rails were slippery. They bumped up against the standing wagon near her and she was killed. The colliery manager promised to make arrangements so that girls would not need to cross the line in future. At a nearby pit Maria Greenall was on her way to the brow one lunch-time.[18] She needed to cross the private driving road which was intersected by three lines of rails. After passing over the first set she found her way blocked by some wagons on the middle lines. Not realising that they were being shunted, she carried on. At her inquest it was explained that shunting was avoided as much as possible when the women had their breaks. The engine driver had been unable to see her. A verdict of accidental death was pronounced. Such a case demonstrates how it was quite possible for pit brow women to be involved in fatal accidents without actually working themselves. Unless one moved extremely quickly it was very easy to be trapped by wagons. One seventeen-year-old girl, Elizabeth Prothero, was cleaning the sidings at Ty Trist colliery, Monmouthshire, when the overman told her to move out of the way for some wagons to be shunted. Elizabeth was a fraction too late and she too was quickly crushed to death.[19]

Some accidents occurred to women using wagons though not necessarily moving them. When Margaret Platt (21) had been working for three months at Crompton and Shawcross's Fir Tree House colliery, Wigan, she was busy one day picking out stones on top of a loaded wagon when she was told to get off as it was about to be moved.[20] Not being quite quick enough she was knocked under the wheels. At her inquest the management was censured. It was revealed that the manager had been involved in a similar case at Ince where a boy had died. He had promised that wagons would be entrusted to 'competent persons' in future. Yet once again the result was a verdict of accidental death and the incident was closed. The danger of such work was pointed out in John Monk Foster's story of a pit lass. Kate Leigh twisted her foot on a piece of coal while raking in the wagons.[21] She fell across the road in front of oncoming wagons though, unlike many of her real life counterparts, she was rescued and escaped with a broken leg.

Perhaps the most arduous and dangerous work was that of actually moving wagons which might weigh about six tons. Margaret Knowles (17) was killed at Haydock.[22] She had been about to couple some wagons but, contrary to regulations, she went on to the rails between them as it was easier to perform this awkward task. Her foot caught on a sleeper, she fell and was run over by several wagons. Margaret Barker (17) was a wagon filler at Wigan.[23] She was crushed to death while moving a wagon down an incline. Standing inside it she held on to the brake but got caught inside the buffers. In the same year one of Munby's friends, Sarah Broadhurst of Kirkless Hall colliery, died from injuries from a coal wagon.[24] Not surprisingly, the district inspector Hall was troubled by this cause of death — in this one year there were nine deaths from railway wagons in his district and three of them were women.[25] Juries at inquests were frequently told that girls had been warned against the actions which ultimately caused their deaths though it was of course only too easy to claim this after the event. Mathilda King (16) of Pemberton had been clearing the screens with another girl.[26] She then fetched a wagon under the screen to collect the dirt. Not noticing her, two men pushed others against it and she was crushed. At her inquest it was emphasised that she had not needed to touch the wagon and had been told not to do so. Hannah Anderton of Ince Hall had been greasing wheels when a train of empty wagons appeared.[27] There was a curve in the line and one wagon jerked off and struck the full wagon which crushed her. It was argued at her inquest that it was her fault for having crossed the line. Yet there was no colliery rule on the subject and, anyway, Hannah was only eleven years old.

The young girl who really aroused interest was Ellen Hampson, whose death helped to draw attention to a more general consideration of the ethics of employing young females.[28] On 7 December 1865 Ellen was injured at Moss House colliery, Rainford, Lancashire. She died on 13 February 1866. The eldest of seven children, Ellen was twelve years old (though she had apparently told the overlooker that she was older). She was eager to start work and her mother, who had worked underground herself from the age of ten, had felt that Ellen's work would be comparatively easy. Due to circumstances which were never fully explained, Ellen arrived an hour late for her first day's work. Rather than waiting for her, her overlooker had gone underground to get on with his work. On arrival Ellen was sent to level slack. A young girl told her to fetch an empty wagon. Ellen began moving it over to the screens by herself. On releasing the brake it began moving rather quickly. She attempted to stop it but got trapped between the buffers and another stationary wagon. Within half an hour of her first day of work she had been fatally injured. The overman Rigby was still not even aware that she had arrived at work. When questioned at the inquest about the lack of supervision, he merely replied that 'wench looked after wench'. Ellen's inquest was attended by the inspector, Higson (who later wrote a damning account of the incident) and by William Pickard. It was revealed that four other girls were employed at similar work at this pit, each working a ten-hour day and earning between 1/- and 1/3d daily. A verdict of accidental death was recorded though the coroner and the jury did express regret that such a young girl should have been allowed to move wagons. A letter in the *Manchester Guardian* commented on the case with 'pain but not surprise', portraying Ellen as 'one of the class who are most improperly allowed to be employed on the pit banks in the neighbourhood of Wigan in labour of the hardest description'. It also prompted a question in the Commons. The *Wigan Observer* sounded a warning note:

> It appears probable that the case will cause the whole question of the occupation of women on pit banks which disgraces this district to be brought prominently before the public.[29]

Inspectors continued to deplore the way that qualified managers 'hardly appear to recognize any responsibility for these surface operations and the result is a sad want of system and care'. Hall stressed that 'if the managers will give a little more of their attention to institute a proper system, there need be very few of these accidents'.[30] In 1885 alone there were recorded seven fatal and twelve non-fatal injuries to men and women from moving wagons in his district. It was as a result of the inspectors' insistence that a clause was eventually inserted in the colliery bill of 1887 to prohibit the moving of wagons by any boy, girl or woman.

Although shaft and wagon accidents together accounted for the majority of the 114 cases examined, there were other types of accidents. In some cases machinery failed, scaffolding collapsed or ropes broke — Mary Fell of Kirkless Hall was dragging out a tub from the top of the shaft when a broken rope struck her. At St Helens, Elizabeth Fryer was killed just a few days before her wedding should have taken place — the breaking of a winding rope caused her death.[31] Sometimes underground accidents had unfortunate repercussions on the surface. A firedamp explosion at Oakley colliery, Dunfermline, resulted in Marion Drysdale being struck by timber at the pit's mouth.[32] Four pit head women died and five others were injured at Fordel colliery when the steam boiler burst and they were hit by flying bricks.[33]

It is impossible to compute the exact number of women who were killed in this period, let alone the numbers badly injured. The 1850 Inspection Act, extended in 1855 and made permanent five years later, required that every accident be reported by the manager to the Secretary of State and the district inspector within twenty-four hours. However, the inspectors' reports did not include all the deaths of women and girls in their areas and it would seem from an examination of local newspapers that these overworked men were simply not aware of some of them. Violent pit deaths occurred to females of all ages — from working girls of eleven to women in their sixties, though the majority were aged between sixteen and twenty-five. Forty-eight of the total examined occurred in Lancashire, many of them dying in the 1860s.

Accepting that the figures are incomplete, a few conclusions can nevertheless be drawn from the evidence that the work was physically dangerous. It appears that certain jobs were potentially more hazardous than others — the work done by bankswomen and by those employed in moving wagons was especially prone to dangerous situations. However, others were not free from hazards. Unfenced shafts and the unregulated shunting of wagons could be death traps and might involve any surface worker. Being a pointswoman or oiler required a keen eye for any wagons on the move. However careful the worker, the lack of efficient machinery or explicit instructions and communications between people doing different jobs could result in serious accidents. Conspicuous by its absence was any sort of training or preparation for jobs which in practice required certain skills and experience. Although the pit brow girls and women were not serving an apprenticeship for a trade they were nevertheless expected to be able to perform a number of varied and awkward jobs which involved the acquisition of a certain knack. And in spite of the general verdict of accidental death at inquests it is difficult to avoid the conclusion that a little more concern and money spent by the management might well have saved a number of lives. As it was, the jury's decision neatly exonerated owners from blame and the need to remedy the situation.

These accidents chiefly arose from dangerous work-situations. It was urged that women should not be involved in such hazardous work. But it was not only women who did such work and got maimed and killed. Men frequently fell down shafts and the statistics reveal the possible dangers of surface work for all.[34] Shaft accidents still occurred in districts where no women were employed and, anyway, females only accounted for a small proportion of the surface workforce. Nevertheless, reports of deaths of females carried more sensational value and were better publicised, so encouraging the idea that women should not be involved in such work.

Some arguments inferred that women in fact *made* some jobs dangerous. For example, the Home Secretary, H.A. Bruce, opposed women engine-drivers at collieries on the grounds that 'the charge of an engine required firmness, courage and presence of mind and ought not to be entrusted to a woman'.[35] The inspector Brough suggested that women 'do not possess the presence of mind that often enables men to save themselves in cases of emergency'.[36] He also felt that they lacked the muscular strength which could be vital in saving themselves. Yet it remained true that the males who worked on the surface (lads or old and/or disabled miners) were usually not as strong as the adult women. It is interesting to note that in 1928 the Open Door Council, which opposed any restrictions on women's work (including mining), tried to combat the idea that there was necessarily a direct correlation between the sex of the worker and the likelihood of accidents.[37] This connection had been stressed in the Standing Joint Committee on Women's Industrial Organisations and the ODC emphasised that the chief causes of industrial accidents – bad fencing, slippery floors etc. in factories – were independent of the worker's sex (see Appendix II). Being equipped for dangerous and heavy work was, they urged, a matter of training and selection of the individual whether male or female. Neither sex, *en masse*, could be fitted for dangerous work and the female sex should not be singled out for differential treatment.

A further argument propounded by Brough was that the women's dress was liable to get entangled in machinery. This was true. It is perhaps significant that in Staffordshire, where women wore long skirts, there was a high rate of female shaft-accidents. Long skirts caused several nasty accidents in the St Helens area.[38] At the Hope colliery, Bedwellty, Wales, a sixteen-year-old banker Margaret Atkins was crushed to death when her skirt caught in part of the landing

machinery as she was landing the water barrel one night.[39] Certainly
the much maligned trousers of the Wigan area could be defended as
safer and more practical. Women's clothes could increase the likelihood
of danger but it was, however, simplifying the issue to assume that
women made the work more dangerous in other respects. A female
tally-taker was hardly likely to make her job more potentially lethal
than a male doing the same work. In fact a better criterion for allowing
the continuation of the work would have been experience rather than
sex and in view of the fate of young girls such as Ellen Hampson, age
also seems to have been an important determinant. Colliery deaths
should not be treated in isolation. Most manual jobs could be dangerous
and in spite of regulations about fencing off factory machinery,
shocking accidents did occur. A young girl who stayed at home might
of course also be involved in fatal accidents – there was a high
proportion of deaths from domestic fires. Yet these were at least due to
private negligence.[40] It is not so easy to excuse the accidents which
happened to women and girls at collieries and in the last resort much
of the criticism of physical danger was a reflection of frequent
negligence by the management.

Another way in which the work was attacked on grounds of
physical unsuitability was by claiming that it was injurious to health.
It was argued that the work must be too arduous for women and
growing girls and consequently their health must suffer. Once again
critics failed to differentiate between the tasks performed and tended
to denounce all female colliery work as inappropriate for the female
physique. But, as has been shown, different jobs demanded varying
degrees of exertion – moving wagons, tipping coal and filling barges
all being more demanding in physical terms than sorting at the belts or
slack washing.[41] Stacking timber was heavy work and was generally
unpopular – even with women who did not mind other jobs.[42] The
Lancashire miners were particularly critical of unloading and carrying
full tubs to the tippler. By the early twentieth century they were even
accepting that all the other jobs of the pit bank were suitable for them
except these.[43]

Much would of course depend on the extent to which a woman
would be ascribed to one job and expected to remain at it. George
Gilroy (manager at Ince Hall) told the Select Committe on Mines in
1866 that women were generally put on to the screens picking and
cleaning coal while the men used the shovel.[44] This may have sounded
admirable to the committee but the death of Ellen Hampson in the
same year stresses the gap between theory and practice. By the 1880s,

however, it was true that some pit brow work was actually becoming less dependent on brute strength and the manual kecking of tubs was being reduced.

Contemporary photographs show the pit women to have been strong — in fact strength was an essential prerequisite for wielding some of the heavy spades and rakes. Proud of their strength, former pit brow women have claimed that they could lift nine cwt easily. The degree of assistance they might receive would vary. At some pit mouths a couple of men might help the women unload tubs but this was not always the case. Munby found overlookers who told him that the women were as strong as the men. Not surprisingly he frequently commented on the robust and vigorous activity of his 'muscular maids'. His descriptions suggest their ability to cope, not just when all went smoothly but also when something went wrong:

> Two youngsters rushed down the steep slope, and standing calf deep in loose coal held up the wain with their shoulders, whilst Elizabeth above threw her whole weight upon the upper end and by sheer strength dragged the wain on to the rails again.[45]

A number of doctors in pit areas spoke in defence of the women's ability to perform the work without any unfortunate repercussions on their health. Several attended the meetings held in support of the work and an Aspull doctor accompanied the 1911 deputation. Dr Angior of Wigan, whose practice included four separate colliery districts, stated that in twenty-five years he could not remember ever being called upon to treat a pit woman for 'strain or any internal complication peculiar to women, the outcome of their work'.[46] The image of strength remained. During the First World War a welfare supervisor at Woolwich Arsenal supply stores explained that the work there

> of course cannot compare with the tremendous efforts put forth by the Lancashire pit lasses, who seem to do so easily the work of the average man.[47]

However, while those who attacked the work as being too demanding condemned it without careful examination, those who upheld it were not infrequently guilty of exaggeration. Although there was general recognition that wagon work was not suitable — which suggests the recognition of a point beyond which it was felt that women's strength should not be pushed — they failed to see the toll that pit work might take over the years. One defender of the work claimed in the Commons that pushing tubs must be less fatiguing than the work done by nurse girls carrying heavy babies and propelling rickety perambulators![48] The feminist Miss King-May had boasted about the suitability of pit brow work yet her knowledge was based on a few days spent at the pit one Easter and she was an expert in physical fitness and a member of the Ling Association of Teachers in Swedish gymnastics![49]

Within Parliament the question of women's strength and ability to perform the work became confused with their right to do the work at all. The gap between idealised expectations of women's work and their actual experience was exemplified in March 1886. Lord Thurlow was asked in the House of Lords about the possible creation of female factory inspectors. In reply he expressed doubt as to whether robust enough females could be found to travel the long distances required and brave the bad weather. Meanwhile fellow members in the Commons were busy bemoaning the excessive strength of pit brow girls, complaining they were too like men![50]

Whereas the traducers of pit work tended to concentrate on questioning the strength of women, its defenders argued that such work was physically superior to other types of female employment on health grounds. Munby commented on rich apricot complexions and general fitness while doctors attested that they were much more hardy and healthy than mill girls.[51] Certainly other female workers did face problems – there were dusty rag rooms in paper mills, a warm oily and smelly atmosphere in cotton mills and dusty powder pervaded lead works. The *Daily News* commented that

> A Parliament that suffers women to work for twelve or fourteen hours in the garrets and cellars of Soho while it talks of prohibiting women in Lancashire from working for eight and a half hours in the open air, might strike the Lancashire women as slightly inconsistent.[52]

Such a comment was particularly apposite at a time when the effectiveness of factory legislation was producing an increase in female labour in unprotected outwork.[53] Though in practice the day at the pit might be rather longer than the newspaper suggested, the women were nevertheless working in an employment where hours were subject to some control.

For those suffering from other occupational hazards such as byssinosis (cardroom asthma) it could also be a way of recuperating.

Lancashire and Fifeshire mill girls were sent to the pit to help recover from anaemia.[54] A former pit woman from Aspull explained how she came to work at the pit:

> I started at Dicconson mill but I was only like what they call duffing you know — well it was spinning and it didn't do for me so I had to come out. The doctor said it wouldn't do. He said 'You'd be better working on the pit brow'. He said I'd be better out in the open, he said, on the pit brow.[55]

Another woman in her ninetieth year recalled how as a child she was delicate and found that a spell at the mill did not suit her. After ten months there she was recommended by her doctor to try the pit.

> So anyway they advised me mother to take me out so I went on pit brow for health you see to try and pick me up a bit, it being clean open air you see.[56]

One overman told Munby:

> It's wonderful how t'lasses do get on at this work for health and getting bigger.[57]

Munby found that out of thirty-nine girls who had left mills during the cotton famine, thirty-three preferred pit work and just under forty per cent gave improved health as their reason. One girl told him she would not return to the mill even if she were offered 5/- a day.[58] One of the pit women's meetings at Bryn was told by the local vicar that twenty out of sixty-three women at a nearby pit had had their health restored after leaving the mill.[59] One girl, Ann Higham, told a newspaper that once a mill girl started pit work she never wanted to return to her former employment.[60] And Frank Hird in his *Lancashire Stories* claimed that 'the healthiness of the pit brow lass is proverbial'.[61] Petitions also urged the superiority of women in this respect. However, in Lancashire the effects of the cotton famine doubtless played a more important part in sending women to the pits than any claims of recuperative powers. And once at the pit, the relief of having a job would probably have made complaints fairly unlikely.

Yet while the pit top might be a valuable antidote to the ill health engendered by mill work, it was hardly the health resort suggested by

some advocates of the work and not all pit girls might 'afford a
sculptor fit models for a Juno'.[62] Moreover there was not much
provision should they fall ill — in Wigan most women and girls belonged
to a surface club and subscribed a penny a week to the Wigan Infirmary
opened in 1873 but they were not then members of the Lancashire and
Cheshire Permanent Relief Society.[63] Former pit women do remember
the bitterly cold winters, and snow and rain drenching them. The lunch
break might have to be spent drying out wet clothes and trying to get
a little warmer, though not all pits had proper cabins let alone braziers
or steam pipes.[64] Gloves were not much help when the job involved
deftly sorting coal and stinging fingers would have to be plunged in hot
water on returning home. Few pit brows were covered in the nineteenth
century though this would never be guessed from the romanticised
studio photographs of pit girls set against exotic backgrounds in an
attempt to make them look like peasants from some sunny European
country.[65]

Most probably they would have developed over time some resistance
to the cold and wet. Investigations of the London dustwomen revealed
that 'due to being so much in the open air the women seemed hale and
well-coloured' and contrasted favourably with those working in the
factories or at home.[66] However, for ailing mill workers used to
confined atmospheres it must have taken a while to build up such
immunity. Those who went to the pit from the start of their working
lives tended, however, to be well built, strong and of a healthy
disposition. Munby's friend Becky Price spent much of her life at
Shropshire pits but considered her daughter Polly to be too slight for
such work so sent her into service instead.[67] Those who were strong
might have an extra advantage. Stephen Walsh, MP for Ince, explained
that 'If she is a bonny lass, as we say. . .they will pay a little more.'[68]

There were however some complaints. Backs became strained and
fingers were cut — one woman covered every finger in bandages each
night. Dust flew everywhere, especially if the pit was high up and it was
a windy day. Eyesight (which needed to be good for detecting bits of
dirt) could be affected. The women got particularly dirty in hot
summers when dust would stick to their faces and arms.[69] Some pits
were better than others in this respect — the relatively clean coal at
Aspull Moor no. 5 gave its pit girls the nickname of 'angels'.[70] Coal dust
was, however, at least clean dirt which did not stick in the same way as
wet clay from brickyards or smell like the oil in factories. The
availability of cheap or free coal at many pits also meant access to a
constant supply of hot water. There were, however, some collieries

which did not give coal allowances and at Becky's pit only the men were entitled to this.[71] This was a particularly unfortunate ruling at a time when there were no pit head baths. One woman explained that they got so dirty that 'dirt – well, you could eat it!'[72] For those at the belts the shaker was extremely noisy and some women even learnt to lip read. The positioning of the belts determined whether or not they had to bend much. Some women certainly had to spend much of the day bending low to pick out dirt and to lift tubs, and all had to stand continually.

Yet the women seem to have accepted such inconveniences as just part of the job. Proud if they did not have to spend any time in hospital or 'laaking' (staying away from work or playing), they were members of a society where one was not given to complaining about the details of work, especially on the top of the pit. One witness to the Children's Employment Commission had explained that 'colliers don't take any account of being hurt unless their backs are broken'.[73] The women themselves emphasised that their work was healthy in terms of building up strength and constitutions. One explained:

> Healthy? Oh I'll say. I did five or six weeks with me sister at weaving shed but I didn't like that. I've never looked back behind me – although it's been cold it's been proper healthy weather.[74]

Another explained that 'muckier you got and healthier' and yet another declared:

> Oh I loved every minute of it. Oh, I did. I loved every minute of it. And it was healthy job, it was hard, it was heavy but it was healthy.[75]

One woman who spent thirty years at the surface (mainly operating the tippler) summed up her work as 'active, hard but healthy'.[76] Evidence from Munby and these former pit women who began work at the turn of the century suggest that once some experience had been gained, the work was quite manageable. Much of it depended not so much on what critics liked to call 'Amazonian strength' as on learning a knack, discovering how best to lift and carry tubs and how to minimise difficulties. Once the correct way of kecking had been learned, the job became much easier. Having become inured to such ways and able to demonstrate considerable dexterity, they could even become scornful of other jobs. This, after all, was 'real' work. One woman who spent years at the pit brow eventually got employed in her sixties at a munitions factory. She recalled her days there:

> It were not my work — it weren't heavy enough for me. A plaything
> that were to me because I've not been used to that. I've been used
> to roughing it and going among things you know — but, a little
> paintbrush! It was a plaything! It was murder![77]

A further opportunity for criticising the women was provided by their
physical appearance. Liberally interspersing moral judgement with facts
and figures, the *Morning Chronicle* declared that the work was
'absolutely unsexing the women'.[78] In fact it was 'difficult to conceive
anything more utterly and coarsely unfeminine than the aspect of these
persons. They are lean, haggard and grisly creatures.' When John
Plummer visited Wigan in 1863 he linked the women's clothes to modes
of behaviour — 'they may be seen wearing jackets like the men, smoking,
drinking and behaving as if completely unsexed'.[79] His words were
echoed in Parliament. Mundella's description of pit women though not
attributed to Plummer, sounds suspiciously like his account:

> No sight could be more degrading than to see women in attire almost
> like that of men with coalheavers' hats on their heads, smoking pipes
> with the men, drinking with them in the pubs and he was told,
> sometimes fighting with them afterwards in the streets.[80]

Plummer had emphasised how their masculinity was evident in their
pugilistic exploits, drinking powers and pipe-smoking. Quite apart from
exaggeration (Munby found for example that pit brow women hardly
ever smoked pipes)[81] such ways of describing their external appearance
confused physical and moral criticism.

The main torrent of abuse was reserved for the trousers, described
by the *Manchester Guardian* as 'the article of clothing which women
ought only to wear in a figure of speech'![82] Trousers were seen as a
blatant manifestation of defeminising. One critic indignantly described
them as a 'disgusting kind of male attire that completely unsexes them,
rendering them in most respects exceedingly repulsive' whilst the *Daily
News* simply explained that 'It is acknowledged that the habitual
wearing of the costume tends to destroy all sense of decency.'[83] The
miners' union subscribed to these notions. The Leeds conference of
1863 had reported that it was a

most sickening sight to see girls and women who had been created

and designed for a much nobler sphere of action, clad in men's attire
on the pit banks but it is a much sadder sight to see them, day by
day losing everything modest and unwomanly.[84]

The obsession with these 'fustian unmentionables' disguises the fact
that women only wore trousers in a few of the female-employing
districts. Munby, determined to solve 'the great breeches question'
found that they were confined to a ten-mile radius of Wigan.[85] The pit
girls of St Helens did not wear them, though between Haydock and
Wigan it was the accepted custom. At Ramshead pit, Haydock, women
were not allowed to work unless they wore trousers. The 'boundary' in
the north was Euxton – Coppull and Blackbrook in the south. The
district where they were worn had a long tradition of women's pit work
and after 1842 women had worked illegally – wearing trousers. Their
continued use may have reflected the preference of influential
coalowners for such a costume. It certainly distinguished them from the
mill girls. Some were made of cord, others were of coarse, black cloth
and striped cotton aprons would be looped up over them. Nineteenth-
century pit workers rarely let down these aprons. Open-necked shirts,
patched waistcoats and stout clogs completed the outfit. Journeying to
and from the pit and working in cold weather, short coats would be
worn, generally those discarded by male relatives. They also had
hooded bonnets of padded cotton, generally pink, blue or black. When
working they covered their heads with a scarf. Clothes were frequently
mended and patched – Ellen Grounds had worn a pair of men's
breeches for nine years. They were warmly lined and padded at the
knees and had been patched many times with pieces of cotton and
linen of various colours.[86]

Most women had to supply their own clothes – some made part of
the costume themselves and relied for the rest on relatives' cast-offs.
Staffordshire and Shropshire women made aprons from potato sacking.
Munby was amused to find that they sometimes still bore the dealer's
name. Clogs were essential but got worn quickly especially in wagon-
trimming work. One women explained that she learnt to do the same
as the men – to have two sets of irons put on her clogs.[87] The Blundells'
women were fortunate from the mid-1880s as their costume was made
locally and provided free for those of 'good character'. It consisted of
a dark-blue flannel jacket, serge trousers and a long apron. They had to
provide their own padded bonnets. This 'Blundells costume' was very
distinctive and was used to great effect at the deputations.[88] At
Haydock, Richard Evans provided flannel jackets for the women and

the colliery accounts of the Bankes family show money being spent on flannel for women's dresses.[89] Gradually the Wigan clothes became 'not quite so mannish as they used to be'.[90] The trousers were covered by longer aprons and in some instances disappeared altogether — Fletcher and Burrows claimed that their new screening methods made them unnecessary.[91] Eventually in the final days of female pit brow work the 'bifurcated garb' became popular again as women donned overalls.

Munby, who naturally defended the 'belles in breeches', recognised that trousers were more practical for the sort of work which women were having to perform. The freedom from physical restraint aided agility (a complete contrast to the highly restrictive clothes which were fashionable), they were safer and warmer. Defenders of the practice drew attention to the fact that the women were at least not *déshabillée*:

> When we take into consideration the vagaries of fashion, with all the improprieties involved in low bodices in the drawing room and short skirts on the stage, we cannot refrain from describing the garb of the colliery lasses as comparatively becoming.[92]

Lady Harberton's Rational Dress Society defended them, Mrs Oscar Wilde being one of the objectors to suggestions that pit women should not wear trousers.[93] The women were certainly not alone in being clad in this manner though sartorial comparisons generally concentrated on ballet dancers, bicyclists (the popularity of this sport was helping to revive the bloomer in the 1880s) and horse riders rather than considering lesser-known women workers such as the Paddington dust women and the flither lasses of Flamborough Head. The staging of the International Health exhibition in London made the concern about healthy dress particularly topical in the 1880s though those upholding the women's work recognised that trousers were really being used as a pretext for expressing moral disapproval and a 'Pecksniffian pretence of prudery'.[94]

Munby frequently noted that the women brightened up their clothes (and thereby added a degree of individuality) by wearing coloured shirts, earrings and flowers. Even Plummer conceded the

> latest evidence of feminine weakness in the shape of a coral necklace, a pair of glittering ear-rings, and a bonnet which as regards shape, size and colour, strongly resembled the fantail hat of a London coal-heaver.[95]

In the Tredegar area their headgear was 'bedecked with beads and feathers'. They were also careful to protect their hair from the dust.[96] Lancashire women generally wore head wraps and shoulder shawls. By folding newspaper under their scarves they protected their hair and had an extra layer of insulation. Welsh women wore checked head scarves and turnovers (shoulder shawls). One Pembrokeshire woman explained:

> We was very particular, us girls, about our hair, tie it tight, tight. . . that there should not have dust touch our hair.[97]

They were proud of their clogs. One woman recalled that hers 'shone like a raven' and a Westhoughton man who used to see the women on their way to work commented that after polishing their clogs

> you could shave through them. You'd see brass nails. . .they'd polish them they would that. . .it were which could be nicest in pit clothes.[98]

Screen lasses at Whitehaven 'prided themselves on arriving at work each day with aprons and shawls clean' and with their clogs 'shining like armour'.[99] Those critics determined to see the women as unsexed and degraded probably only saw them as they left work 'in their dirt'.

Beyond the Wigan area few women wore trousers. There were occasional exceptions − Sal Madge, the Whitehaven horse-driver, was well known for her 'rationals'.[100] Dressed in a cloth peaked cap, scarf, shirt, waistcoat, jacket and trousers her employer, the Earl of Lonsdale, once mistook her for a man. Belgian mining women wore off-white trousers of mid-calf length. Van Gogh's spell in the Borinage in 1879 familiarised him with the *logues de fosse* (pit rags) worn by men and women alike and prompted him to do several drawings of the *hiercheuses* who worked underground. The *rachaneuses* who were employed on the surface wore long, blue skirts as their *haillons* (pit costume).[101]

Some areas of Britain were proud that their pit women did not wear trousers. Alexander MacDonald was quick to point out that Scottish women 'dressed like ordinary females, they do not dress like the Wigan ladies'.[102] These Scots pit head workers wore heavy shoes, 'huggers' (thick stockings), skirts, petticoats, shirts, jackets and 'mutches' (caps). The inspector for South Wales, Thomas Evans, explained that Welsh pit girls did not wear trousers so were 'respectably dressed'.[103] Some few Welsh women did, however, dress in trousers as photographs of Bwllfa colliery, Aberdare in the 1870s reveal.[104] Most Welsh women, though, dressed in long, flannel frocks or skirts, with leather aprons known as 'brats' (the Welsh word for pinafore).[105] In Pembrokeshire they wore canvas aprons made from bags. They also had scarves, plaid shawls, black woollen stockings and hob-nailed boots. Some tip girls wore 'clappers' (loose cloth shields) over the back of their hands to keep them warm and protect them and girls in the Blaenavon area wore leather straps round their wrists and pads on their hands. An article in the *Bristol Mercury* in 1865 described the 'peculiar' style of dress worn by the women employed at the patches around Tredegar. It consisted of

> a short frock and apron, tight to the neck, made of a material somewhat resembling hop cloth or fine sacking, red worsted stockings and lace up boots heavy with hob nails, tips and toe caps that would pull the legs off some of the ploughmen of the Midland counties.[106]

This description can be placed alongside the photographs taken by Clayton, a Tredegar photographer. Forty-nine of his studio portraits of patch girls survive and show how visual representation not only reflected but consciously and deliberately extended a particular image (see jacket photograph). These were sold to a collector and demonstrate the contrasts which critics delighted in stressing, the superhuman strength combined with studio scenes of alpine splendour. Photographic techniques would be used to great effect – especially controlled lighting and the use of a long lens. High skirting boards, large shovels and riddles accentuated the strength and squat appearances. Thus the physical image of the pit women was exploited through photography, enabling the women to be presented as objects of curiosity. The miners' conference of 1863 was shown photographs of Wigan pit women as was the 1866 Select Committee which was also treated to a photograph of all the Ince Hall women in their Sunday clothes.[107] Eager amateurs such as Dr Albert Dingley of Wednesbury photographed the women actually at work but only too frequently the photographs were far removed from the actual scene of work and a bizarre contrast was suggested by a black pit girl in her work clothes and the romanticised studio background.[108] The Wigan photographers Dugdale, Craig, Little, Millard and Cooper all developed a good trade in selling photographs of pit brow women. They were displayed in the studios and shop windows of Wigan, Burnley and other Lancashire towns. John Cooper told Munby in 1865 that he had sold hundreds of *cartes de visite* of the collier girls. He would enlarge any picture to life-size and colour it if requested. Miss Millard told the same story and Mrs Little had a set of photographs displayed in the main street of Wigan showing the girls in their work clothes. Sometimes the pit girl would be shown dressed for work on one side and wearing her Sunday clothes on the reverse. They were chiefly sold to commercial travellers who bought them as curiosities.[109]

Some pit women visited the photographer because they enjoyed being exhibited and receiving a free copy. Munby, who claimed to be worried about the 'sentimentalists and sensualists', frequently recognised photographs of his friends. On 18 August 1863 he wrote:

> Saw Jane Horton and one or two other cartes de visite of girls in pit clothes hung up in the streets by photographers: one of whom in Clarence Yard told me they often come to her to be taken.[110]

Munby constantly encouraged them to have their photographs taken and by this action unconsciously stimulated further the publicity which he so deplored. He generally gave a shilling to the girls who accompanied him to the studios and not surprisingly did not often meet with resistence. In fact, he remained remarkably free from parental intervention though very occasionally a girl's father forbade her to visit the photographer with him. On his travels he would visit studios (for example, Lee in Pewfall and Andrews in Swansea) to see if there was the chance of purchasing additional pictures for his collection. There were also postcard sets of pit brow women – Starrs of Wigan produced a series of hand-coloured cards. The Milton Facsimile series which depicted the Douglas Bank pit women succeeded in making them appear very untypical of English workers. Large shawls and the occasional use of handkerchiefs over the mouth (to keep the dust away) added to the exotic image.

The pictorial representation of pit women in middle-class journals was initially rather different. The *Illustrated London News* of the 1850s did depict women about coal mines but as the mourners at the scenes of disaster, the sufferers plunged into sudden widowhood. As in the traditional art world, it was woman in the family setting or as the heroine in joy or grief who captured attention. Twenty years later, however, due partly to the publicity given to the mines legislation of 1872 and the fashion for commissioning artists to work 'on the spot', the women were depicted as workers. Eight wood engravings of the 1873 lock-out in South Wales showed tip girls (highly stylised), accompanied by imprecise descriptions of the work and rather more positive indictments of it.[111] A further fourteen pictures followed in 1875. Munby was 'struck all of a heap' when he saw representations of the pit brow women of the Mesnes colliery, Wigan, in the *Pictorial World* (1874).

> What right had this artist to poach on my manor, to exhibit my heroines thus and perhaps send people to see and spoil them or to try and 'put them down'?[112]

Once again the sketches were accompanied by a denouncement of the work as a relic of barbarism. The expansion of popular illustrated journals in the 1870s provided a glimpse of the pit brow women for the uninitiated but it was one which emphasised that her strength was gained at the expense of her femininity.

The desirability of depicting pit lasses was not recognised by the world of art. Subjects such as coalmining, even without women, had only become acceptable in paintings by being suitably dramatised. Miners, like gypsies, had acquired a romantic touch but in British art circles the fusion of women and hard pit work in serious painting marked a radical departure from tradition. When the Lancashire artist, Eyre Crowe, exhibited 'The Spoil Bank' showing women and children collecting coal from the slag heaps, all the *Athenaeum* could say was that

> We admire Mr. Crowe's conscientiousness in painting such uninviting subjects as these but we submit that he might often have used his time more wisely, and that photography was made for such work as recording all that these pictures tell us.[113]

It was Crowe who immortalised the Wigan mill girls with his 'Dinner Hour. Wigan' (1874). And in spite of the popularity of the work of French artists such as Millet and Courbet and the vogue for the lunch-hour theme — Steinlen painted the Parisian factory girls at their lunch break and Meunier also did a lunch-hour picture — Crowe's effort was judged as truthful rather than as pleasing.

By the time of the pit brow debates a picture of the Lancashire pit lasses had eventually found its way to the Royal Academy. It was exhibited in the Summer exhibition, conveniently being on view during the time of the deputation. Painted by Arthur Wasse II of Manchester it was entitled 'Lancashire Pit Lasses at Work' and was praised by Munby as 'good and accurate'.[114] Meanwhile photographs of the

women were on show in the Strand and were handed round at the
Home Office.[115] At Southport a life-size cork model of a pit girl had
been displayed at a bazaar.[116] At worst they were presented as
androgynous Amazons and even when there was an attempt to depict
them more accurately they were still curiosities, fascinating aberrations
who were often deliberately presented away from the workplace.
Pictorial representations thus provided ammunition for the debate
about the disturbing physical and moral implications of the work.

Literature parallelled this. Colliery stories usually depicted women
as the silent heroines, patiently bearing children and grief, the victims
of society who kept the community going – distributors of food and
warmth locked in a perpetual battle for survival in a world dominated
by the pit and male colliers. Whilst the non-working, long-suffering
collier's wife continued and was reinforced by the later Lawrentian
image, there developed also a lesser-known counterpart to the pit wife,
the toiling pit lass who was depicted as a defeminised creature. She
appeared as Joan Lowrie, the heroine of Frances Hodgson Burnett's
first full-length novel. Published in England in 1877, this story of a pit
brow girl of Riggan was an immediate success. *That Lass O'Lowrie's*
opened with a comment on the physical appearance of pit girls and the
immediate impression that they created:

> They did not look like women, or at least a stranger new to the
> district might easily have been misled by their appearance, as they
> stood together in a group by the pit's mouth.[117]

They were women who

> wore a dress more than half masculine, and who talked loudly and
> discordantly, and some of whom, God knows, had faces as hard and
> as brutal as the hardest of their collier brothers and husbands and
> sweethearts.[118]

Yet we are told that it was not to be wondered at that they had lost all
bloom of womanly modesty and gentleness. Their physical appearance
was such that

> At first one shrank from them but one's shrinking could not fail
> to change to pity. There was no element of softness to rule or even
> influence them in their half savage existence.

Punch seized the opportunity for a burlesque of the story.[119] Its serialisation of 'That Lass O'Towrey's' parodied the descriptions of unsexing by unfolding the tale of Emmeline Beerie and her father Bitter Beerie! Though a pit brow heroine was at first sight an unlikely subject to engage the attention of Mrs Burnett's middle-class readers, the situation was eased by Joan's transformation and by the fact that, like Mary Barton, she was somewhat different from the rest of her class. Her less pleasant characteristics were balanced by redeeming features — though extremely strong she possessed a superior will and mind and the other women half-feared and half-revered her. The novel contributed to the fascination for 'discovering' working women — the *Ladies* journal in 1872 had embarked on a series of investigatory articles to determine how tip girls and other women unknown to readers lived and worked.[120] *That Lass* helped build up the stereotype of the aberrant pit woman on whom attention became centred in the 1880s.

In some respects the story provided a familiar tale of colliery life. It contained the stock ingredients. There was a cruel collier father 'living. . .as most of them do — drinking, rioting and fighting' and a pit explosion which supplied a sense of drama and a convenient excuse for Joan to help rescue and then nurse the engineer Derrick back to health and thus display her suppressed qualities![121] As the story develops so Joan gradually shows signs of disenchantment with the apparently uncivilised world of the pit brow woman and begins to disentangle herself from it. A corresponding refinement emerges. Joan becomes increasingly self-conscious — she sees the unsuitability of her work and as she encroaches into the 'other' and, by implication, better world beyond the pit, so she softens and becomes increasingly disdainful of her former work and habits and painfully ashamed of her shortcomings. She receives elementary instruction from Anice, the Rector's daughter, and tries to follow more feminine pursuits such as sewing since

I'm tired o'bein' neyther th'one thing nor th'other. Seems loike I've allus being doin' men's ways, an I am na content.[122]

The idea that pit work could not be reconciled with being feminine was reinforced by the pit girl Liz. Here physical degeneration merged with moral decline (though we are told that Riggan was more rigid in its criticism than in its morality). Liz has an illegitimate child for whom she feels no interest. Yet, as the tale develops, so Joan displays increasingly maternalistic feelings towards this baby and eventually is forced to ask herself 'Is na theer a woman's place fur me i' th' world?'[123]

At the same time Mrs Burnett was careful to emphasise that the metamorphosis would not be immediate or easy — 'from the pit's mouth to the kitchen would not be a natural transition'.[124] At the end of the story it is Joan's awareness of her inadequacy and her subsequent humility which is stressed. Even leaving Riggan and beginning to work for Anice's grandmother cannot remove her sense of not belonging and belief that she is not worthy of Derrick:

> give me th' time to work an' strive: be patient with me until the day comes when I can come to you an' know I need not shame you.[125]

Though the authoress conceded that the 'barbarity' of the pit was partly caused by other people's abdication of their responsibility (the pompous Rector could not 'get down fro' his perch') she was at greater pains to show how deference should replace a pit girl's defiance. With over fifty novels and children's stories to her credit, an international success who crossed the Atlantic thirty-three times and helped to promote changes in the international copyright laws, Mrs Burnett had herself moved far away from the image of the Victorian lady of leisure.[126] Yet though so successful in a world dominated by male professionals, it was the incongruity of women at the pit rather than their ability to work alongside men which was stressed in the novel, physical criticism giving way to moral probing.

Her story had considerable impact in America and Britain and her outsider's interest, value judgements and indictments were imbibed wholesale. Munby, however, was able to comment that 'the authoress knows Wigan but not the Wigan pit girls'.[127] He and Hannah enjoyed the story but were critical of the way Joan was made to behave outside the pit. Mrs Burnett originally came from Lancashire having spent her childhood in Manchester and Salford. Her inspiration for Joan was apparently the result of watching a group of mill girls from her window when she was ten. Six years later she emigrated with her family to Tennessee and only made one brief return visit to Manchester between then and the publication of her book in England. Her visit was, however, in 1873 and it would seem that she probably based much of her evidence on the *Manchester Guardian*'s series on 'The Lancashire Collier at Home' which was published in that year and included a section on Wigan and pit girls.[128]

Four dramatisations were made of the novel and Mrs Burnett also wrote a stage version herself. Munby saw the play in 1877.[129] He acknowledged the attempt to 'act Lancashire' and blackening of the arms but was relieved to note that her dress 'happily was all wrong and the scene absurd to one who knows'. Yet Munby was one of the few with such esoteric knowledge. For the majority of the middle-class readers or play-goers this story might be the first acquaintance with a pit brow lass yet it was an acquaintance via a writer who it seems had no actual knowledge of the women based on first-hand experience. As with the pictures of pit brow lasses it was only too easy to ferment criticism. In the concern to cleanse society both physically and morally, it was forgotten that dirty faces did not necessarily denote degraded souls.

Plummer had felt that there was something abhorrent in seeing the pit girls 'begrimed with dust and placed in the way of temptations which might lead to immorality'.[130] Much of the debate about the pit women revolved around the question of morals. There was an assumption that the work environment (and particularly pit language) must coarsen the women and make them immoral and irresponsible. The Third Report of the Children's Employment Commission commented on the pit women of Staffordshire and South Wales 'hardly distinguishable from men in their appearance and begrimed with dirt and smoke'.[131] It went on to explain that they were 'exposed to the deterioration of character, arising from their loss of self-respect which can hardly fail to follow from their unfeminine occupation'. The wearing of trousers, the rough nature of the work and dirty appearances all played a part here and were seen to result in a lack of shame and the likelihood of immoral behaviour. Field work was seen to have disastrous results for women for similar reasons. The choice of words of one farmer giving evidence to the 1867 Royal Commission on Agriculture is particularly revealing. He claimed that field work would

> almost unsex a woman, in dress, gait, manners, character, making her rough, coarse, clumsy, masculine; but it generates a further very pregnant social mischief by unfitting or indisposing her for a woman's proper duties at home.[132]

Such vitiation of the character of outdoor women workers was prompted by the belief that they were neglecting their natural roles of housekeeper and mother. This fitted in with the wider argument against working women and was a chance to urge the importance of family life. It was particularly strongly emphasised in this instance as the women were not only working away from home but were employed in what was seen as a particularly unsuitable environment. As in 1842, intervention was considered expedient due to the dangers which the present held for the future. Both Plummer and Lever urged legislative interference

> for the sake of future generations yet unborn, for the sake of the future mothers of our mining population and for the sake of the moral, social and physical welfare of the present generation itself.[133]

The *Manchester Guardian* felt that it was a disgrace to the men that wives and mothers of the future should be allowed to engage in a 'coarse and degrading occupation'.[134]

Thus while the women were accused of being unfeminine and rough, they were also portrayed as immoral, perhaps a recognition that though sexuality was primarily associated with men, this might not be so for the working class where the sexes were employed together. Outdoor working women therefore constituted a threat to the stability of the family. The double standard of morality appeared to work well for the middle class. There the dependent wife and mother was desexualised, ensconced within the shelter of the home, which in Ruskin's words was supposed to be 'a sacred place, a vestal temple, a temple of the hearth watched over by household gods'.[135] Prostitution reinforced the status quo. Thus, while the sexuality of the middle-class woman was not recognised but saw 'the mutation of the Eve myth into the Mary myth, of temptress into redeemer', at the same time her labouring counterpart in the working class was in a very different situation.[136] Though unfeminine, she was not desexualised but seen as behaving more like a man.

It was generally assumed that the pit women always worked in close proximity to the men but this was not necessarily the case. At the Atherton pits men were strictly forbidden to enter the place where the women worked and even the men on the brow did not see much of them. At the Wigan Coal and Iron Company's pits only those who examined the tubs as they reached the surface had any contact with the men.[137] Sorting at the belts was done almost entirely by women in female employing districts though there might well be a male overlooker supervising. Munby always commented on how well-behaved the women were at work. Many of the criticisms of immorality emanated from those who were applying their own standards and preconceptions about social behaviour to a group of workers about

whose lifestyle they knew very little and whose customs they did not
appreciate. They noted that the illegitimate birth rate for Wigan
between 1873-83 was almost double the national average. Certainly a
number of pit women did have illegitimate children — Ellen Meggison
had eight — but not only did pit women form only a tiny percentage
of Wigan's female population but critics failed to recognise traditional
customs. Munby constantly rebuked the girls for their former sins and
was puzzled by the way that parents (who looked after children while
their daughters worked) were not ashamed. Munby found, however,
that there was such a premium on children in mining districts that a
woman had first to be proved capable of bearing children 'before she
is taken for good'.[138] He had discovered that though there were a
number of young unmarried pit girls in Wigan with a child or children,
they generally eventually married the father.

Upholders of the women's right to work marshalled evidence from
the clergy which laid stress on the pit women's Christian outlook, their
contributions as district visitors and their strong moral disposition.[139]
The morality argument was also inverted. It was pointed out that
exclusion could lead to even more unfortunate results. Josephine
Butler cited the example of Irish women expelled from ropeworks in
Liverpool.[140] Forced to leave their employment they had resorted to
coal-heaving at the docks, picking oakum in the workhouse and street
walking. Once again the lesson of 1842 was remembered. A letter to the
Wigan Times reminded readers about the act's

> pitiful and withering results: the youthful female was scattered in all
> directions for a livelihood; families were broken up never to be
> united again; sent to procure employment in towns where they were
> exposed to temptations in forms that had never assailed them
> before.[141]

Those opposed to the women's work concentrated not so much on the
results of the 1842 legislation as on its philosophy. They argued that
not working constituted respectability and therefore presumed that
work led to ruin. The north-east was cited as an example of superior
home comforts. A letter from this area to the *Mining Journal* claimed
that pit women could not make the best wives since 'the delicacy and
affection which constitute the charm of women are invariably
destroyed by the performance of hard manual labour.[142] A letter to
the *Women's Union Journal* from South Wales exclaimed:

But the other sex — the tender! the fair! Who that has not seen it and is outside of Bedlam, could even in his wildest dream have imagined woman (and those dapper Welsh women too), the very handiwork of nature, designed for mothers in the incongruous position of a beast of burthen — hauling about huge trucks of coal?[143]

Miners' conferences reiterated the belief that domestic duties should be the chief concern of women. The Leeds conference pointed out that at last the miner was in a position where he could afford to maintain his wife at home so now 'the wife and mother can take the place of nature intended for her and a collier's home has now the possibility of comfort being realised'.[144] In Belgium opponents of women's work in the pits were echoing similar sentiments. It was hoped that exclusion would mean that 'ses qualités de ménagère ne tarderons pas a s'améliorer' (it would not be long before her housewifely skills improved).[145] Neddy Rymer, who became the agent of the St Helens Miners' Association in 1866, wrote and spoke on female pit brow work, denouncing it as a 'dark blot on our national character' and 'an eternal disgrace to all who uphold the iniquity or in any way reap profit from its abominations'. Coming to Lancashire from a non-female employing area, he was concerned about the disturbing effects on society — 'the evil entered more into the social, mental and domestic relations of the people'.[146]

There is no denying that pit women had a very heavy day and they had no labour-saving devices in the form of servants or gadgets to facilitate domestic tasks. Yet they were familiar with the organisation of shift work and the peculiar demands of the mining industry which at least placed them in a position to be able to cope with the demands of collier families. Where married women did work, it could be argued that this prevented the home from becoming even less comfortable than it might have been had there not been the additional wage. Anyway much of the criticism of home and family by those outside the industry was based on a fallacy. It was assumed that most women were married and had young children. Yet this was not, in fact, the case. The majority of pit brow women were single girls. At the Lilleshall pits in Shropshire in 1866 only forty out of 592 women were married.[147] In the Pemberton district twenty years later 131 of the 164 pit women were single (and there were seven widows).[148] The inspector, Dickinson, told the 1866 Select Committee that 'when a woman is married and with children you do find her staying at home'.[149] At some Lancashire pits the management forbade the employment of married women. In Whitehaven only single women were allowed to work and in South Wales it was extremely rare to find any married women working, the colliers being as opposed to the practice as the employers.[150] Yet the single woman, so feared by the Victorian upholders of 'respectable society', was barely acknowledged and indeed has only recently been given serious consideration by historians.[151] There was also an increasing emphasis on motherhood which was linked to the physical effects of the work. Some critics argued that the pit women's constitutions must suffer and therefore 'puny weaklings will be the result for the succeeding generation'.[152] With an eye to the future of the race, it was feared that the women might not be fit to fulfil their 'real' role in life. In the 1840s the domestic ideology had stressed the woman's position as a wife, her need to acquire domestic skills and her importance as a pacifier in the home. Towards the end of the century this ideology was beginning to shift its emphasis to place greater weight on the woman as mother, the guardian of the race, responsible for future generations. Set against the recognition of the need to maintain the Empire in the face of rival master races, social Darwinistic ideas became particularly important, especially as there was evidence of a falling birth rate from the time of the census of 1881. Thus the *Spectator* could argue in 1886 that if the work was as severe as was claimed, it would mean that the women were unfit to be mothers and so injured the future of the race.[153]

Those who did have children appear to have been more fortunate than many of their urban counterparts. Coalmining seems to have perpetuated strong family links. Socialisation of children was often shared in the Wigan coalfield (see Chapter 4) and in more remote and monolithic mining communities dependence on relatives may have been even greater. Defenders of the pit brow argued that being out of doors all day made the women appreciative of home life. Investigators examined a number of homes — the *Manchester Guardian* compared their houses with those of factory workers and concluded that in no district around Wigan could anything approaching a bad opinion of pit girls be found.[154] Yet in this area pit girls and mill girls resided within the same families and newspapers tended to differentiate too sharply between the two. Interpretations of what constituted 'good' homes would anyway vary from one individual to another and in the case of Wigan, most pit girls' homes were tended by mothers who were not themselves working. In considering the attacks on morals and accusations of neglect of the home, the question of where blame ultimately lay is inevitably raised. Critics might find the colliery houses to be far from perfect but these pit lasses, frequently daughters helping to bolster their family's income or colliery widows struggling on a single wage, were not earning much anyway. Their homes were hardly likely to be abounding in luxuries and it is hardly surprising that arguments about the home were joined to economic considerations of their work.

It was the question of wages which formed the third major concern of critics. Upholders of the work pointed out that the women's wages formed their sole capital and source of material well-being and strongly resisted attempts to marginalise the importance of the work.[155] For those who were supporting families on their own, the wages were clearly much more than 'pin money'. Opponents, however, viewed the women's wages in relation to those of other workers and could not help concluding that the women were cheap labour. As one miner put it:

> Strip the women of their clogs and flannel trousers and let the unemployed men of Wigan step into them, and take their places on the pit heads, and instead of the women receiving 1/6d let men have 2/8d or 3/- for the same labour and see if Wigan does not improve.[156]

It was the economic exploitation of the women by the coalowners which formed the main thrust of the miners' argument against the women. Whereas non-miners who criticised the work concentrated on physical and moral denunciations, those within the industry had different grudges. Their criticisms provoked a cynical response from their opponents who suspected their motives. The Conservative MP, Sir Richard Temple, commented:

> The amount of specious humbug that was uttered on this point amused me much. The real object was, by excluding the cheaper female labour, to raise the wages of the men: a real instance of masculine selfishness. It was a bare-faced instance of the worst part of labour unionism.[157]

In order to unravel the economic arguments it is necessary first to consider the allegations that the women were cheap labour by looking at their wages. It is no easy task deciphering female wage rates. They varied considerably — not just according to the state of the market but they also depended on the area and type of work performed. Age was a vital factor and some pits had an age scale for women employees though there was no standard policy. At other pits there was a 'setting on' rate which would be improved by 2d once a girl had proved herself capable.[158] At some other pits there might be five or six different rates being paid depending on size and the number of years' experience rather than age. Most women were paid by the colliery but others received their wages from butty miners or even the browmen. Welsh patch girls for example were paid by contractors. After 1872 there were a number of Lancashire day wage women doing odd jobs. The one consistent and indisputable factor was that women always earned less than men even if they were doing exactly the same job. In the 1840s wages were especially low and hours long.[159] Banking paid only about 1/- a day in North Wales while in South Staffordshire the butties paid girls of twelve to thirteen between 4/- and 4/6d a week which rose gradually to between 7/6d and 9/- for seventeen to eighteen year olds. Yet this top rate remained the ceiling for a long time. In the mid-sixties women were still paid between 1/- and 1/6d a day. Those at the brow got slightly more than screeners – at Deep pit, St Helens, in 1863, the brow workers received on average 8/6d for a week's work but those screening and loading wagons got only 7/-.[160] The average wage for Lancashire women was between 1/- and 1/2d a day but men were getting 2/6d to 3/- for the same work. High wages at the mills had drawn some women away in the fifties but the cotton famine soon reversed the situation. Those at the brow and coke ovens continued to earn more than others. Sarah Fairhurst working at Ince Hall was paid by the browman and got 2/- a day. By 1878 she was getting 2/6d daily though most pit women received between 1/8d and 1/10d. In 'T' Pointswoman' Munby explained how the brow worker would get the tubs and 'rowk em eawt o' t' caage' and for this she could command a decent wage – "aaf a croon a daa'.[161]

In South Wales in the mid-sixties women brickworkers might earn just under 7/- a week and stonebreakers 10/- though fillers, unloaders, pilers and dram girls got only 5/- to 7/-.[162] Wages would depend on a regular flow of orders and Welsh women faced the extra problem of the truck system. At Blaina a young orphan Janet James who earned 6/- a week for two years pushing tubs at the brow never actually received her wages. They were confiscated by her employers Levick and Simpson in order to pay off a debt which her dead father was alleged to have owed the company shop. She explained,

I have never received a farthing in money, but all goods at the shop. The whole of my wages were swallowed up in shop bills for bread or tea, on which I lived.[163]

W.P. Roberts brought an action against the colliery owners who were eventually ordered to pay the 'Welsh orphan' several hundred pounds. Wages in Wales were still generally paid monthly. Elsewhere the fortnightly pay day had been adopted. Munby described the Saturday afternoon 'reckoning' at Middle Place, Ince Hall in 1866:

> It was a picturesque sight, this reckoning. Our group stood at the entrance of the yard, and round the office in the middle pitmen were standing in scores, and with them dozens of pit girls, in coaly trousers, and in fustian coats of blue or in waistcoats and pink and lilac sleeveless shirts, were sitting on logs and coalheaps till their turn came. At last as the crowd of men thinned, we all rushed forward to the little brick building. A clerk within called out the names, and the gaffer, standing in one of the two doorways, repeated it aloud for those outside. John Royds! Maggie Turner! Ellen Jones! and then he or she, pressing in through the good natured crowd received a fortnight's wages wrapped in paper at the counter and passed out at the other door.[164]

There would be some stoppages — money for 'coffin clubs', perhaps payment for cheap coal and rent for colliery houses. Girls were expected to 'tip up'. When Mrs Holden's wages were increased at Duxbury Park colliery when she reached the age of eighteen, she got 6d a week spending money instead of 3d as she was now earning 2/- a day (minus 3d for sick pay).

> I began to think I was a millionaire. I kept turning it over and studying, how to spend it for the best. I had my own clothes to buy and very seldom, never to[o] many tasty bits in my basket, we were to[o] poor.[165]

Wages varied considerably between coalfields. In the early 1870s the West Lancashire colliers were for a time the highest paid in coalmining and this found some reflection in the women's wages. This period also witnessed less overt opposition from Lancashire to the women's work than in the less prosperous mid-sixties and eighties. By the 1880s the Lancashire pit women were averaging 1/8d to 1/10d daily with forewomen receiving a few pence extra. At Atherton wages were 9/- weekly while Wigan Coal and Iron Company paid 10/-.[166] At J. and R.

Stone's New Railway pit at Garswood Park in 1888 a browman earned 3/6d daily but the women only between 1/4d and 1/8d (depending on age).[167] In July and August of that year Sarah and Elizabeth Shaw (both brow women) got 8/- and 10/- respectively for their six-day week yet Robert Davies earned £1.1.6d for the same work and time.

Nor was it easy to remedy the situation. In 1891 the Wigan paper, the *Comet*, which supported miners' causes drew attention to the fact that Pearson and Knowles had not fulfilled a promise of a ten per cent advance to the pit women.[168] Yet lacking any union protection for the whole century, the women were in a very vulnerable position. Employers and workmen in the Midlands had agreed in 1888 that advances should be paid to all manipulating coal (therefore including females) but this never materialised.[169] As late as 1908 some Lancashire girls were starting work at 10d a day.[170]

Wages in other parts of the country were low. In the 1880s the average pay for Whitehaven women was between 1/3d and 1/8d daily and Scottish pit head workers were only getting 1/4d to 1/6d. The 1892 Report of the Royal Commission on Labour revealed that Welsh women got between 6/3d and 10/6d weekly for oiling trams, 4/6d to 10/- for unloading coal but still only about 1/- a day for screening.[171] Martha Jane Waters and eight other trammers and screeners earned only 1/- a day at Lower Level colliery, Kilgetty, Pembrokeshire in the 1890s. Twenty-three days' work gave them £1.3.0d but men doing the same work and working for half a day less got £2.5.0d. Filling cobbles paid only 9d a day.[172] West Wales mining families remained closely tied to the land and low incomes were supplemented by keeping some livestock and growing vegetables. Munby also found that they followed an old tradition of knitting and selling woollen stockings. In the eighteenth century Welsh women, generally the daughters of small farmers from Tregaron and surrounding districts in Cardiganshire used to walk two hundred miles to London following the drovers' roads, knitting stockings as they walked. The proceeds from their sales helped to pay for their lodgings whilst they worked in the market gardens.[173]

A summer season in market gardening in fact remained one way for Staffordshire and Shropshire pit women and nail and chain makers to supplement their incomes in the nineteenth century. Their wages at the pits were poor — Becky Price was getting only 7/- a fortnight at Ketley Bank in 1888.[174] Some women worked in the Martley area of Worcestershire and in the Vale of Evesham though the majority travelled to Middlesex to the gardens at North Hyde, Brentford, Hounslow, Twickenham and Isleworth. Market gardening had a long

season which began in May and required a large number of helpers.
Most women stayed about three months. By the late-1880s Middlesex
was becoming less popular as the three-monthly railway ticket to
Southall now cost 15/-. Masters in Gloucestershire (where fruit was
sent direct to jam works and thus eliminated some of the intermediary
processes) were however prepared to pay rail fares so many transferred
there.[175] The work was varied and in the London area included
carrying fruit to Covent Garden. Women helped weed and plant early
in the season, also pick pears, apples, strawberries, gooseberries and
strip currant bushes. Others gathered beans, picked peas and dug
onions. It was strenuous work even for those accustomed to demanding
outdoor employment and in the 1860s field work paid only between
6/- and 8/- a week.[176] Becky got 10/- for a week of dunging and digging
in 1885. Fruit picking was paid by the piece and so gatherers were
dependent on the weather and type of crop. In the 1870s the highest
wages were over £1 a week but involved working from 3 a.m. until
8 p.m. The women lived simply − at Isleworth some paid 1/- to stay in
rather cramped lodgings but others preferred to save money and sleep
in empty haylofts and sheds. There were some clashes between the
Shropshire women (known as 'Sloppies') and the Irish as the latter were
prepared to work for lower rates. The police had to provide protection
for the pit women after one incident which involved an attack on their
shed.[177]

The women were generally able to save about four or five pounds
and some sent additional money home. The work was apparently seen
as a welcome break and nest egg to help them and their families
through the.year.[178] The visits would depend on the state of the coal
market. In 1872 for instance, wages at the pits were comparatively
high and few women went south. Those who did so found that it did
not cover expenses so few went the following year. A strike in 1874 at
Shropshire pits resulted in many returning to the market gardens. Some
went time and again − in 1891 Munby found one woman who had been
going regularly to Wilmot's gardens at Spring Grove for twenty two
years.

The seasonal absence of a number of women did not seem to disturb
seriously the labour supply at the pits.[179] Munby was told that
alternative girls were always available to do the work and at the
Lilleshall pits men replaced the fifty or sixty women who went away
for the season. Yet for some miners the possibility of replacing women
by men was a crucial consideration. Even though the product of the
women's labour was equal in value to that of the men's they were

generally paid only about half of the men's wages. This encouraged
the continued employment of female workers and could be interpreted
as a means of keeping down the price of the men's own labour. When
women were prevented by law from doing nightwork at Nantyglo in
South Wales, men replaced them and were paid double the women's
wages.[180] Relations between male and female workers were soured by
the consciousness of this discrepancy in pay. The miners sought to
remedy the situation by urging female exclusion. Although they viewed
surface labour as less skilled than underground employment (and work
at the belts in particular might be seen as appropriate for women), the
high incidence of pit accidents ensured that there was a supply of
disabled miners who deserved the opportunity to continue working.
The women were seen to be usurping the rightful jobs of men.

Such cheap labour was felt to be particularly unfair in an already
overstocked labour market. The *Iron and Coal Trades Review* deplored
the fact that 'in this overcrowded country, for every woman employed
in any occupation other than in those exclusively suited to her sex, a
man must be left idle'.[181] George Howell who accompanied miners'
representatives to the Home Office in 1887 argued in *The Conflicts of
Capital and Labour* that those who wanted liberty for women were
really meaning liberty for the employer 'first, to pit one woman against
another, and secondly, to put them in antagonism to the men'.[182] He
believed that the less they competed with men in the coal mining
industry, the better it would be for both sexes. The miners' fears were
reinforced by local incidents. At Haydock local coalowners voiced their
opposition to the erection of a mill. It was feared that this would
threaten to remove cheap labour, i.e. women, from the surface. At a
pit near Leigh where men could earn 19/- a week there was a deliberate
policy of replacing these men with women.[183]

The experience of 1842 had helped formulate an official union
response to women's work at pits.[184] Yet recognising that complaints
couched in terms of wage differentials would simply produce
criticisms of economic self-interest, the miners carefully emphasised
other aspects of the work, particularly their belief in the moral code of
domesticity. This was most clearly expressed in the 1860s at the Select
Committee on Mines. The questions and duration of interviews varied
but female labour featured prominently with thirty-five of the
witnesses being quizzed on this subject. Those miners connected with
female-employing districts were especially encouraged to air their views
and all six West Lancashire miners spoke against female pit work with
conviction and a striking uniformity. It was denounced a⌐ degrading to

the sex. When pressed for further explanation, the witnesses remained adamant and their arguments consistent. They urged the moral opposition to the work, arguing that it prevented a woman fulfilling her domestic duties. Peter Dickenson of Aspull Moor echoed the general sentiment when he claimed that a woman with children could not carry out her duty to them. William Pickard was more explicit:

> Their absence from home leaves domestic duties entirely in a jumblement and when the husband comes home it leads to much unpleasantness and altercation and leads the men to go and spend their time elsewhere.[185]

He emphasised that if a mother lacked the means of teaching her children she could not make them 'take the road to greatness'.[186]

Looking back on the controversy in 1889 the ex-miner John Monk Foster felt, like others, that the real motives for urging exclusion had been suppressed — deliberately.

> No feelings of charity actuated the men who took up the cry; they had not chivalrous regard for the weaker sex; it was not that they deemed the labour too arduous or that it had a tendency to demoralise the worker; it was because they regarded pit brow women as rivals in the labour market and wished to have the field to themselves.[187]

Certainly the miners were not seeking to remedy the problem by asking that the women be paid more — the idea of equal wages was only being acknowledged very tentatively by some TUC members in the mid-1880s. Instead they were wanting them to be removed. Yet in one sense they were being no more than realistic in their demands. They knew only too well that they faced a huge stumbling block. Colliery owners were hardly likely to entertain even the possibility of increasing the wages of one section of their workforce, particularly during the difficult years of the mid-sixties and eighties, especially since they knew that the women were not in a position to protest via union channels.

The miners' cautious and controlled emphasis needs to be seen as more than a contrivance by which they could forestall criticisms. They did genuinely worry about the effect of the work on women and the family, a worry which forced them to see this conflict in terms of gender rather than class. But their fears were to a large extent prompted by their employers' attitudes towards the women. It is interesting to note how the coalowners' belief in a woman's natural place being in the home broke down at this point. They applied it to their own wives but did not extend it to their female employees. As with work below ground, they could say that they did not engage the women directly or personally. Now the double standard which operated against all women was re-doubled in the case of working-class women. The employers did not recognise that a conscience or responsibility could be their concern. This had been clearly demonstrated in the aftermath of 1842. It was only when the livelihood of the pit lasses was threatened, and thereby cheap labour and the strong economic position of the masters placed in jeopardy, that they began to evince an interest in the women's cause.

They too were highly conscious of the economic difficulties. George Gilroy, manager of Ince Hall, explained to the Select Committee that women were earning between 1/2d and 1/9d a day. Prohibiting their work would mean that men would have to replace them and be paid considerably more. Male workers on the surface were already getting 2/6d to 3/- a day. The heavier work could not be done by boys (an admission that the work was not all of a light nature as was frequently claimed!) so any alteration would be costly. According to one Shropshire manager, female exclusion would mean a thirty to forty per cent increase in the wages being paid out to ten per cent of his colliery workforce.[188]

The pit brow controversy was, in a number of respects, convenient for the coalowners. It provided an excuse for 'union bashing'. It was questioned whether a nation which had 'cast off the tyranny of Kings was now to obey meekly to dictates of the trades unions'. The *Church Reformer*'s interest in the pit brow issue was directed against what it called 'socialism of the benevolent policeman kind' which was used against the weak and unprotected:

> the trades unions feel that they are not strong enough permanently, even to save themselves; they are feeling after a true socialism but they have not yet found it nor yet openly acknowledge that they are seeking it.[189]

At the same time the existence of a moral code which argued that woman's true place was in the home encouraged both the women and men to see female employment as transient. Though in practice the coalowners ignored the domestic ideology, they recognised its value in helping to justify the women's wages as supplemental. The men reacted to the women's work in terms of sex solidarity rather than seeing them as part of the working class which must collectively resist capitalist exploitation. A workforce which was not completely united (particularly since the women were not union members) was less of a threat to the employers. Keeping the women employed was therefore not only advantageous in economic terms but also served a useful purpose in driving a wedge between sections of the workforce.

The miners' union recognised these problems and so justified their endorsement of exclusion proposals in terms which showed concern for the women and at the same time protected themselves. They also had to meet the criticism that they had not prohibited the work voluntarily. They did this by urging the necessity of legislation in order to make measures effective. Recognising that not all miners subscribed to a policy of excluding women, they countered attacks by claiming that miners might be divided into two classes, the 'thinking' ones and the rest.[190] William Pickard argued that the latter were too fond of spending the pit women's money for them — at the pub.

The union official's position was becoming increasingly professional and the gulf between him and the rank and file was widening appreciably. Pickard's career, in fact, demonstrates this effectively.[191] He had moved a considerable way from the pit he had entered at the age of seven and had become distanced in outlook from many of the men he claimed to represent. A temperance advocate and Wesleyan Methodist lay preacher, he had in 1863 been a delegate with his brother George to the Leeds conference and was chosen as Vice-President. He then became the treasurer of the Miners' National Association. The miners' agent for the Wigan area, he was in later life made one of the first workmen-magistrates, a member of the Board of Guardians and of the School Board and a director of the Mechanics Institute. A close associate of John Lancaster he even had £365 invested in shares in the Wigan Coal and Iron Company and was a director of a North Wales colliery. A successful autodidact, it was said that he would rather see the miners possessing a higher degree of intellectual ability than even an advance of twenty per cent upon their wages — 'a man's happiness does not consist of pounds, shillings and pence but in the honourable performance of duties that were calculated to benefit mankind'. A witness before every House of Commons committee of coalmining from 1860 until his death in 1887, Pickard became the official spokesman for the Wigan miners. Yet his caution and increasingly conciliatory behaviour in strikes made many miners disenchanted with their agent. No doubt his indisputable bravery and relentless effort in mine rescue work (he led a number of rescue teams personally) saved him from becoming even more unpopular. Nevertheless, his tendency to urge restraint and gradual desertion of the working class were spelt out in a Wigan Broadside of 1880:

> It is quite time we should see that his aim is personal gain. His interests are not ours. How can he devote his time to us while acting as a political agent?[192]

In the strike of the following year his efforts to get the men to agree to the owners' demands severed his connections with the union.

Pickard was the most outspoken opponent of the Wigan pit work yet, though influential, his beliefs were not fully representative of the views of the local miners. Not only were many men not even union members but even within the union, many would not subscribe to the official attitude of opposition towards the women. Munby found critics of Pickard's attitude towards pit women. One miner at Barley Brook colliery told him that the agent had exceeded his instructions in 1866 and did not always tell the truth.[193] For the ordinary miner the fears about cheap labour would have had a more direct relevance than the sort of arguments he adduced. In fact for miners with daughters working, a very different type of argument might hold sway. The prospect of forbidding women's work raised another kind of economic problem, the possibility of cutting off a vital source of income. This was a possibility which seemed all the more worrying when the consequences of 1842 were borne in mind.

The divisions between the official union attitude and local sentiment became even more marked in the 1880s when physical, moral and economic arguments about female pit work were viewed as symptomatic of wider problems about women's right to work.[194] A miners' conference at Manchester in 1887 showed clearly these internal divisions. Although a number of delegates spoke in favour of exclusion, Sam Woods pointed out that although he personally felt that female labour ought to be allowed to die out by itself, as a Lancashire representative, he felt obliged to mention that he had no authority from his members for speaking for or against abolition.[195] He admitted that the predominant feeling in his coalfield was against it and that the reactions of the girls themselves were so strong that he could not feel justified in advocating their exclusion. Thomas Oakes of Hindley substantiated this by pointing out that Lancashire would be badly handicapped by such a step and an already glutted market in the

colliery and mill district would be placed in an even worse position.
Thomas Burt and Benjamin Pickard (North Riding) were both from
non-female-employing areas and were embarrassed and disturbed by
the split. Pickard pointed out that it would be misleading for both the
government and the country if the miners expressed doubt at the
eleventh hour. Burt reminded them that a resolution had previously
been passed at the Birmingham conference with an overwhelming
majority against female employment. Moreover the miners' deputation
to the Home Office in 1886 had not shown dissension. To re-discuss
the subject and even hint at a lack of approval of earlier trades union
activity now that the mines bill was about to go into committee would
be cutting the ground from beneath them. Several representatives then
spoke about the awkward position of the Lancashire miners and it was
explained that it was not that there was a lack of unanimity but that
the situation was such that the Lancashire delegates wanted it known
that they did not represent people whose views were united on this
question. The chairman then ruled that no new resolutions could be
drafted in view of previous conference discussions on the matter and it
was then dropped.

The truth was that opinion was not as unanimous as the miners
wanted people to believe. Quite apart from differing viewpoints
between rank and file union members and the labour aristocrats, the
divisions within the ranks of the union officials were only concealed
because Lancashire miners were not represented in Parliament.[196]
Union opposition in the Commons emanated from representatives of
non-female-employing colliery districts. Here differences between
miners were restricted to the question of how long it might take to
enforce exclusion rather than considering whether it was a wise move in
the first place. In spite of the conference statement smoothing over the
dilemma of the Lancashire delegates, miners did have a duty to
represent the views of the people in their districts. Moreover some
unease had been expressed about the decisions taken in 1886. Thomas
Glover, a miners' representative for St Helens, had complained that the
Birmingham resolution against female employment had been rushed
through without discussion after he and other Lancashire delegates had
left the conference. Some of the miners who attended the union
deputation to the Home Office regretted that they had not spoken out
against the views uttered by Burt and later disclaimed any desire for
prohibition of the women's work.[197] The inspector for West Lancashire
explained that although trades union agents had pledged their support
for exclusion they had had 'good reason for stating that this wish was

far from being unanimous or even general.[198] Letters to the local press bear this out — one from a miner who claimed to know 150 pit women commented that he and the people of Ince were deeply grieved by the exclusion proposals.[199]

In their localities both Woods and Oakes supported the pit women. Sam Woods had been agent for Ashton since 1881 (and was the son of a woman miner). He sent a letter to a Bryn meeting in support of the women where he pointed out the considerable differences of opinion which existed among the miners.[200] Although reluctant to commit himself fully, he did stress that in the present state of depression, any repressive legislative interference would be wrong. He explained that he had worked for many years as a checkweighman and could bear testimony to the good character, morals and industrious behaviour of the women. Thomas Oakes, agent for Hindley and Westhoughton, was more positive in his support and for this was denounced by the Miners and Checkweighmans Association of Hindley in 1887. He had condemned the idea of female prohibition at a meeting of about fifty West Leigh miners. After explaining the disastrous results it would cause for them and their families, a resolution had been unanimously adopted by the miners in favour of the retention of the pit women and condemning any proposals for legislation to the contrary. Oakes, along with several other miners' agents, accompanied the pit brow women to the Home Office in 1887.[201]

Oakes and miners such as Kay, Wogan, Tranter, Battersby and Glover were in an awkward position and were hesitant to voice too strongly viewpoints which could be interpreted as divisive for their union. They did, however, express themselves more forcefully at local meetings. William Wogan, President of St Helens Miners Association, had worked with pit girls at Pemberton. He admitted that not all trades unionists had been appealed to on this subject and was convinced that if the miners of south-west Lancashire were polled, ninety-nine out of every hundred would vote for the women to continue at work.[202] Stephen Walsh who became Vice-President of the Miners' Federation spoke on behalf of the pit brow women in 1886. He married Ann Adamson, a pit brow girl from Ashton, and in 1911 became the leading Parliamentary spokesman in defence of their work.[203] Opinion was also divided in South Wales. Whilst Will Abraham (Mabon) could declare that the 'angels of humanity' should not be seen among the grease and dust of the mine, and Merthyr Trades Council could pass a resolution condemning the work, Tredegar working men were urging active support for the local pit women.[204]

The economic argument was a complex one and could not easily be divorced from physical and moral criticisms. It hinged around the undeniable fact that the women were cheap labour but it was complicated by other issues, local pride and family situations making a considerable difference to the way the miners themselves viewed the work. The comment made by Sir John Burnett, Labour correspondent to the Board of Trade, about chain and nail-makers was also appropriate for the pit brow lasses.[205] He explained that they were caught between 'the devil of cheap labour competition and the deep sea of family poverty'. In the last resort the miners, both male and female were dependent on the owners' policy. This policy was neatly summed up by their organ the *Colliery Guardian*:

> If women perform the work better than men, for wages they are content with and glad to receive, why should men be employed at somewhat higher wages and yet not so high as they might obtain at other branches from which women are very properly excluded?[206]

The campaign against the women's work needs to be seen against the network of relations existing between the male workforce and the employer. By viewing the implications of female exclusion in this light the opposition which the women encountered from some, though by no means all, the miners becomes more comprehensible.

This opposition reached its climax on 20 June 1887 when the mines bill reached the committee stage. Wry comments were made about the stony heart of the Home Secretary having been touched by the visit of the pit brow women. Worried by the speed with which the bill was being rushed through Parliament, opponents now sought to delay its progress. John Ellis, Liberal member for Rushcliffe, Nottingham (a colliery owner from a non-female-employing area) made one last bid to curb female pit work.[207] He wanted to prevent the engagement of girls other than those who were already at work. His amendment proposed that no newcomers under sixteen should be permitted. On 23 June after some discussion a test division was taken on this amendment. A majority of 76 prevented its acceptance — 188 voting against altering the bill and 112 supporting the amendment.[208] Examination of the division lists shows that although there was a split along party lines (147 in favour of the women were Conservatives and only 29 were Liberals), nevertheless a significant determinant was whether or not a member represented a female-employing district. In the last resort Lancashire members overwhelmingly supported the women — sixteen

Lancashire MPs and the Manchester members voted in their favour
with only two Lancashire MPs voting against them. Opposing the
women were 72 Liberals (and some Irish Nationalists) and only twelve
Conservatives, the latter largely representing areas of non-female
employment.

Following the failure of Ellis's amendment there was some discussion
about the age at which girls might start work. Twelve was chosen in
preference to ten though this could hardly be said to represent a
triumph for the exclusionists as only two girls below thirteen were
actually at work and those already in employment were allowed to
continue. Concentration on such issues does however suggest the
continued ignorance of many members of the actual situation at
collieries. The Durham MP John Wilson, who had sought the total
exclusion of women from any kind of pit work in his maiden speech in
Parliament in 1886, later admitted that quite apart from never having
visited Wigan, he had never seen pit brow women at work.[209] In the
words of one woman chain-maker, 'It's very 'ard upon the pore
gentleman to 'ave to make the laws, and not to know nothing about
it'.[210]

After passing its third reading on 3 September the bill's passage
through the Lords was rapid. The Mines and Collieries Act (50 and 51
Vict c 58) received the Royal Assent on 16 September 1887 and any
female over twelve could still be engaged to work at the pit top. The
case of the pit brow lasses had demonstrated that outdoor work for
women was not to be easily or hastily swept away. Ironically when
female pit work did end many years later, it was due to mechanisation
and decline in the industry rather than as a result of pressure for the
removal of the pit brow lasses by legislation.

Notes

1. These are compiled from the inspectors' reports on mines 1854-91 and
from newspaper sources.
2. PP 1858, XXXII, p.75.
3. PP 1861, XXII, p.8. See also PP 1839, XII, p.93.
4. PP 1867, XVI, p.179.
5. *Morning Chronicle*, 21 March 1850.
6. PP 1868, XIX.1, p.97.
7. PP 1866, XIV, p.206, qu.6842-5.
8. PP 1864, XXIV.1, p.103.
9. PP 1863, XXIV, p.46. The Children's Employment Commission had
provided some early examples – for example Ann Jenkins (12) at Graig Colliery,
Merthyr Tydfil. PP 1842, XVII, no.49, p.513.

10. PP 1854-5, XV, p.105.
11. PP 1864, XXIV.1, p.165; 1870, XV, p.129.
12. T.E. Lones, *A History of Mining in the Black Country* (Dudley, 1899), p.58.
13. PP 1861, XXII, p.29.
14. PP 1874, XIII, p.76.
15. *Liverpool Weekly Chronicle*, 7 April 1906.
16. PP 1861, XXII, p.106.
17. PP 1885, XV, p.247. Robert Woodward, a collier from Haydock, explained to the Select Committee on Mines (1866) that lowering wagons and braking could be particularly dangerous on wet mornings. PP 1866, XIV, p.1886, qu.2963. *The Wigan Examiner*, 16 January 1886, reported the case of a sixteen-year-old wagon-trimmer from Hindley being run over by six wagons on a wet day when the rails were slippery.
18. PP 1891, XXII.1, p.11.
19. PP 1879, XVIII, p.430.
20. PP 1887, XXII, p.208. Mary Golding of Wood pit, Pemberton, was killed in 1856. Horses pulled the wagons at her pit and they moved as she was dressing the coal so she fell between them. PP 1857, XVI, p.92; *Wigan Observer*, 30 August 1856.
21. *Comet*, no.9 (4 May 1889).
22. PP 1865, XX, p.55.
23. PP 1867, XVI, p.56.
24. Ibid., p.50; Munby MS, Diary 33, 5 October 1865.
25. PP 1867, XVI, Preface.
26. PP 1882, XVIII, p.86.
27. *Wigan Observer*, 25 February 1859.
28. See Ch.3. *Wigan Observer*, 1 December 1865, 24 February, 10, 17 March 1866; PP 1866, XIV, p.86, qu.2964; PP 1867, XVI, p.60.
29. *Wigan Observer*, 11 December 1865. The *Observer* later defended the women's work, thus upholding the coalowners' interests and reacting against the slur being cast on Wigan by other newspapers.
30. PP 1886, XVI, p.256.
31. PP 1855, XV, p.75; Munby MS, Diary 6, 29 September 1860.
32. PP 1864, XXIV, p.86.
33. PP 1877, XXIII, p.155.
34. The peak years for deaths from surface accidents were 1866 (107 recorded), 1873 (109), 1876 (111), 1883 (108).
35. Hansard CCXII, House of Commons, 26 June 1872, p.183.
36. PP 1858, XXXII, p.64.
37. Open Door Council, *Restrictive Legislation and the Industrial Women Workers* (February, 1928).
38. At Garswood Hall a woman got suctioned down the shaft when a rush of air caught her skirt. Lancashire and Cheshire Joint District Committee, 'Arbitration on the Scale of Minimum Wages for Females' (NUM, Bolton, 1919), p.29. See also PP 1856, XVIII, p.35.
39. PP 1858, XXXII, p.96.
40. See P.E.H. Hair, 'Deaths from Violence in Britain. A Tentative Secular Survey', *Population Studies* (1971), p.20.
41. Edgar Wakeman felt tipping to be the most strenuous and cumbersome job yet he admitted that women did this in a way which 'would electrify even an American woman's rights promoter'. *Wigan Observer*, 12 September 1891.
42. Interviewed 25 October 1974.
43. Joint District Committee, 'Arbitration', p.26.

44. PP 1866, p.365, qu.10836.
45. Munby MS, Notebook IV, 1869.
46. Hansard XXXII, House of Commons, 5 December 1911, p.1255.
47. Women's Work, Box 1. Munitions 6, 7. Imperial War Museum. I am grateful to Deborah Thom for this reference.
48. Hansard CCCXVI, House of Commons, 23 June 1887, pp.795-7.
49. *Wigan Observer*, 7 October 1911.
50. *Illustrated London News*, LXXXVIII, no.2447 (1886).
51. *Globe*, 3 July, 1896.
52. Quoted in *Wigan Observer*, 20 May 1887. See, for example, A. Foley, *A Bolton Childhood* (Manchester, 1973), pp.51-3 for descriptions of mill work. See also J.O. Foster, *Class Struggle and the Industrial Revolution* (London, 1974), p.92 which discusses consumption and women mill workers in Oldham.
53. See J. Schmeichen, 'State Reform and the Local Economy', *Economic History Review*, 2nd series, XXVIII, no.3 (1975).
54. *Women's Industrial News*, October 1911.
55. Interviewed 24 August 1978.
56. Ibid.
57. Munby MS, Diary 41, 12 September 1873. The inspector Dickinson told the Select Committee on Mines that the women were 'a picture of health'. PP 1866, XIV, p.228, qu.7372.
58. Compiled from Munby's diaries and notebooks for the 1860s.
59. *Wigan Observer*, 17 April 1886.
60. Ibid., 9 February 1886.
61. F. Hird, *Lancashire Stories* (London, 1912), p.414.
62. *Manchester Guardian*, 31 March 1886.
63. Letter from former collier about Alice James BEM (colliery worker of Tredegar), kindly supplied by Tredegar council.
64. The Wigan Coal and Iron Company had its own scheme. At the Ince Hall pits a woman paid half the rate of other members. Ince Hall Sick and Burial Society rules, 1852, Wigan Public Library.
65. See jacket.
66. T. Oliver, *Dangerous Trades* (London, 1902), p.280.
67. Munby MS, Visits to Hannah, 10, 14 January 1890, 16, 24 November 1891.
68. Joint District Committee, 'Arbitration', p.21.
69. Interviewed 25 August 1978.
70. Interviewed 24 August 1978.
71. Munby MS, Visits to Hannah, 17, 19 January 1892.
72. Interviewed 24 August 1978.
73. PP 1842, XVII, no.36, p.230.
74. Interviewed 23 July 1974.
75. Interviewed 25 August 1978.
76. Interviewed 6 March 1974.
77. Interviewed 25 August 1978.
78. *Morning Chronicle*, 3 January 1850.
79. J. Plummer, *Once A Week*, XI (1864). The Select Committee on Mines heard in 1866 that the trousers 'drowned all sense of decency'. PP 1866, XIV, p.21, qu.679.
80. Hansard CCXII, House of Commons, 21 June 1872, p.31.
81. Munby MS, Diary 37, 18 August 1869; Notebook III, 1866.
82. *Manchester Guardian*, 17, 18 April 1873.
83. *The Times*, 16 May 1883; *Daily News*, 1 August 1868.
84. Transactions of the Iron, Stone, Coal and Lime Association of Great

Britain (1863), p.141.
85. Munby MS, Diary 17, 1 March 1863; 38, 25 June 1870; 40, 7 June 1872; 42, 4 June 1874.
86. Ibid., Notebook III, 1866.
87. Mrs Holden, *True Story of a Lancashire Pit Brow Lass* (n.d.).
88. Interviewed 25 August 1978.
89. J.M. Bankes, 'A Nineteenth Century Colliery Railway', *Transactions of the Historic Society of Lancashire and Cheshire*, 114 (1966), p.173. Ebbw Vale women were provided with canvas aprons and stout shoes. A. Gray Jones, *A History of Ebbw Vale* (Risca, 1977), p.118.
90. Hird, *Stories*, p.414. This eventually turned full circle – the last women wore overalls.
91. *Wigan Observer*, 12 September 1891.
92. Quoted in ibid., 25 March 1884.
93. *Woman's Signal*, 9 July 1896.
94. *Wigan Observer*, 25 March 1886.
95. Plummer, *Once A Week*, p.279.
96. *Bristol Mercury*, 29 April 1865.
97. Interviewed by R. Keen, 8 June 1970.
98. Transcript from Ken Howerth of Bury Museum to whom I am indebted.
99. I. Hunt, 'The Lakeland Peddlar' in R. Samuel (ed.), *Miners and Quarrymen* (London, 1976), p.196.
100. *Cumberland Pacquet*, 13 April 1899. A photograph of Sal Madge was issued in the R and N postcard series.
101. *Complete Letters of Vincent Van Gogh II* (London, 1958). See letter 325, 1885, p.144, where he compared the pit men and women of Courrières with those of the Borinage. See also letter 277, 1883, p.17. His drawing of miners and pit girls returning from work was followed by a smaller version sent to his brother Theo in August 1888. 'Tekening mijnwerkers', Rijksmuseum, Amsterdam.
102. PP 1866, XIV, p.206, qu.6851.
103. Ibid., p.301, qu.19166.
104. Aberdare Public Library. See also L. Simonin, *La Vie Souterraine* (translated by Bristow as *Mines and Miners or Underground Life*, London, 1868), p.243. The candle in the girl's hat suggests that this stylised engraving was depicting work in the pit. Munby MS, Notebook I, 1866.
105. Interviewed 13 April 1976. I am grateful to Mrs Brown and Mr Griffiths, of Tredegar for information. Some wore hats on top of scarves like Welsh fisherwomen.
106. *Bristol Mercury*, 29 April 1865; Anon., *Tredegar Workmen's Hall 1861-1951, pp.16, 157.*
107. Ibid., Notebook III, 1866.
108. See the photograph by Dingley of women bankers at the Blue Fly pit, Ridding Lane, Wednesbury, in Dudley Museum. I am grateful to Michael Hiley for identifying this.
109. Munby MS, Notebook I, 1865. Little's studio was in Clarence Yard, Wigan. Sarah Fairhurst did not want to be 'draw'd aht in pit clas'. Diary 37, 10 October 1869; Diary 33, 4 October 1865. Another girl was worried about having her photograph displayed in a shop window because 'if mah feller should see it, he'd abaht kill ma'. Diary 6, 29 September, 1860. By the end of the century photographs taken at work were becoming popular.
110. Munby MS, Diary 21, 18 August 1863.
111. *Illustrated London News*, LXII, 18 January, 1, 8, 15 February 1873. The lock-out was described as a strike.
112. Munby MS, Diary 47, 20 April 1874. *Pictorial World*, 1, nos. 6, 7 (11, 18

April 1874). See also Cassell's *History of England*, IX (London, 1871), p.619. *Graphic*, no.460 (21 September 1878), no.463 (12 October 1878).
113. See H.E. Roberts, 'Marriage, Redundancy or Sin' in Vicinus (ed.), *Suffer and Be Still* (Bloomington, 1973), pp.45-76 which discusses painters' views of women in the mid-nineteenth century; *Athenaeum*, no.2428 (9 May 1874); F. Klingender, *Art and the Industrial Revolution* (London, 1968), illustration 113. I am grateful to Doug Gray for discussion on this subject. The Royal Academy exhibited 'The Lunch Hour Wigan' in 1874.
114. Arthur Wasse II was the son and father of Manchester artists with the same name. He exhibited in Manchester, Liverpool and London from 1878-95. A member of the Manchester Academy of Fine Arts from 1882, he exhibited for them and at a number of Lancashire galleries, painting chiefly in oils. Twelve of his pictures were exhibited at the Royal Academy and one at the Society of British Artists. He had studios in Manchester and London and eventually moved to Bavaria. His 'Lancashire Pit Girls' was exhibited at the Garswood Hall collieries in 1887. *Echo*, 17 May 1887; Munby MS, Diary 55, 1887. I am grateful to Arnold Hyde and Jeremy Maas for information.
115. *Lancet*, 30 July, 1887.
116. Munby MS, Diary 25, 19 May 1864.
117. The story was accepted in 1876 by the American journal *Scribner's Magazine* for serialisation on the strength of the first few chapters. F.H. Burnett, *That Lass O'Lowrie's* (London, 1877), p.1.
118. Ibid., and following quote.
119. *Punch*, 73, 13, 20, 27 October 1877; 3, 10, 17 November 1877.
120. *Ladies*, 1, no.25 (14 September 1872). It commented how 'as a rule their lives are kept out of sight and women's work is seen as trifling'.
121. Burnett, *Lass O'Lowrie's*, p.1.
122. Ibid.
123. Ibid.
124. Ibid., pp.102-3.
125. Ibid., p.165.
126. See *Wigan Observer*, 11 May 1877. A. Thwaite, *Waiting for the Party* (London, 1974), pp.14-15. Many of her stories, for example, *Seth*, the tale of a young miner in Tennessee (who eventually proved to be a girl) were based on Lancashire workers in the United States.
127. Munby MS, Visits to Hannah, 19, 22 September 1893.
128. *Manchester Guardian*, April 1873.
129. Munby MS, Diary 45, 19 September 1877.
130. Plummer, *Once A Week*, p.280. His article included pictures of Elizabeth Hunter and Caroline Jones which had been on sale in Wigan in 1863.
131. PP 1864, XXII, p.14.
132. See J. Kitteringham, 'Country Girls in Nineteenth Century England', *History Workshop*, Pamphlet II (1973), p.71; *Mining Journal*, 31 October 1885.
133. E.A. Rymer, 'The Martyrdom of the Mine' in *History Workshop Journal*, 1 (Spring, 1976), pp.220-44 (edited by R. Neville). A petition from Northumberland and Durham signed by 4,965 miners described the work as a 'foul blot on the civilisation and humanity of the Kingdom'. Appendix to 6th Report on Public Petitions (1865). Appendix 128, p.64.
134. *Manchester Guardian* in *Wigan Observer*, 11 May 1867.
135. K. Millet, 'The Debate over Women. Ruskin versus Mill'. Vicinus, *Suffer and Be Still*, pp.130-1.
136. F. Basch, *Relative Creatures* (London, 1974), p.8. See also K. Thomas, 'The Double Standard', *Journal of the History of Ideas*, XX, 2 (1958).
137. *Leigh Journal and Times* in *Colliery Guardian*, 5 February 1886.

138. Munby MS, Diary 6, 29 September 1860.
139. *Shafts*, IV, no.12 (December 1896).
140. *Women's Suffrage Journal*, II, no.21 (1 November 1871). Mrs Butler had previously visited Wigan in 1871 to speak about women's poverty and oppression. She attended the deputation and wrote to the *Pall Mall Gazette* about the dangers of swelling the ranks of prostitution through female pit exclusion. *Wigan Observer*, 13 May 1887.
141. *Wigan Times*, 7 April 1860.
142. *Mining Journal*, 31 October 1885.
143. *Women's Union Journal*, V, no.5 (March 1880).
144. Transactions of the Iron, Stone, Coal and Lime Association (1863), p.XII.
145. *Revue Industrielle de Charleroi*, 5 September 1886.
146. Rymer, 'Martyrdom'.
147. PP 1866, XIV, p.227, qu.7351.
148. See *Wigan Observer*, 20, 27 March 1886.
149. PP 1866, XIV, p.450, qu.12973.
150. *Wigan Observer*, 2 July 1886. See evidence of Miss Orme to the Royal Commission on Labour, PP 1892, IV, p.238: 'I came across no married women in the coal, iron, slate and tin trades, nor in the brickyards. There are some widows, and I saw a few very old women. The employers and residents agreed that married women were never employed in these industries in Wales.' A few married women were employed in the Tredegar area – E. Powell, *History of Tredegar* (Newport, 1902), p.116, and O. Jones, *The Early Days of Sirhowy and Tredegar* (Risca, 1975), p.118.
151. For recent consideration see L. Tilly and J. Scott, *Women, Work and Family* (London, 1978) and Basch, *Creatures*.
152. *Woman Worker*, 12 June 1908.
153. *Spectator*, 27 March 1886. For a discussion of the early-twentieth-century attitudes see A. Davin, 'Imperialism and Motherhood', *History Workshop Journal*, 5 (Spring 1978) pp.9-65.
154. *Manchester Guardian*, 18 April 1873. See A. Kessler-Harris, 'Women, Work and the Social Order' in B.A. Carroll (ed.), *Liberating Women's History* (Urbana, 1976), where American trades union attitudes towards nineteenth-century female factory labour are discussed. A report of 1836 from a National Trades Union Committee explained that the female 'in a measure stands in the way of the male when attempting to raise his prices, or equalize his labor, and that her efforts to sustain herself and family, are actually the same as tying a stone around the neck of her natural protector, Man, and destroying him with the weight she has brought to his assistance. This is the true and natural consequence of female labor when carried beyond the family.' Quoted on p.335.
155. See W.C. Lubenow, *The Politics of Government Growth* (Newton Abbot, 1971), p.158. In the 1830s arguments defending women's factory work had drawn upon the writings of economists such as Ricardo and Smith in stressing the women's labour as their sole form of property.
156. *Wigan Observer*, 9 December 1859.
157. Sir R. Temple, *Letters and Character Sketches from the House of Commons* (London, 1912), Letter CXCII, pp.385-6.
158. Joint District Committee, 'Arbitration', p.22. A story in the *Wigan Observer*, 12 August 1887, explained that it was customary in Lancashire colliery villages for girls to be paid 1d for each year of their life until they were 18 when their wages remained at 1/6d.
159. PP 1842, XVII, no.247, p.374; XVI, p.12, nos. 23 and 24 HB.
160. Munby MS, Diary 20, 18 August 1863.
161. *Idem*, Notebook III, 1866, 110[7].

162. T.A. Owen, *The History of the Dowlais Iron Works* (Risca, 1977), Appendix B, pp.117-18.

163. *Miner and Workman's Advocate*, 23, 30 April 1864. Rymer, 'Martyrdom'.

164. Munby MS, Notebook III, 1866.

165. Holden, *True Story*.

166. *Wigan Observer*, 3 February 1886.

167. Garswood Colliery Surface Time Books show deductions of 6/- and 7/6d monthly for coal and 2/2d and 2/7d for rent. NCST 23/1, 24/2, Lancashire Record Office, Preston.

168. *Comet*, no.1 (12 January 1889).

169. Joint District Committee, 'Arbitration', p.7.

170. Interviewed 24 August 1978.

171. PP 1892, IV, pp.38, 186.

172. Grove and Lower Level collieries Time Book, March 1897. Wales Tourist Board, Kilgetty, Dyfed. Transcript of interview with Mrs Richards.

173. J. Williams-Davies, *'Merched y Gerddi. A* seasonal migration of female labour from rural Wales', *Folk Life*, 15 (1977), pp.12-21.

174. Shropshire women had worked there in the late eighteenth century. M. Ramelson, *The Petticoat Rebellion. A Century of Struggle for Women's Rights* (London, 1972), p.25. Munby MS, Visits to Hannah 6, 3 April 1886.

175. R. Samuel, 'Comers and Goers' in H.J. Dyos and M. Wolff (eds.), *The Victorian City*, 1 (London, 1973), pp.137-8; R. Samuel (ed.), *Village Life and Labour* (London, 1975), p.12; *Edinburgh Review*, 117 (1863), p.436.

176. Munby MS, Visits to Hannah, 5, 24 April 1889; 8, 1 October 1885. Some Black Country women went hopping but this does not appear to have been popular with pit women.

177. *Idem*, Diary 19, 23 May 1863; Visits to Hannah, 5, 2, 5, 10 October 1888; Diary 38, 25 June 1870; Diary 40, 28 June 1872; Diary 42, 4, 6 June, 14 August 1875; Diary 44, 4 June 1876; Diary 45, 8 June 1877.

178. Visits to Hannah, 5, 10 October 1888. A.T. Pask, *The Eye of the Thames*, pp.148-9 in Dyos and Wolff, *Victorian City*, p.137. A story of an 'Oakengates Wench' by Mrs Lucy Cameron (n.d.) told how the women brought fine clothes as well as money to the Oakengates Wakes, some gained by 'London industry alone but many, it is feared, in a different way', in B. Trinder, *The Industrial Revolution in Shropshire* (Chichester, 1973), p.354; Munby MS, Diary 40, 7 June 1872; Diary 41, 17 June 1873; Diary 42, 4 June 1874; Visits to Hannah, 14, 4 June 1891.

179. PP 1866, XIV, p.450, qus. 13037, 13045.

180. Munby MS, Diary 38, 4 October 1870.

181. *Iron and Coal Trades Review*, 32, no.941 (12 March 1886).

182. G. Howell, *The Conflicts of Capital and Labour* (London, 1890), p.341.

183. *Leigh Journal* quoted in *Wigan Observer*, 3 February 1886.

184. See Ch.2.

185. PP 1866, XIV, p.21, qu.201.

186. Ibid., p.49, qus. 1750, 1773-5. See also p.37, qus. 1311-3; p.60, qus. 2257; p.86, qu.2987.

187. *Comet*, no.9 (4 May 1889).

188. PP 1866, XIV, p.364, qus. 10801-9.

189. In *Colliery Guardian*, 29 July 1887.

190. For example, 'The thinking men belonging to the mines abominably hate it', PP 1866, XIV, p.51, qu.1801; p.174, qu.5711. Female prohibition could be interpreted as evidence of progress. A miners' petition to the House of Commons in 1859 had placed it as part of an improvement programme along with

educational and inspection demands. *Wigan Observer,* 3 December 1859.

191. Born in Burnley in 1821, Pickard moved to Wigan and worked in the pits at a young age. He later became salesman to the executors of James Diggle of West Leigh. He investigated 24 colliery disasters and worked hard for the dependents of those killed in accidents. In 1862 he became Vice-President of the Miners National Provident Society and in 1873 was Vice-President of the National Permanent Relief Society. He was treasurer of the Wigan district of the Miners Association (1848) and was miners' agent from 1862. In 1874 he contended the Wigan seat as a 'Labour candidate' and came fourth. His first wife worked underground and his step-sister Ann Johnson was a pit brow lass. I am grateful to Messrs F. Smith and J. Smethurst for letting me use their unpublished material on Pickard.

192. Wigan Broadsides Collection. Wigan Record Office, Leigh.

193. Munby MS, Notebook III, 1866.

194. It is impossible to know the full extent of discussion in these conferences as edited accounts do not necessarily reflect the total amount of discussion and/or disagreement. The amount of alternative pressing business and the attitude of the person chairing each meeting would obviously influence the degree of discussion.

195. Reported in *Women's Suffrage Journal,* XVII, no.209 (2 May 1887).

196. See Epilogue.

197. Hansard CCCXVI, House of Commons, 23 June 1887, p.811.

198. PP 1887, XXII, p.190.

199. *Wigan Observer,* 23 April 1886.

200. *St Helens Newspaper,* 8 May 1886.

201. *Wigan Observer,* 20 May 1887.

202. *St Helens Newspaper,* 27 April 1886.

203. See Epilogue.

204. *Labour Tribune,* 18 June 1887. *Dictionary of Employment Open to Women,* no.1 (London, 1898), HD 6058, TUC Congress House; *Wigan Observer,* 7 May 1886; *Manchester Guardian,* 28 May 1886.

205. PP 1888, XCI, pp.12-19.

206. *Colliery Guardian,* no.1299, 20 November 1866.

207. Hansard CCCXVI, House of Commons, 20 June 1887, pp.643-6. For those who spoke in the debates of 20, 22, 23 June 1887 see A.V. John, 'Women Workers in British Coal Mining 1840-90, with special reference to West Lancashire', unpublished PhD thesis, University of Manchester, 1976, Ch.8, Section C, Appendix 1. Sixteen MPs, mainly Conservative, are known to have attended the deputation.

208. Parliamentary Divisions (1887), pp.699-701. F.W.S. Craig, *British Parliamentary Election Results 1885-1918* (London, 1974).

209. Miners Federation of Great Britain. Standing Committee B, House of Commons, 2 August 1911, pp.889-91.

210. Quoted in R. Strachey, *The Cause* (London, 1978), p.237.

CONCLUSION

The attention paid to the pit brow women in the 1880s did have some beneficial side-effects. The publicity helped to reveal differences in conditions, the press praising those collieries where screening methods were most advanced (for example Fletcher and Burrows Atherton pits in Lancashire). It also revealed the continuation of illegal practices. It had been only too easy to bypass the law. Munby had found that colliery wages were still being paid at Wigan pubs in 1860 although this had been prohibited in 1842.[1] Now further evasion of the law was exposed. For example, the *Leigh Journal* revealed in 1886 that a girl of eighteen had been employed locally to do night work although this had been made illegal in 1872.[2]

There had been a danger that concentration on the small number of pit brow women might emphasise them as a self-contained group and thus divert attention away from the need to improve conditions for all colliery workers. The enquiries, however, at least revealed deficiencies which in turn underlined the need for more general improvement. The inspector, Hall, urged that in order to forestall further criticism, employers should

> now take care that the women's occupation should be made as little liable as possible to the charges which were urged as a reason for its discontinuance.[3]

He suggested that greater protection from the weather might be secured at very little cost. At the time that he was writing (1887), only five pit-heads were covered in the whole of Lancashire.[4] However, although this provision (like supplying decent cabins for the women) was not costly, it was only very slowly adopted, as oral testimony has borne out. Investment in modern plant was potentially a much more profitable exercise and, prompted by competition, change tended to be in the direction of mechanisation. This did initially help by lightening the women's tasks, though in the long run it helped to remove them completely.

The pit brow debate of the 1880s succeeded in exposing a myth about women's pit work. Despite the empassioned rhetoric (which too often disguised a lack of knowledge), and some wildly inaccurate accounts, by the end of 1887, the overall impression was one which suggested that there was a vast difference between the work formerly performed by women below ground and that on the surface. The former, even divested of the outpourings of outraged moralists, could not be defended easily. Justification of work at the pit top was somewhat simpler, and the influence of its upholders eventually won the day. Quite apart from Munby's biased accounts, contemporary evidence does seem to suggest that, on the whole, the women were physically fit and strong (especially in comparison with many other women workers). Nevertheless it would be misleading to suggest that their work was therefore anywhere near the ideal that its powerful defenders claimed. Many of the latter were far removed from the pit themselves and even though oral testimony from former pit lasses emphasises the happy days at the picking belts, their evidence must be tempered by a recognition that memory is usually sweetened by time.

A closer look at the defence of female surface work reveals that, in the main, altruism was most definitely not the key to the debate. Women's evasion of the law after 1842 had not been an indication that the work was in any sense pleasant or enjoyed. Rather it had demonstrated exploitation, a desperation born of necessity and a double standard of values which generally exonerated the coalowner from culpability if his activities were discovered. This in turn contributed to the resistance of many miners to any form of women's colliery work whilst it also increased the women's dependence on their employers. In a similar way coalowners found it useful to retain female surface work and thereby antagonised male miners who saw the women as cheap labour. Moral critics meanwhile were concerned to assert the sanctity of the home. Thus the debate became a test case for them to disprove the rights of women as much as it provided an opportunity for upholders of women's rights to use it as a platform for their demands. Though both sides spoke loudly and at length about what was best for the women, little effort was made to listen to the latters' views. Admittedly the deputation was a concession to their feelings, but the sentimentality surrounding the occasion and its novelty value clearly removed it from the reality of everyday working life. Even after travelling to London, the women were barely given a chance to express their reactions. Atherley Jones later recalled how 'picturesque photographs of women carefully washed, doctored and dressed' were distributed and, as has been shown, they were placed in prominent positions on platforms at meetings where, of course, they wore their pit clothes.[5]

In fact, contemporary accounts of the pit brow women emphasised the idea of dressing up and at times they suggest the atmosphere of a carnival. The language used by both attackers and defenders of the work to describe the women frequently drew upon similar analogies and is extremely revealing as an indication of the ways in which they were perceived. A Royal visit to Lancashire was described by the press.[6] Commenting on the day's events, it was noted that one float in the procession had a 'curious prominence'. Coal proprietors had got two women 'dressed in those unmentionable nether garments' sitting in coal carts:

> As a part of the public procession, they were certainly a significant illustration, not so much of local trade as of Lancashire civilisation.

Mrs Burnett referred to their 'half savage existence' and an article in the *Morning Leader* commented on the 'hardy race' who pushed and handled trucks like 'industrial Amazons'.[7] Such imagery (which suggests that attitudes towards coalmining had not really progressed since the 1840s) extended beyond Britain. A book on the Belgian Borinage by the art historian Lemonnier referred to those 'rudes amazones du travail charbonnier' (those rough Amazons of colliery work).[8] The brute strength of the woman surface worker was stressed. She was like a wrestler and was robust and masculine in appearance. Her simple clothes were imprinted with coal from the tips which looked like the yoke of an ox. At the local *Kermesses* or fêtes she was the chrysalis transformed into the butterfly. On her way home from work, her singing, carefree behaviour and independence made her like the birds.

Edgar Wakeman's 'Beauties in Black' compared the women slack washers of Wigan with birds, though this time they were caged birds and the women were described as 'prisoned'.[9] Thus, although a common imagery had been employed, Wakeman's symbolism invoked the obverse of the qualities suggested by Lemonnier. Yet in both instances, their language was in part a response to their unfamiliarity with their subject matter, the product of a voyage into the unknown. Lemonnier described the pit girl as blacker than a negress. Munby frequently made this comparison and many of the women he sketched were given negroid features. Fascinated by the Christie minstrels and Ethiopian serenaders whom he saw in London, the symbolism of black versus white must have been further stimulated by the fact that Wigan was a trade victim of the American Civil War.[10] Contemporaries also associated white with cleanliness, purity, home, civilisation and order whereas black meant dirt, sexuality, distance, the Empire, slavery and chaos.

There was frequent use of the animal as metaphor. As John Berger has argued, this was part of a very old tradition, anthropomorphism having been in the past an expression of the close economic and productive relationship between man and animals.[11] Animals had been 'with man at the centre of his world'. Now their centrality had been challenged, the encroachment of industrial capitalism altering their significance for man. Yet there were important residual connections. In the first stages of industrialisation, the animal was used as a machine. Women and children too were increasingly reduced to being mechanical assets. The early women pit brow workers, the mines' alternatives to beasts of burden, were soon endowed with the qualities of animals. Those in the mining industry were seen to be near to nature and Darwinist theories about evolution now reinforced the process of animalisation. Wakeman described the women wagon-fillers as possessing the 'agility of monkeys'.[12] Some of Munby's drawings were little more than caricatures, the women being portrayed in apish terms, their size exaggerated and their arms elongated. An account of Tredegar tip girls in the *Bristol Mercury* told how a stranger to the district had enquired what were the animals he could see moving about on the mountain tops. Munby provided frequent analogies with horses.[13] In his long, unpublished narrative poem *Leonard and Elizabeth*, he compared the woman miner Elizabeth to a horse, thereby using the opportunity to emphasise the qualities he most admired in woman — devotion to duty, to hard work and to man:

> She thinks it sweet
> To walk all day upon her hands and feet,
> With a full wain behind! To rejoice
> In being a quadruped? To give her voice
> For such a degradation? Let her go,
> Disgusting creature! — Ah, you little know
> The ways of women and the might of love.[14]

Badly disfigured in a pit accident, Elizabeth wanted to spend the rest of her life hidden with the cattle rather than among 'higher beings'. Until rescued by Leonard, she lived underground in the horses' stable.

It was not really surprising that employment underground prompted equine comparisons. Women had been performing haulage jobs, had been harnessed and travelled on all fours. Helen Paterson (17) had told the Children's Employment Commission that 'We are worse off than the horses; for they draw on level rails, and we on rough roads.'[15] Zola's *Germinal* described Catherine trotting along 'like one of those dwarf animals in a circus'. The haulage girls were 'steaming like overloaded mares'. Such imagery suggested sexual overtones – Zola referred to the 'waves of bestiality that ran through the mines'.[16]

Comparisons with horses were also extended to surface work. Munby called the pit brow girls 'galloping draught horses' and 'coach horses steaming with sweat and rain'. A poem about a girl loading coal on to the barges began with the line 'She was a splendid animal.'[17] At a time when the horse had replaced the human beast of burden underground and was gradually giving way to machinery both above and below ground, it was ironical that the language used to describe the pit women achieved the same unfortunate results that critics deplored in the process of industrialisation and dehumanised them.

As with Richard Ayton's account of the William pit in 1813 (see Chapter 1), the initial encounter with a pit – even above ground – was sufficient to provoke emotive language. Pit terms were taken up and, by implication, the women were seen as tainted by their environment. One article described their surroundings as 'the very dross and scum of nature'.[18] Both attackers and defenders of pit brow work could take their comparisons to ridiculous extremes. One paper claimed that factory girls were 'angelic creatures' compared with the pit lasses who kept their eyes on the ground 'as if they were conscious of their degradation'.[19] The women were either portrayed as pariahs or else they were highly romanticised. Wakeman described how first impressions on seeing them

> fill you with a feeling of revulsion and dread of contact with such apparently saturnine creatures, and a thrill of indignity that women were enslaved by such seemingly degraded work.[20]

Yet morbid fascination soon gave way to sweeping claims:

> the lasses are superb athletes and models for the sculptor – Healthy, contented and harmless.

Those who set themselves up as the defenders tended to portray their lives as less complicated than those of other people. One account told of the 'uncaring childlike happiness of the brave girl'.[21] So they felt justified in responding to criticisms of the work on behalf of the women.

It was an ex-miner of Wigan, who had worked for many years with pit brow women, who produced a more realistic and balanced account of the pit lasses. John Monk Foster sought to provide this in his story *A Pit Brow Lassie*.[22] He avoided the presentation of a stereotype by showing the heroine Kate Leigh as 'frank-eyed and sure footed, even graceful' but a fellow worker, Moll Sheargold, was 'rather coarse, decidedly fast, and her reputation was of the most shady nature'. They were active and healthy workers, doing their job as well as men but this did not mean that the pit girl was a 'bold masculine type' – an allusion to Mrs Burnett's Joan Lowrie. And whereas *That Lass O'Lowrie's* had demonstrated how literature might help shape public opinion, Foster showed how public attitudes could in turn influence the writing of stories. His tale (published in the *Comet* and never as well known as Mrs Burnett's) was designed to show how the pit brow lass had been over-exposed and unfairly treated by critics in recent years. It was published in 1889 just after the pit brow debate reached its height though Foster set the story in 1878 'before the cry against female labour about mines had grown strong enough to deserve notice'.

Although it contained a liberal dose of Victorian melodrama – the plot becoming increasingly far-fetched as it unfolded – the detailed explanations of pit work helped by comparison to show the over-simplifications of many critics who had failed to distinguish between various surface jobs. Foster's use of everyday pit terms also provided a direct contrast to the image of the noble savage and emphasised still further the remoteness from the pit of many of the protagonists in the pit brow debate. In his stories he had adopted the device of giving characters surnames which were local place-names (for example, Kate *Leigh* and Luke *Standish*) and located his descriptions by using a combination of actual places (for example, Holland Green, based on Upholland and Lamberhead Green in *That Wench O'Ballin's*). Such techniques reminded readers that these stories were not intended to be purely fictional. Foster believed that the movement against the pit women had its origins in the worst of motives but he was particularly concerned to register his opposition to any interference, either ostensibly for or against the women, by those who did not understand the coal industry and the local situation.[23] This he achieved through the medium of the plot. Although eventually there was a happy ending, from the point that a stranger entered the pit district the relationship between the pit workers Kate and Luke appeared to be doomed.

Foster's story helps draw attention to the way in which the pit brow debate had become translated into a conflict of interests which placed the coalowner, suffragist, individualist and others in a seemingly unlikely alliance ranged against the miners' union and certain devotees of moral order. For the supporters of the work, the chief anxiety lay in the dangers and problems which would be posed by the removal of the women from their work. The coalowners were certainly not prepared to replace the women with male labour or machinery which would threaten their profits. Although in terms of the work performed by the women, the 1880s were vastly different from the early 1840s, when it came to the motives of the employers, attitudes had not really changed. The upholders of women's rights opposed exclusion above all because it conflicted with their hopes for women's legal and political equality in the future.

Opponents of the work concentrated not so much on the future as on the evils engendered by the present situation. Miners recognised that exclusion would not produce a sudden increase in wages — quite apart from anything else, the number of women was too small — but women's employment at the present time represented a condonement of the policy of cheap labour. The few coalowners who supported exclusion did so because they felt the present situation to be unfair since, coming from non-female-employing areas, they were not able to benefit like their competitors, from this source of cheap labour. For moralists, the women's presence at the pit was a constant threat which must be eradicated. So, for both sides, the issue became a yardstick for measuring their wider concerns. For the mining industry it was one more facet of the conflict between capital and labour. Beyond the coalfield, the pit women became a mere symbol, an impressive spectacle which enabled others to adduce arguments about the rights and wrongs of women's work. In the final analysis the pit brow lasses became caught up in a larger debate which confronted fundamental questions about late-nineteenth-century attitudes towards women, the family, work and class.

Notes

1. Munby MS, Diary 6, 29 September 1860.
2. In *Wigan Observer*, 3 February 1886.
3. PP 1887, XXII, p.190.
4. MFGB Coal Mines Bill. Standing Committee B, 2 August 1911, p.887. Evidence from Stephen Walsh MP for Ince.

5. Ibid., p.891.
6. *Wigan Examiner*, 11 October 1872.
7. In *Manchester Guardian*, 26 June 1901.
8. C. Lemonnier, *Le Borinage* (Brussels, 1902), p.95.
9. *Wigan Observer*, 12 September 1891.
10. For example, Munby MS, Notebook VIII, 1882. Hannah's pet name for Munby was 'Massa' based on the negro slave's term for master. See L. Davidoff, 'Class and Gender in Victorian England. The Diaries of Arthur J. Munby and Hannah Cullwick', *Feminist Studies,* vol 5, no.1 (1979), pp.91-2; also C. Bolt, *Victorian Attitudes to Race* (London, 1971), especially Chs. 1 and 11.
11. See J. Berger, 'Animals as Metaphor', *New Society*, 39, no.783, (10 March 1977), p.504; no.756 (31 March 1977).
12. *Wigan Observer*, 12 September 1891.
13. *Bristol Mercury*, 29 April 1865. Munby referred to the 'grotesque weird black figures in the white mist' of Tredegar. Munby MS, Notebook II, 1869.
14. A.J. Munby, *Leonard and Elizabeth*, unpublished MS, formerly in the possession of Dr A.N.L. Munby.
15. Quoted in ibid.
16. E. Zola, *Germinal* (London, 1973 edition), pp.43, 53.
17. Munby MS, Notebook III, 1866; Notebook VIII, 1882; 'Heaving Day' in Jones Brown (Munby's pseudonym), *Vulgar Verses* (London, 1891), p.185.
18. *Women's Union Journal*, V, no.5 (March 1880).
19. In *Wigan Observer*, 29 June 1867.
20. Ibid., 12 September 1891.
21. Lemonnier, *Borinage*, p.97.
22. See Ch.4 for details of Foster. *Comet*, no.9 (4 May 1889). It was also printed in the *Blackburn Standard*.
23. J.M. Foster, *That Wench O'Ballin's. A Mining Sketch of Lancashire Christmastide* (n.d.), Wigan Public Library, sought to provide a more accurate account than *That Lass O'Lowrie's*. Like Joan Lowrie the pit brow heroine risked her life by going underground after an explosion but Foster used the occasion to draw attention to the appalling safety standards.

EPILOGUE

After 1887 the issue of female pit labour lay dormant for some years. The Seventh International Conference of Miners at Aix-la-Chapelle did pass a resolution against female labour *about* coal mines in 1896 but in Britain women continued to work on the surface and in a number of countries they still worked above and below ground (see Appendix II).[1] In the same year and again in 1908 the pit brow women were briefly discussed in connection with proposed mines legislation but recruitment was not affected adversely. In fact at the end of the nineteenth and during the first years of the twentieth century the number of British pit brow lasses was on the increase — by 1909 there were 6,168 at work.[2] They had been used as a test case in the 1880s. Now the pit lasses and other outdoor work for women appeared to be secure.

There was, however, a final attempt to remove pit women in 1911. Significantly this was the year in which underground female exclusion was finally achieved in Belgium. At a time of high unemployment in Britain the idea of protective legislation was particularly attractive. The women chain-makers of Cradley Heath had gone on strike in the previous year, their refusal to work at lower rates than those established by the new minimum wage once again redirecting attention towards those areas of work which in the past had been dubbed as unsuitable for the female sex. The concern about female pit brow work in 1911 was the product of concern about minimum wage demands and of an intensification of opposition to married women working. Sir Arthur Markham, Liberal MP for Mansfield and a colliery owner, proposed an amendment in the Commons to prevent the future recruitment of females to colliery work. A Grand Committee considered this in August and the women's cause was once again upheld by Stephen Walsh MP for Ince who boasted thirty-seven years' experience of mining and was a veteran from the anti-exclusionists of the mid-1880s.[3] There were other familiar names — Atherley Jones was once again pressing for a prohibition of the work and was concentrating on the neglect of children. The *Wigan Observer* commented wearily on the attempts to reiterate old issues — after letting them slumber for twenty five years 'their pent-up emotions have now flashed forth. . .such belated indignation will doubtless be assessed at its full value'.[4]

On 2 August the committee decided by fifteen votes to thirteen to endorse Markham's amendment. However, this was immediately threatened by the resumption of the tactics of 1887. The very next day a deputation of forty-seven pit brow women from Lancashire (chiefly from Wigan collieries) visited Masterman the Liberal Under-Secretary of State. It had been hastily arranged though it was estimated that two thousand supporters attended a meeting convened at the skating rink in Wigan. A number of pit girls actually spoke here.[5] Eliza Neal of West Leigh moved a resolution against interference and asked local MPs for help. The Conservative mayor, Sam Wood (son of the wealthy coalowner William Wood), the mayoress, a local vicar and doctor then travelled to London with the women. Once again they appear to have created a favourable impression. Masterman appealed in the Commons against the decision of the Grand Committee. It was actually reversed in November when two hundred and ninety seven members voted against it, only seventy one declaring in its favour.[6] As a concession Masterman put forward an amendment designed to protect the women against injury. This forbade the 'lifting, carrying, or moving anything so heavy as to be likely to cause injury to the boy, girl or woman'. This extremely vague clause was accepted after a more specific bid to prohibit the pushing of tubs failed. Critics were, however, still not satisfied and expressed their concern about over-exertion to the new Home Secretary McKenna. There was some unease in Scotland where there were now about 2,000 female pit head workers, reflecting the recent increase in Lanarkshire. The Scottish TUC had been voicing opposition to the work for several years and in August 1911 the Scottish Miners Federation had passed a resolution against it at its annual conference at Edinburgh. The President Robert Smillie reiterated arguments about the unsuitability of such employment for the mothers of future generations.[7] However, the eventual act (1 and 2 Geo V c 50) incorporated Masterman's amendment along with the 1887 prohibition on wagon work and still permitted all females over thirteen to be employed at the pit top.

As in 1887 opinion was deeply divided. The Scottish miners were not unanimous — four of their representatives attended and supported a meeting in defence of the women. The majority of the opposition still came from non-female-employing areas. Midland miners' representatives, such as W.E. Harvey of Derbyshire, opposed the work but since Lancashire miners were now represented in Parliament they were able to state the other side of the argument. And although the *Wigan Observer* might complain about the exhumation of old platitudes, the context for this debate was clearly very different from that of the late nineteenth century.[8] This was a time of overt militancy by the suffragettes. Interestingly, Wigan had assumed a particular importance in the demand for suffrage since, in 1906, the borough had been chosen by the textile committee of the Women's Social and Political Union as a suitable constituency in which to fight an election on the issue of women's rights. The position of Wigan's vast workforce of women in the cotton trade had improved since the 1890s. Though traditionally low paid and unorganised, they had benefited from the work of Helen Silcock as President of the Wigan Weavers' Union. Although in the useful position of being on the executive of the local trades council, she found that the miners' own interests counteracted any real support for the suffrage candidate, Thorley Smith.[9] However persuasive radical suffragists such as Helen Silcock might be, they inevitably suffered from the delicate situation in which they were placed. Unlike earlier feminists, they were personally acquainted with the practical problems facing working-class women. This might initially win them respect yet in the last resort their demands brought them increasingly into conflict with the labour movement, forcing an embarrassing confrontation of priorities. Ironically, such women had usually espoused the women's cause after an early background of trade unionism.

It was hardly surprising that in 1911 a deliberate attempt was made to harness the pit brow issue very firmly to the suffrage movement. The Wigan Cooperative Hall was the scene of a meeting in October where twenty-one pit brow lasses sat on a platform beneath slogans such as 'We Claim the Right to Sell Our Labour Even as Our Brothers' and 'Working Women Need to Vote in Order to Protect Themselves in the Industrial World.'[10] All the pit women spoke briefly and defended their work. Resolutions were passed against the 'misleading and unscrupulous attacks made upon their labour' and in support of votes for women. Further meetings followed in London and Manchester. One held at the Albert Hall, Manchester, was organised by the National Industrial and Protective Women's Suffrage Society, the Lancashire and Cheshire Women's Textile and Other Workers Representation Committee and the Manchester and Salford Women's Trades and Labour Council. Esther Roper spoke and also wrote a leaflet for the Men's League for Women's Suffrage entitled 'The Case for the Pit Brow Worker'.

The pit brow workers' employment was in fact changing – not only was there the eight-hour day but most pit heads were mechanised and the majority of the women's work (Walsh claimed as high as nine-tenths) was now at the belts.[11] They were also joining trades unions.

In 1914 women in the Lancashire colliery districts were being recruited to the National Federation of Women Workers.[12] By August the Wigan and district branch had over five hundred members and branches were soon being organised at Ashton-in-Makerfield, St Helens, Sutton, Sutton Heath and Platt Bridge. Ada Newton and Helen Silcock (now Mrs Fairhurst) worked hard to improve the women's situation. The union intervened in several disputes and helped negotiate shorter hours and increased wages.

The numbers of pit women were swollen during war time – from 6,500 in July 1914 they rose to 11,300 by November 1918.[13] Temporarily wages were high – in South Wales women could earn 30/- a week though by 1921 they were getting only half this amount. The end of the war marked a turning point in relations with the miners' union. The Lancashire and Cheshire Miners Federation for example now recognised that women should be union members though this was not accepted without serious reservation. The President, Thomas Greenall, explained that

> There is a feeling in Lancashire we ought not to take women in, upon the opinions of our people, that colliery work is not suited for them.[14]

At the same time it was appreciated that the women's very lack of rights necessitated incorporating them for their own protection –

> We were forced in the end to take these women to see justice done to them with regard to their wages.[15]

Intrinsically linked with this decision was a recognition of the need for uniformity in hours, ages and wages. The Minimum Wage Act of 1912 had only applied to underground work and although surface men eventually got an increase, the women had not been able to achieve this. A Sub-Committee now drew up a scale of minimum wages and hours and this was then considered by a Joint Committee of the Lancashire and Cheshire Coal Association in October and November 1919. Failing to come to any agreement, the coalowners formed their own Sub-Committee but when the two sides met again in February 1919 there was still a difference of 1/- per day between the two sides for top rates and there was no consensus about the definition of an adult worker.[16] The issue was therefore submitted to arbitration and the case was heard before His Honour Judge Mellor at Manchester in

June 1919 with eight representatives for the owners and twelve for the miners. The latter based their claim on the advances gained under the Conciliation Board set up in 1894 and argued that if the women had received the full value of wage advances they would now be earning between 2/2d and 4/7d daily.[17] The owners concentrated instead on a minimum wage fixed on an average related to present rates.[18] They wanted to fix the top rate and then work downwards whilst the miners wanted to start from the bottom.

The award was made on 1 July. The rulings of the Conciliation Board were to apply to all women manipulating coal in the same way as men. A scale graduated according to age (thereby accepting a direct relationship between age and strength) was deemed most suitable. A minimum wage was fixed (to which was added the war bonus, war wage and Sankey award). This was higher than the owners' demands though lower than the miners' claim, starting at 1/2d as the basic rate for fourteen to fifteen year-olds and rising to 3/4d for those over twenty.[19]

The miners therefore now recognised a right which had not been conceded earlier and were trying to redress the balance. Whereas in the past the union had officially opposed the women's work and the owners had upheld it, the need now to support fellow union members was producing a change in the way they were arguing. Yet although they now claimed higher rates for the women rather than their exclusion, the old doubts which had dogged miners for many years persisted. Several times they had to be reminded that they were straying from the question of arbitration and were instead taking issue with the owners over the right of the women to perform certain jobs. In fact they partially reconciled their apparent *volte face* by drawing a distinction between types of work, i.e. screening and the rest, and thereby accepted the women as workers but with certain marked reservations. While they were prepared to accept that conditions had improved and that 'there is a different feeling to what there used to be with regard to the women', they justified their inconsistency by protesting against tipping and any work other than that at the screens.

The increased mechanisation of the industry was inevitably challenging employment opportunities. Ultimately it was forcing 'progress' but in a way which was very different from that envisaged by nineteenth-century exclusionists. Eventually mechanisation performed the job which man-made laws had failed to do. By 1953 there were only 956 females left at collieries (two-thirds of them in Lancashire), working in a post-war industry which was now nationalised.

But the old debate was to be resurrected once more during the discussion on the mines legislation in 1954.[20] The women's work was opposed by Walsh's successor, the miner Tom Brown, and by a miner's daughter Margaret Herbison, Labour MP for North Lanark. She suggested that no new female recruits should be allowed, arguing that changes in social and economic circumstances had made it possible for women to get (and travel to) alternative employment in factories. A long discussion in committee resulted, however, in a decision not to support an amendment against the women. The Mines and Quarries Act (2 and 3 Eliz.II c 70) allowed females to continue their work though the debate had helped promote the idea that there were men available who could and should do the work instead of women. The National Coal Board and National Union of Mineworkers came to an agreement whereby disabled miners should be favoured for these jobs and as women retired they were not replaced. In some cases they were made redundant. By the mid-1950s women remained at only two Lancashire collieries. Wherever possible they were given alternative work at the canteens and switchboards or more frequently in cleaning.

In 1894 a contributor to the journal *Science and the Art of Mining* had predicted a 'millenium of dealing with coals' at the pit brow:

> I believe the time will come when the hutches will run off the cage, empty themselves, and return back to the cage, ready for another journey whilst the coal will be screened, cleaned and loaded, and the wagons shifted, if not altogether automatically, at least with only a fraction of the manual labour now expended on the work.[21]

The use of gravity washing-methods from the 1920s and later the adoption of power-operated machinery which loaded coal on to conveyors, helped to realise this millenium. At Bickershaw colliery for example, where pit brow lasses used to sort coal, a new screening plant was erected in 1955.[22] The capacity of the coal washery was 400 tons per hour and a £90,000 surface rapid loading scheme speeded the movement of coal to the power stations. Continuously-coupled wagons each capable of holding 30 tons of coal could be loaded or unloaded with 1,000 tons of coal in less than thirty minutes.

Colliery closures helped put the finishing touch to the work of the pit brow woman. By the mid-1960s only eleven collieries were still at work in the Lancashire coalfield. The last woman left Golborne colliery in 1966. Although she had spent her later days cleaning, whenever somebody was needed on the screens she returned to help. The

Lancashire pit brow lass, so frequently attacked in the past, now became a quaint and romanticised memory. In Scotland women were ceasing to 'pick brasses' — the last Scots pit head woman left Minto colliery, Fife, when it closed in 1967. Women had ceased to do pit work in South Wales though a few had been retained as cleaners. It was in Cumberland that the screen lasses' work continued for a little longer.

Yet mechanisation eventually overtook them. Eleven women who had been employed at Haig colliery, Whitehaven, had to leave the screening plant in March 1970. This left just two screen lasses, both working at Harrington no.10 Lowca where, although the colliery as such was abandoned, a washery was still in operation. These last two British female surface workers were made redundant and left their work on 1 July 1972, 130 years after legislation had forbidden the employment of women below ground.[23]

Twenty years after the Mines and Quarries Act of 1954, the last major mines legislation to reconfirm the ban on women miners below ground, a government white paper on sexual discrimination in Britain set out proposals for equal opportunities. These included the intention to 'retain for the present' the exclusion of women from working in mines though an amendment of the hours that women might work on the surface was proposed.[24] The eventual legislation of 29 December 1975 embodied these proposals. A slight modification to the mining act has, however, permitted the employment of women in disused mines and their occasional work in active mines as long as their jobs do not ordinarily take them below ground for a significant proportion of time.[25] This, for example, allows a woman doctor to work below ground if necessary as long as her main duties lie elsewhere. In August 1978 the NCB made their first appointment of a woman as deputy medical officer for their South Wales area.[26] However, a report of March 1979 based on a three-year investigation by the Equal Opportunities Commission has not resulted in a recommendation to relax the law any further in so far as it relates to female manual workers in mines. Representatives of both miners and management have stressed the difficulties of introducing women into mining work. They have pointed to continued unsavoury conditions particularly as far as sanitation is concerned and also emphasise the fact that recruitment is carried out on the basis that all recruits should be capable of progressing to facework and believe that

> this kind of work would be beyond the capabilities of almost all women.[27]

Since most jobs are seen as either preparation for facework or are reserved for incapacitated miners, it is felt that to introduce women would 'disturb an employment policy based on social considerations'. The EOC, particularly concerned about sanitation problems, endorses the present arrangements though it believes that the situation should be kept under active review both by themselves and by both sides of the mining industry. At the same time it does recognise clear discrimination against women in the sections of the 1954 legislation which deal with the duties of the male person in charge of winding or rope-haulage apparatus. It recommends that where these duties are carried out on the surface women might perform these jobs and the word 'male' should therefore be deleted from the clause.

There is, however, a final postscript. In parts of present-day China — for example, in Yungan county — women work in the coal mines and lead coal-cutting teams. Meanwhile in the United States, pressure to comply with anti-discrimination legislation resulted in 1974 in the largest coal companies (mostly owned by steel or oil concerns) taking the unprecedented step of hiring women to work underground. The first and largest employer was Beth-Elkhorn, a subsidiary of Bethlehem Steel in Jenkins, Kentucky. Other states followed suit. By mid-1979 there were over 2,500 women miners in the States.[28] They are initially employed as trainee 'GI's (General Inside Laborers) doing jobs such as shovelling the beltline (scooping up coal which has fallen off the belt and replacing it) and rock-dusting (spraying crushed limestone on the walls to keep down the dust level). Some have progressed to being shuttlecar operators (transporting coal from the face to the belt).

Others bid to do highly dangerous facework and in joining the longwall crews have already proved that it is not beyond their capabilities. They carry timber and as chocksetters help move up the chocks or supports after the coal has been cut and do vital cribbing work (placing timber in a criss-cross pattern on top of the chocks to provide extra support). They also shovel up the débris after the chocks have been moved. A few women are now entering welfare and union positions and are becoming Presidents of United Mine Workers' 'Locals'. Lacking the British tradition of female underground work, their employment can be seen as a progressive move. Yet despite the fact that Britain is also witnessing a revitalised women's movement, the historical background of women's colliery work in this country militates against the likelihood of Victorian legislation being repealed in the near future. Here the possibility of having women coal miners is more easily equated with retrogression than with progress.

Notes

1. *Wigan Observer*, 1 August 1911.

2. Hansard DXXIX, House of Commons, 1 July 1954, p.1687. Women were also now working in areas which had previously not had female surface labour. For example, in 1905 women began working at Fletcher's Outwood collieries at Ringley, Lancashire (where they had originally worked below ground). *Wigan Observer*, 4 March, 25 November 1905. See also L.R. Haggard (ed.), *I Walked by Night. Being the Life and History of the King of the Norfolk Poachers* (London, 1935), p.81 for an account of 'picken cole' in the Manchester area.

3. Stephen Walsh had worked in the pits from the age of thirteen. He became a miners' agent and was MP for Ince from 1906. See Ch.5. *Science and the Art of Mining*, XXI, no.20 (13 May 1911). A petition from 700 men working at two Wigan pits opposed interference. Hansard XXII, House of Commons, 5 December 1911, p.1275.

4. *Wigan Observer*, 5 August 1911.

5. Ibid. Once again they were shown the sights of London.

6. Hansard XXI, House of Commons, 15 November 1911, p.362; 5 December 1911, p.242.

7. S. Lewenhak, *Women and Trades Unions* (London, 1977), p.139; *Votes for Women*, 27 October 1911; *Women's Industrial News*, October 1911, pp.137-8.

8. *Votes for Women*, 27 October 1911.

9. J. Liddington and J. Norris, *One Hand Tied Behind Us* (London, 1978), pp.97-8. See also D. Brown, 'The Labour Movement in Wigan 1874-1967', unpublished MA thesis, University of Liverpool, 1969.

10. Arncliffe Sennett collection, Add. MS C121, British Library. At one London suffrage meeting twenty pit brow women were present.

11. C.M. Percy's work on colliery mechanisation published in 1905 explained that within the last twenty years practically the whole of the banking-out and screening and sorting arrangements had undergone considerable change. In *Wigan Observer*, 4 March 1905.

12. National Federation of Women Workers. 7th PA Report, August 1914, p.33; 8th PA Report, August 1915, p.29, HD6079 TUC. In 1915, for example, there was a dispute at the Wood pit, Ashton, where the women refused to tip slack into the fire holes — an extremely demanding job in terms of physical strength and one normally performed by the men. The company offered an extra 5d for this work, the women refused and after union negotiation, eventually the management agreed to introduce lighter tubs.

13. Report on the Increased Employment of Women during the war. WS Emp. 25[1] Imperial War Museum. See also G.D.H. Cole, *Labour in the Coal Mining Industry* (Oxford, 1923), pp.15-19.

14. Minutes of the Lancashire and Cheshire Miners Federation, 9 February, 6 April, 14 May 1918, NUM Bolton.

15. Lancashire and Cheshire Joint District Committee, 'Arbitration on the Scale of Minimum Wages for Women' (NUM Bolton, 1919), p.6.

16. Federation minutes, 9 February, 8 July 1918.

17. Ibid., 14 October 1918, p.2; 15 November 1918, p.7; 10 February 1919, p.1. The employers' representatives suggested 1/8d per day at entry rising to 3/- whereas the miners proposed 1/8d which could rise to 4/- a day.

18. Joint Committee on Arbitration, 7 July 1919, pp.2-3.

19. Ibid., 19 June 1919, p.35.

20. Hansard DXXIX, House of Commons, 1 July 1954, p.1689.

21. *Science and the Art of Mining*, V, no.25 (1894-5), p.583.

22. Bickershaw Colliery, 1877-1977, Centenary Brochure NCB Western Area.

Warrington, 1977.
23. Interviewed 25 October 1974; *Whitehaven News*, 26 February 1970.
24. HMSO White Paper on Equality for Women 5724, September 1974. The original proposals forbade the work of male midwives which, along with women's work in mines, had been singled out as an exception to the rule. The eventual act did however allow males to become midwives.
25. To date there has been no test case on Section 21 of the Sex Discrimination Act, so no authoritative interpretation of it can yet be provided. It states that 'No female shall be employed in a job the duties of which ordinarily require the employee to spend a significant proportion of her time below ground at a mine which is being worked.'
26. *Western Mail*, 22 September 1978.
27. EOC Health and Safety Legislation. 'Should we distinguish between men and women?', pp.202-16.
28. Interviewed West Virginia, 20 November 1978; *The Times*, 5 August 1974. Some women had worked in small 'country bank' mines in the past. In Appalachia they helped during the depression. In 1935, Ida Stull won a court case which gave her the title of 'America's First Woman Coal Miner', *United Mine Workers Journal*, December 1977. The first two modern women miners began work in Kentucky in December 1973. The first conference of women coal miners was held in Virginia in June 1979.

APPENDIX I: MUNBY'S VISITS TO PIT WOMEN

1853-4	First visit to Wigan though details not recorded
1859	Wigan
1860	Wigan
1861	South Wales, Wigan
1862	Belgium
1863	Staffordshire, Shropshire, Wigan
1864	(working women in France)
1865	Wigan (twice), South Wales
1866	Wigan, Whitehaven
1867	Wigan
1868	Belgium, Wigan
1869	Wigan, South Wales
1870	Market gardens Middlesex, Wigan, South Wales
1871	Market gardens, Belgium
1872	Market gardens, Shropshire
1873	Market gardens, Wigan
1874	Market gardens, Wigan
1875	Market gardens
1876	Market gardens, Wales
1877	Market gardens
1878	Market gardens, Wigan, Shropshire
1879	Market gardens, Shropshire
1880	Market gardens, Belgium
1881	Market gardens, Belgium
1882	Shropshire, Wigan
1883	Market gardens, Belgium
1884-6	(some periods of ill health. Visited European working women. Sorted out collections on female labour. Negotiated about Lancashire defence of pit brow exclusion plans)
1887	Shropshire. Attended deputation of pit women in London, Wigan
1888	Shropshire
1889	Shropshire
1890	Shropshire

From 1890 to 1898 Munby spent much of his time with
Hannah in Shropshire. He still visited local pits there but
no more visits to Wigan were recorded. His written accounts
cease in 1898. His eyesight was deteriorating. He contracted
chronic glaucoma (hardening of the globe) and had an
irridectomy performed on one eye. In old age the acute
observer was almost blind.

APPENDIX II: THE OPEN DOOR POLICY

Founded in 1925 the aim of the Open Door Council was that 'a woman shall be free to work and protected as a worker on the same terms as a man'. Three years later it took the revolutionary step of attacking not just opposition to female surface work but the exclusion of women from underground colliery employment. There had been no serious challenge to this since the Commons debate of 1843 when the chief concern had been the preservation of the rights of colliery owners rather than recognising the rights of women. Now the ODC defiantly proclaimed:

> the right of the adult woman in mining districts to decide for herself what manner of work she feels fit to undertake, even if her choice should lead her into the mine.

It was only in the context of the operation of very different social forces that it was possible eighty-five years after 1843 to make such a claim. Even then it provoked hostile reactions including a Memorandum to the Women's Advisory Committee of the Labour and Socialist International which explicitly attacked such a view.

In 1935 the Open Door International (which had been founded in 1929 and published a pamphlet on 'Women and the right to work in mines') actually claimed that current unrest in the British coalmining industry was due to the female exclusion of 1842. Without this the public conscience would have insisted on improvements in the industry which it had ignored since only men were employed below ground. Such an argument however failed to recognise the omnipotence of the nineteenth-century coalowner.

The concern of the Open Door organisation with something which in Britain had long ceased to exist and had, through time, been obliterated from peoples' direct experience was not as anachronistic as it might at first sight appear. The 'sham protection' against which these women railed was of topical concern in other parts of the world. Admittedly most countries had forbidden such work — the early twentieth century witnessed a spate of laws which consolidated earlier legislation and forbade the work in Europe, Australia, Canada and elsewhere. In fact the only countries where women were still employed in large numbers were India and Japan where the custom of engaging workers by families survived. Opponents of Open Door policies feared that attempts were being made to drag Britain 'down to the Indian and Japanese level'. In these two countries attempts were, however, being made to restrict female employment. In 1928 draft regulations to this effect were drawn up in British India where at the beginning of the decade females had accounted for 37 per cent of the total colliery labour force. Generally of low caste, they worked seasonally both above and below ground. The coal mines of Bengal, Bihar, Orissa and the Central Provinces were to have the law gradually enforced over a ten-year period. In 1932, however, there were still over 11,000 employed at the Bihar mines alone. Japan was also slowly making changes. In 1930 she had over 44,000 women mine workers. An order of 1928 forbade employment under certain conditions (for example in high temperatures) after September 1933 but there were many exemptions and women continued to be employed in thin seams.

The International Labour Organization passed resolutions against women's work in mines in 1929 and 1931 and at its eighteenth conference in 1934 a Mines Committee reported on the situation. The prospect of intervention prompted action from the ODC which deputised the Ministry of Labour and sent written complaints to the ILO. Yet in spite of opposition from this and the new ODI, the ILO accepted by 117 votes in June 1935 that 'No female, whatever her age shall be employed on underground work.' It was, however, recognised that national laws and regulations might exempt some and that non-manual labour might be permitted. Meanwhile the ODI made some direct appeals — in 1935 letters were sent to Stalin (now that Russia was a member of the ILO) urging him not to adopt restrictive policies in this sphere. Elsewhere however, the influence of the ILO was being felt. The employment of women in mines in India was prohibited in 1937 though the difficulty of securing adequate replacements and the problems of alternative work for the women delayed change. By 1939, the ILO was declaring that underground labour for women was 'now absolutely forbidden in every country in which the existence and exploitation of mineral resources might give rise to such employment'. It did however have to admit that Japan was the exception (here women were still employed in the early 1970s) and during the Second World War the situation changed again temporarily — in India for example the ban on women's work in mines was lifted in 1943 until February 1946.

INDEX

Abraham, Will 154, 206
accidents 25, 39, 57, 72, 166-74
 passim, see also disasters, Hampson,
 Ellen, safety
Acts of Parliament: Agricultural
 Gangs Act (1867) 159n5;
 Brickfields Act (1871) 76;
 Contagious Diseases Acts (1866,
 1868, 1869) 156; Education
 Acts (1976, 1880) 76; Employers
 Liability Act (1880) 157; Factory
 Act (1833) 28-9, 33, 36; Factory
 and Workshops bills/Acts (1874,
 1878) 136, 150; Inspection Acts
 (1850) 172; (1855) 168, 172;
 (1860) 144, 168; (1872) 168,
 172; Minimum Wage Act (1912)
 227; Poor Law Amendment Act
 (1834) 51; Reform Act (1884) 151;
 Sex Discrimination Act (1975) 230;
 Workshops Regulation Act (1867)
 76, *see also* Mines and Collieries
 bills/Acts
ages (of pit women) 21, 38-9, 72,
 75-6, 113-18 *passim,* 158 195-6,
 228
agriculture 33n20, 40, 53, 60n3, 91,
 114, 151
Alexander, Sally 14
alternative employment 12, 50-5
 passim, 59, 92, 114-15, 192, 229
Ambler, Ann 47, 77
Anti-Beef agitation 126
Anti-slavery 20, 155
art/artists 26-7, 80, 100, 105, 143,
 185-6
Ashley, Lord (7th Early of Shaftesbury) 19, 28-9, 44-55 *passim*
Atherley Jones, L.A. 145-6, 217, 224
Ayton, Richard 30-1, 43, 220

balance pits 79
Bald, Robert 30
Banks, Frederick Charles 156
banksmen/browmen 79-80, 196 *see*
 also overseers, pit brow women
Barnsley 32, 38
bearers *see* haulage

Becker, Lydia 148-50, 152
Belgium 34n25, 41, 80, 82, 92n61,
 105, 137, 143, 183, 193, 224, 234
Benson, John 118
Berger, John 219
Bilston 78
Binney, E.W. 46
Blackmore, R.D. 104
Blaenavon 184
Blastfurnacemen's Association 152
Board of Trade 28, 207
Boer War 90
Bolton 124, 147
Bolton Chronicle 126
Booth, Charles 146
Bradford 37, 151
Bradford Women's Electoral
 Association 151
Bradlaugh, Charles 153
brickmaking, 52, 72, 85-6
Bright, Jacob 153
Bright Lucas, Mrs 148-9, 153
Bristol Mercury 184, 219
British Women's Temperance
 Association 153, 155
Broadhurst, Henry 136-7
Brophy, Peter 58, 78
Browning, Elizabeth Barrett 145;
 Robert 98
Bruce, Henry Austin 92, 173
Budworth, Joseph 21
Burnley 97, 106, 184
Burnett, Frances Hodgson 187-190,
 218, 221
Burnett, Sir John 207
Burt, Thomas 93n1, 138, 144-6,
 154, 205
Butler, Josephine 50, 148, 156, 192

canals 27, 107
carpet weavers 182
Cavendish Bentinck, G. 146
census 24-5, 70, 73, 75, 106, 108,
 110, 113-18 *passim*
chain-makers 48, 151, 198, 207-8,
 224
Chartism 42-4, 47-58
checkweighers 80, 144, 206

239

125-6, 166, 195-202, 204, 207;
moral arguments 15, 50, 52, 147,
166, 221-2 – and defeminisation
11, 166, 180, 186, 217 – and
immorality 50, 52, 191-2; physical
arguments 14, 166 – and appearance 137, 180-187 *passim,* 190,
217 – and health 14, 39, 140,
147, 174-9, 221 – and strength
173-6, 179
factories 24, 28-9, 62n39, 150, 176,
180-220; in France 63n65, 186;
safety 173-4; Ten Hour Movement
28, 62n60, *see also* Acts of
Parliament, mills
Fairhurst sisters 89, 196
Faithfull, Emily 112, 149
family: and employment 20, 26-7,
59, 114-8, 150, 193, 201; and
industrialisation 43-6, 112;
economy 25; life 105, 113, 190,
194-5; support 15, 118-19; wage
26, 40, 58, *see also* domestic ideal
Fawcett, Mrs 148, 150
Fenwick Miller, Mrs 149
fines 56, 93
fisher women 33n20
flither lasses 182
Fortescue, Earl of 157
Foster, John Monk 103, 115, 121,
170, 201, 221-2
Franks, Robert 37, 41, 43, 46 *see also*
Sub-Commissioners

Gentleman's Magazine 21, 90
gin pits 35n44, 77-9
Girls' Club and Home 157
Girls' Friendly Society 157
glass-makers 34n30
Glover, Thomas 205
Gore-Booth, Eva 154
Grounds, Ellen 125, 181

Haigh Moor brewery 54, 114
Hair, P.E.H. 34n26
Halifax, 37, 46
Halliday, John 145
Halliwell, Elizabeth 146-7
Hampson, Ellen 87, 170, 174
Handloom Weavers 37
Hardcastle, F. 153-4
Harrison, Brian 155
Harvey, W.E. 225
haulage: below ground 19-21, 23, 30,
39-40, 42, 69, 86, 115; above

ground 79-80, 85-7, 136, 174 *see
also* horses, Madge, Sal
Head, Sir George 35n47
health 39, 182, 220-1 *see also*
exclusion: above ground
Herbison, Margaret 229
hewers 22, 33n23, 39-40 *see also*
women miners
Hine, lewis 85
Hird, Frank, 177
hiring of colliery workers 20, 40
Hirwaun 37
History of Collieries round Haigh 108
Holden, Mrs P. 91, 197
Hopwood, Charles 156
horses 21, 23, 30, 219-20
hours of work 39, 90-3, 136, 150,
171, 176; shift work 43, 26, 120
houses/homes 27, 51, 117, 119,
194-5, 197; lodgers 116 *see also*
domestic ideal
housework 90, 91, 120
Howell, George 200
Hudson, Derek 99
Hutchinson, Thomas 135
Hyde Women's Liberal Association
151

Illustrated London News 47, 185
India 33n16, 236-7
industrialisation 43, 106, 217
individualism 154, 157, 222;
Individualist club 157, *see also*
Personal Rights Association
informers 56, 59
Inspectors of mines 56, 58, 69-70,
94n22, 129n38, 166, 168, 171,
173, 183, 193, 205, 216, *see also*
Acts of Parliament
International Health Exhibition 182
International Labour Organisation
237
Irish 106, 112, 119; Nationalists 208
Iron trade 72, 78, 92, 151; methods
of work 71-3, 85-6, 88, 91

James, Janet 196
Japan 95n61, 236-7
jobs *see* pit brow women, women
miners

Kennedy, J.L. 39, 46, *see also* Sub-
Commissioners
Kidderminster 152
King-May, Miss 154, 176